IMAGES
of America

SHENANDOAH COUNTY

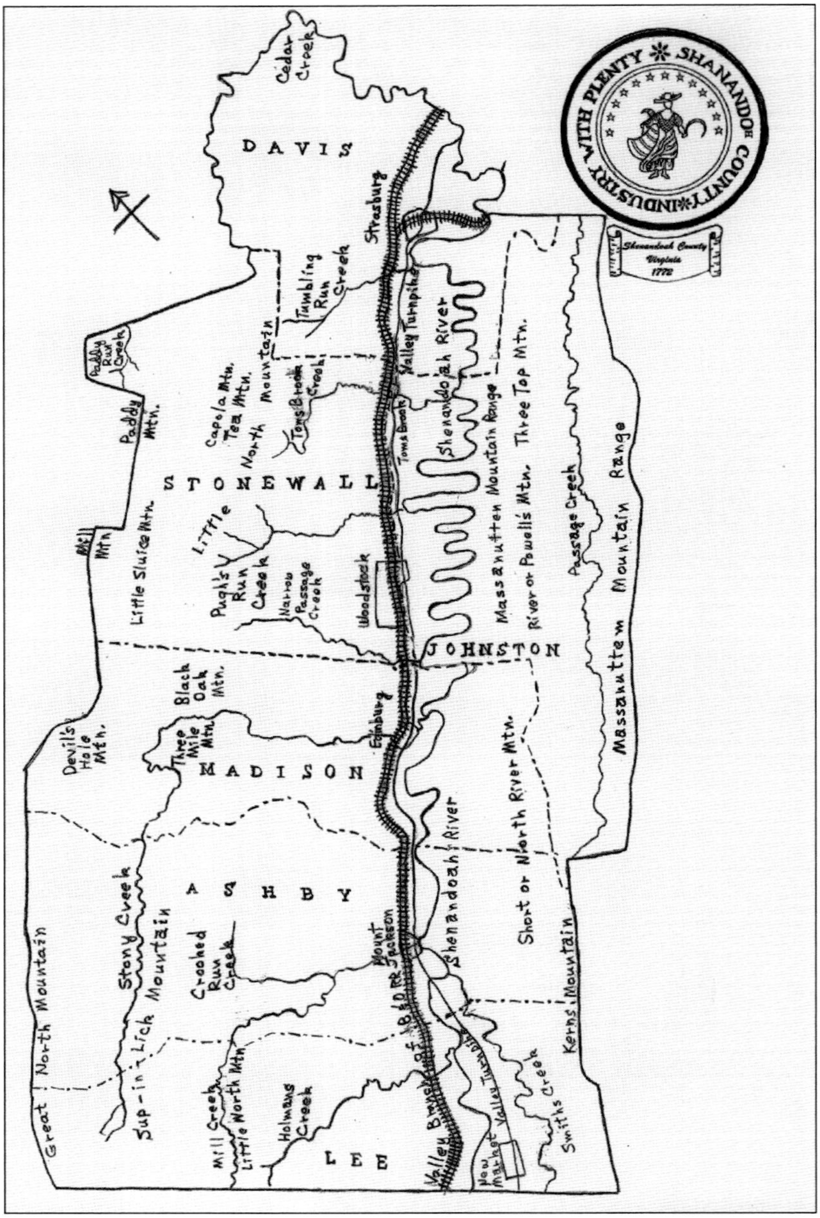

Map of Shenandoah County. Beckford Parish, laid out in the colony of Virginia at the southern end of Frederick County, was founded in November 1769. In 1772, using the same boundaries as those for the parish of Beckford, the county of Dunmore was established. In 1778, the county name was changed to Shenandoah. Before 1830, the area included approximately 800 square miles. The map made for this book is not intended to be accurate in all aspects. (Courtesy of John Adamson, Charlie Martin, and Shenandoah County.)

On the Cover: Shenandoah County has always been an agricultural region. Over the years, the equipment used to work the fields and the number of farmers and animals has changed. These horses are bringing in the wheat on the John Connor farm, on Buck Hill Road off Back Road. (Courtesy of David and Joyce Connor Hamrick.)

IMAGES
of America

SHENANDOAH COUNTY

Jean M. Martin in association with
the Shenandoah County Historical Society

ARCADIA
PUBLISHING

ISBN 978-0-7385-6654-2

Published by Arcadia Publishing
Charleston, South Carolina

Printed in the United States of America

Library of Congress Control Number: 2009931193

For all general information contact Arcadia Publishing at:
Telephone 843-853-2070
Fax 843-853-0044
E-mail sales@arcadiapublishing.com
For customer service and orders:
Toll-Free 1-888-313-2665

Visit us on the Internet at www.arcadiapublishing.com

This book is dedicated to the men and women of Shenandoah County who have loved this place and dedicated their lives to its care. One person in particular has exemplified the love of place; Rosalie Jennings is a poet and a good neighbor. She has written poetry to honor its beauty; one poem in particular came to mind when I started to think about this book. She has graciously allowed me to share the last part of Into that Lacier Dome of Thought. *"Let me find the truth, feel God's will. Let me hear songs a mountain can echo! Let me be carried into the music a whole valley dreams." I hope you will enjoy the book, and thank you, Rosalie.*

Contents

ACKNOWLEDGMENTS

The people of Shenandoah County have created this book over the past 300 years. They have shaped and planted the land to provide a way of life that appeals to succeeding generations. Those who come for a short stay often return to their favorite part of the Shenandoah Valley and make it their home. As the archivist/genealogist for the Shenandoah County Library for the past seven years, I hope this book will contribute to the ongoing education and preservation of traditions. Members of the Shenandoah County Historical Society have been most helpful. I wish especially to thank John and Barbara Adamson, Nancy and John Stewart, C. F. and Janet Wagniere, and John Wall. Patty Heubusch has been of invaluable assistance. Thanks also to the staff of the Shenandoah County Library in Edinburg and to my husband, Charlie. Without the following lenders of photographs the book would not have been possible. Thank you to all of you.

The institutions that provided photographs for this book include the U.S. Department of Agriculture Forest Service (USDAFS); Shenandoah County Historical Society (SCHS); Shenandoah County Library (SCL.); Shrine Mont, Inc. (SMOC); and the Woodstock Museum of Shenandoah County, Virginia, Inc. (WMSC).

The private collectors who provided photographs for this book include Margaret Fravel Carte (MFC); Holley Cooley (HC); Judith McVicar Copenhaver (JMC); Cheryl Dellinger; Olivia Bland Gentile (OBG); Perry Crabill collection (PCC); Donald and Joyce Conner Hamrick (DJCH); Jacob Haun (JH); Fay Helsley Kidd (FHK); Dr. James and Patricia Kiser (JPK); Ann Laing (AL); Mark Loving (ML), Jeremy D. McCleary; Jean Painter Miller (JPM); Harriett and Ronald Miller (HRM); Marvin Polk Jr. (MP); Beatrice Johnson Ritenour; Patricia Phillips Shelton (PPS); Gloria and Ralph Stickley (GRS); Linda Dellinger Varney; the Wakeman family (WF); and Beverly Ward.

INTRODUCTION

The earliest images of the region now called Shenandoah County are hand-drawn maps. The main features are the mountains, the river, and the streams. Between the ridges of the mountains and along the river is a natural corridor from the more populated areas of northeastern America to the less or unsettled regions to the south and southwest. This pathway is often named on those early drawings as "Indian Trail" or "Wilderness Road." The religious settlers who came by this road were predominantly Pennsylvania Germans looking for limestone-rich land and religious freedom. Today mountains on both sides of the valley are within the George Washington National Forest and are covered with trees planted in the 1930s by the "boys" of the Civilian Conservation Corps (CCC). The roads they made are lined with rock walls or guardrails, and their stone bridges cross the streams. The people who have lived along these roads, as well as the streams, river, and mountains themselves are the main focus of the images in this book.

The Blue Ridge Mountains form the eastern band of Shenandoah County, and the Great North Mountains of the Appalachians form the western boundary. Part of the Northern Neck Land Grant from Lord Fairfax in 1737, the county was formed from Frederick and Augusta in 1772.

Since 1873, the county has been divided into six magisterial districts. Locals go "up" when they travel south and "down" on the northward trek. When asked, they say, "That's the way the river flows." Beginning at the southern border with the Rockingham County line are Lee, Ashby, Madison, Stonewall, and Davis Districts. The last district, Johnston, includes both sides of Powell's Mountain. The earliest maps label it "Powell's Fort." The western line for the county meets Hardy County, West Virginia, near the top of the North Mountains. Along the north, Cedar Creek provides a beautiful and meandering border between Shenandoah and Frederick Counties. The creeks, streams, and springs run into the North Fork of the Shenandoah River as it flows north and meets the South Fork, as the mighty Shenandoah River empties into the Potomac River at Harper's Ferry, West Virginia. Most agree that the river needs to be protected as it runs on between the steady mountains in this place of God's majestic beauty.

This verdant region, loved by its nearly 40,000 occupants, offers diverse religious, cultural, and educational opportunities. Agriculture has always been the main occupation in Shenandoah County. Recently there has been an increase in vineyards in the county; the dairy farms are decreasing as the wine makers work their magic on the pastures and rolling hills by planting and caring for their special grape vines. According to the latest U.S. Census figures released in 2002, nearly $70 million in farm receipts was brought into the county for poultry, eggs, cattle, dairy products, fruits, vegetables, and nuts. To do this, 549 full-time and 440 part-time farmers used modern planting methods and equipment for harvesting. Some of the images will reveal the older machinery and the creativity of the farmers, as they found new ways to do old jobs.

These religious and enterprising citizens have gradually made of this wild and beautiful place a county that successfully uses its natural resources in a conscientious way and provides for the material, spiritual, and cultural needs of its citizens.

The individuals and organizations that provided these photographs are proud of their heritage in Shenandoah County and offered to share their memories of the people and times of the past. The images reveal the natural beauty of the valley and the courage and creativity of the people. It is hoped that readers will enjoy seeing the past through these images and that they will be inspired to search for and identify the photographs of their own families.

One

This Hallowed Space

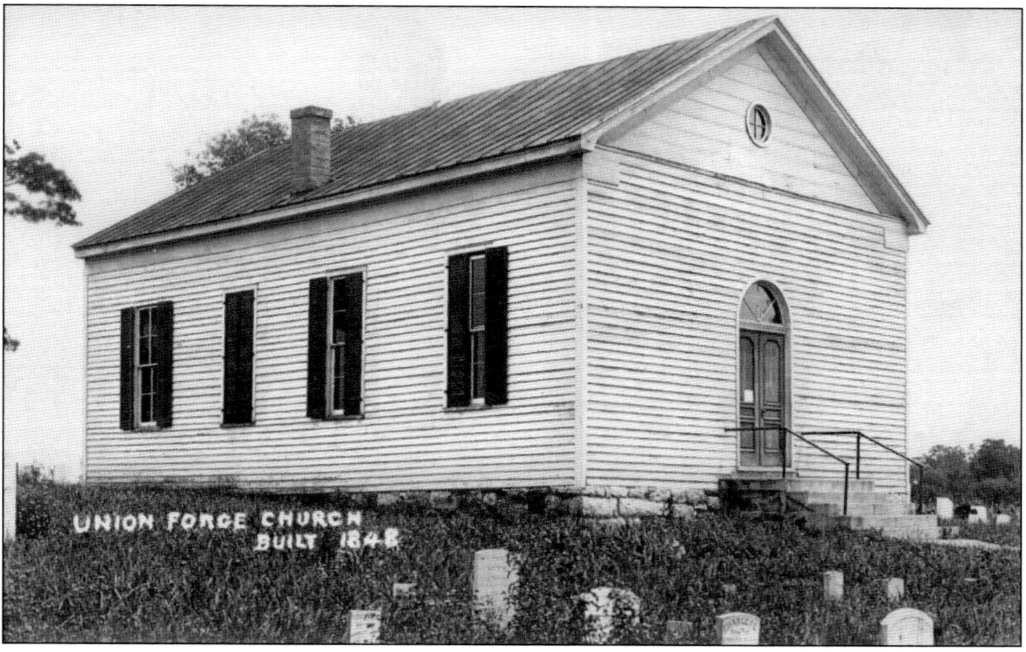

Early Church. The first Episcopal congregation was made up of English- and German-speaking members. The first log church was built at the center of Woodstock. There is no known image of the first church, but it was probably similar to early homes. The early Union Forge Church was built on land donated by Augustine Hollar in 1815. It is seen before changes were made in later years. (SCL.)

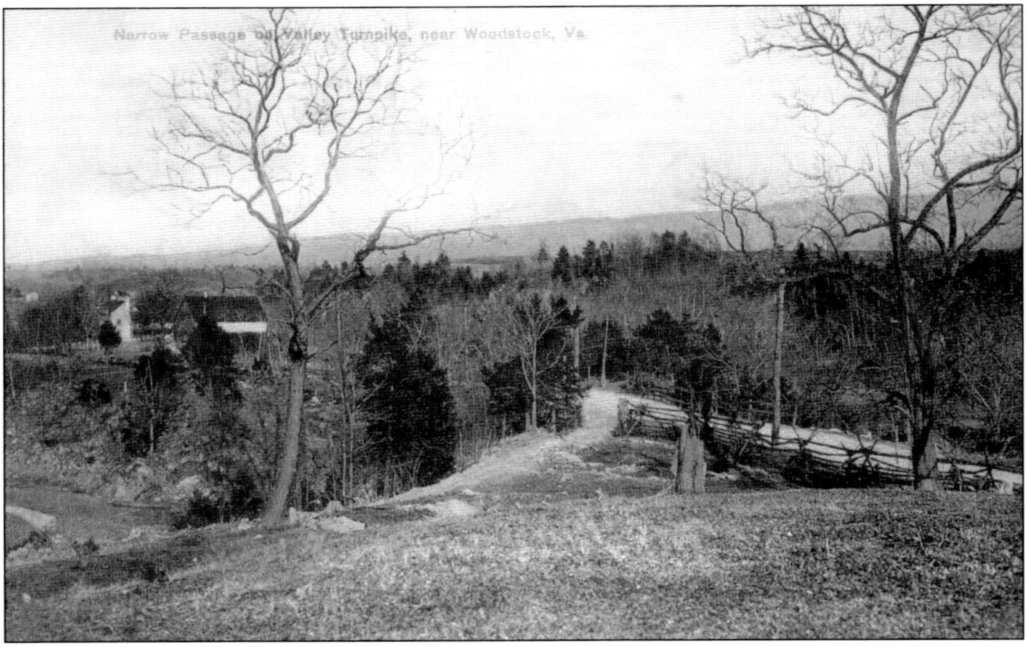

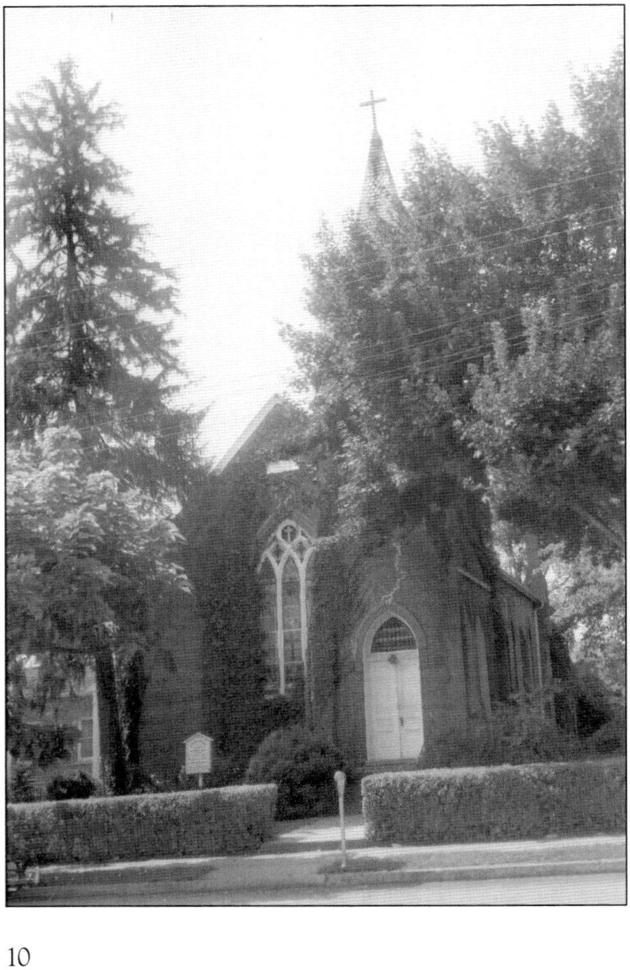

Narrow Passage on Valley Turnpike. Many of the settlers to Shenandoah County came because of religious intolerance in the Palatine region of Europe. Seeking to worship God according to their own conscience, they settled in Pennsylvania and then moved to this area. This view is near the center of Shenandoah County. The North Fork is close to the Valley Turnpike here, and travelers stopped at the Narrow Passage Inn. (SCL.)

Peter Muhlenberg's Church. At the center of Woodstock, the first church was one block behind the courthouse, but it disappeared by 1880 due to neglect after Muhlenberg's departure. Services were held in the stone courthouse until the new brick church could be built in Woodstock. Records for Shenandoah County are kept here. The first service was held at Emmanuel Church in 1882, and it was consecrated in 1883. (SCL.)

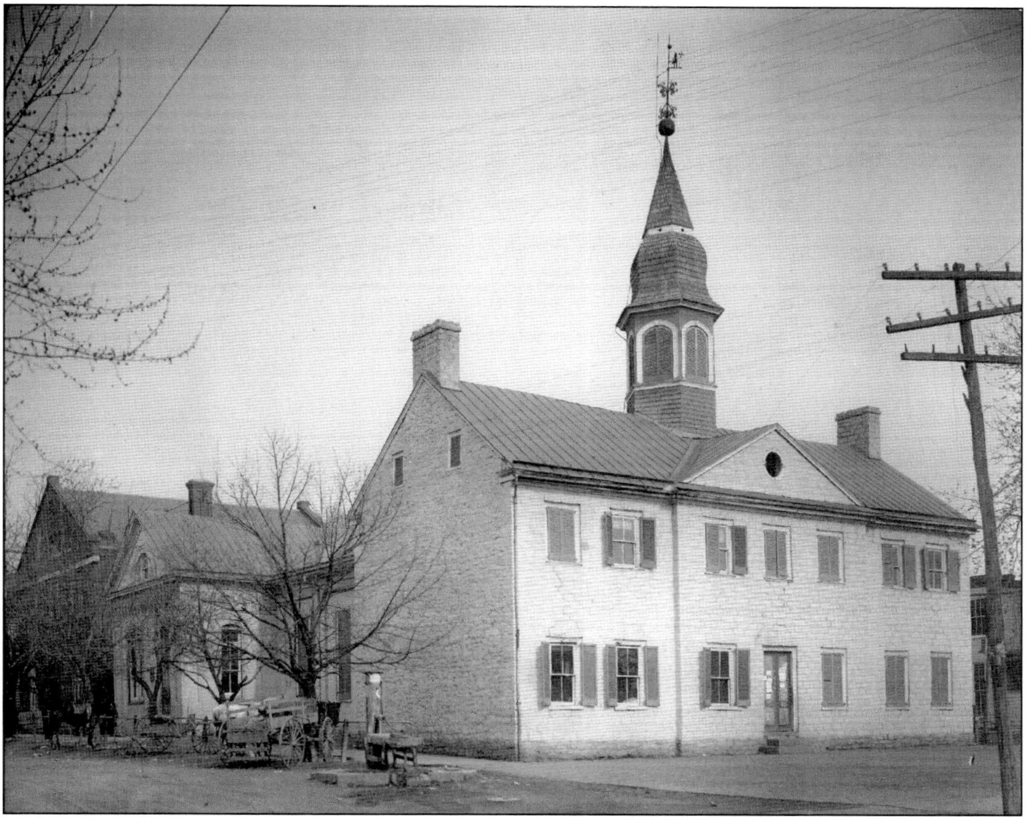

COURTHOUSE ON VALLEY TURNPIKE. The present courthouse, built in 1795, replaced one in use since 1774. It was enlarged in 1871 and again in 1886. A portico with four tall columns was added in 1927. The cupola with a weather vane and a Swiss Army Guard testify to the respect of the residents to their ancestors in Europe. The county's population increased from 13,836 in 1800 to 18,925 by 1820. (SCHS.)

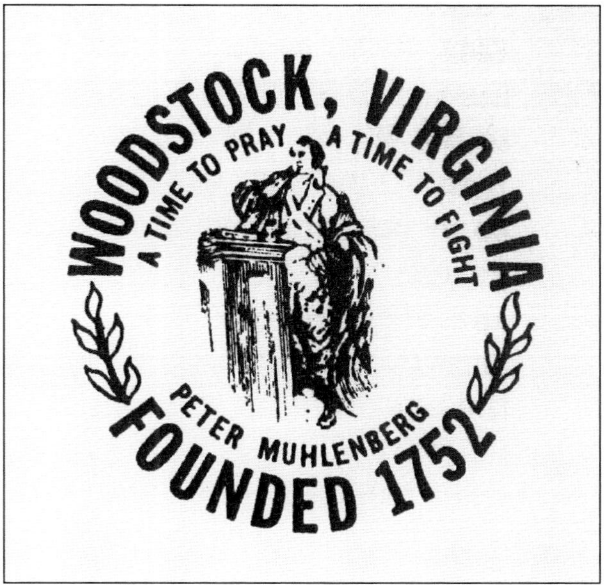

WOODSTOCK TOWN SEAL. In 1774, John Peter Gabriel Muhlenberg moderated a meeting that formed a resolution for independence. In Woodstock on January 23, 1776, he proclaimed at the end of a fiery sermon: "The time for war has come." The fighting parson was wearing the uniform of a Continental soldier under his clerical vestments. This image is part of the Woodstock Town Seal. (Courtesy of the Town of Woodstock.)

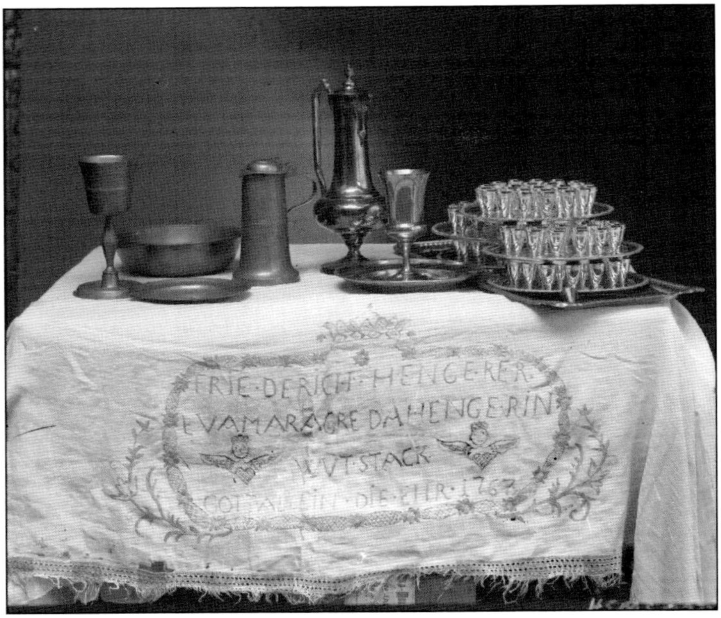

Glory and Praise to God. Woodstock Lutheran Church owns a cloth made in 1767, celebrating the wedding of German missionary couple Friedericht Hengerer and Eva Margagre Dahengerin. Similar designs are found on early local Fraktur. Research by Klaus Wust indicates the Stony Creek artist was Anna Christina Helzel Willy, wife of the first minister of this church. Peter Muhlenberg may have used the baptismal basin and communion vessels. (SCHS.)

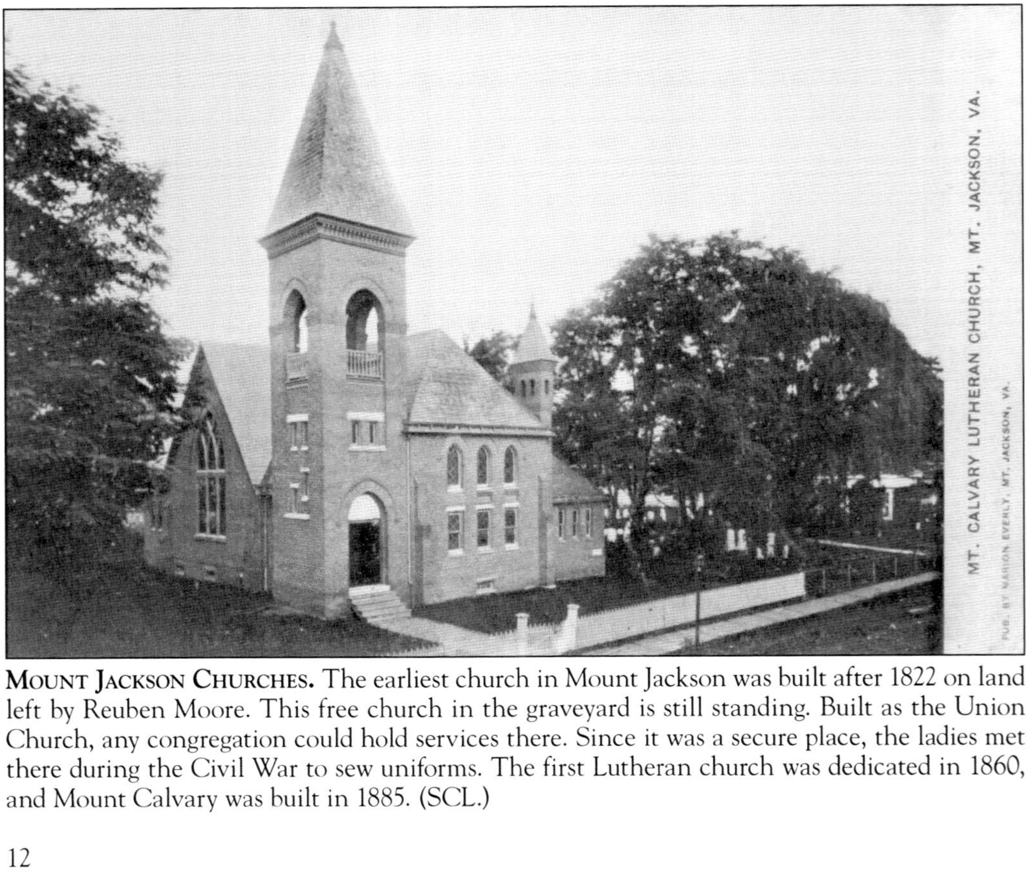

Mount Jackson Churches. The earliest church in Mount Jackson was built after 1822 on land left by Reuben Moore. This free church in the graveyard is still standing. Built as the Union Church, any congregation could hold services there. Since it was a secure place, the ladies met there during the Civil War to sew uniforms. The first Lutheran church was dedicated in 1860, and Mount Calvary was built in 1885. (SCL.)

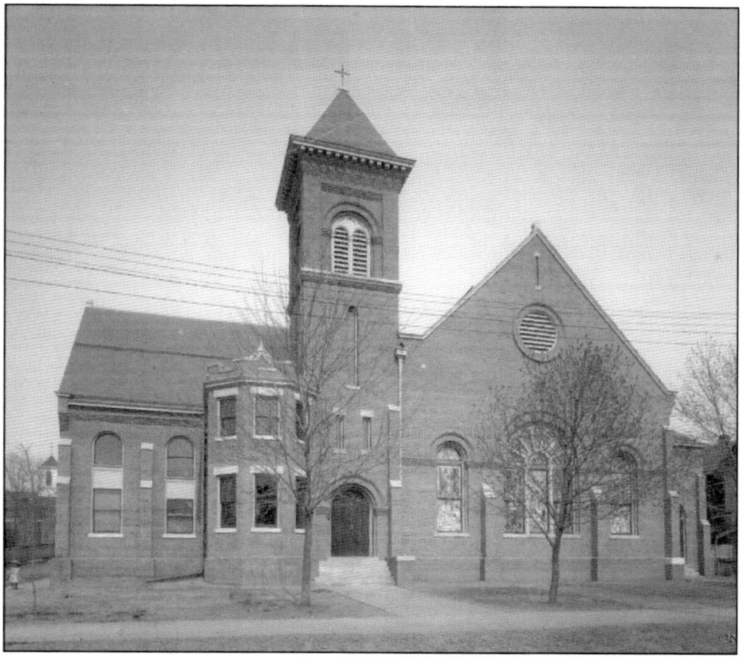

New Methodist Church in Woodstock. According to the journal of Francis Asbury, a Methodist bishop, he conducted services between 1790 and 1809, often in the Episcopal churches. This church is the fourth one built by the Methodists in Woodstock. The first one of logs was built in 1808. The second served from 1830 until 1858. The third church, on the corner of High and Commerce Streets, was built about 1905. (SCL.)

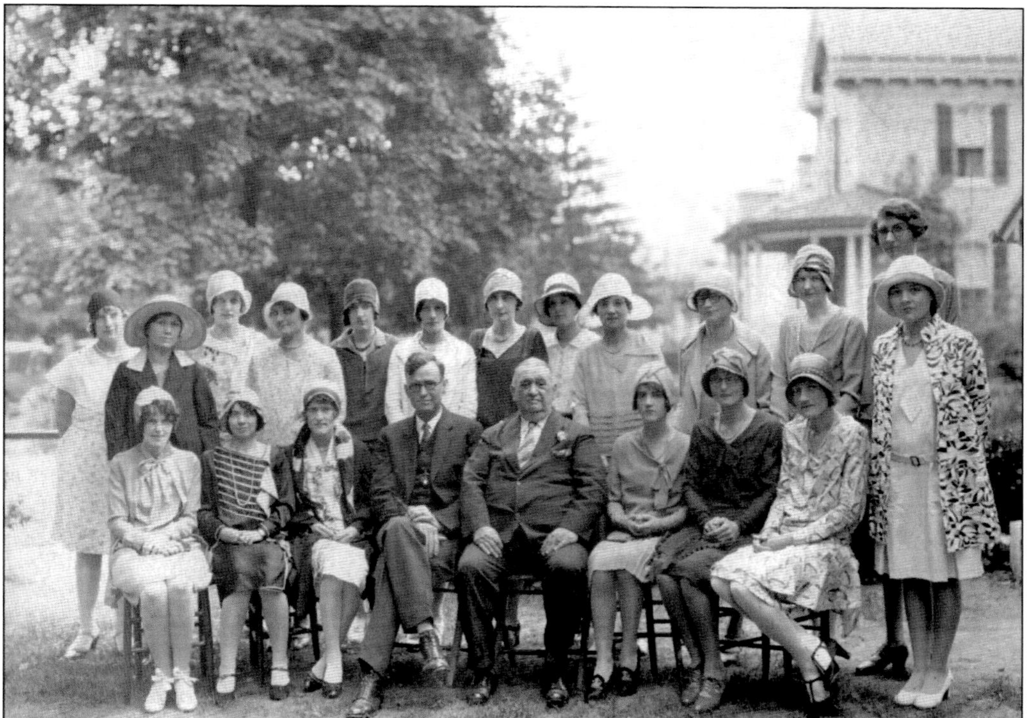

Methodist Ladies. Shown here in the 1920s, ladies from the Woodstock Methodist Church are shown with Rev. Scott Coffee, who is fourth from left on the first row, and Morgan Lauck Walton, who is fifth from left on the first row. Walton was a Virginia state senator from 1891 to 1895. Only two women in the back row are identified: Jesse Smoot and Ethel Johnson (the tall one with no hat). (Courtesy of Linda Dellinger Varney.)

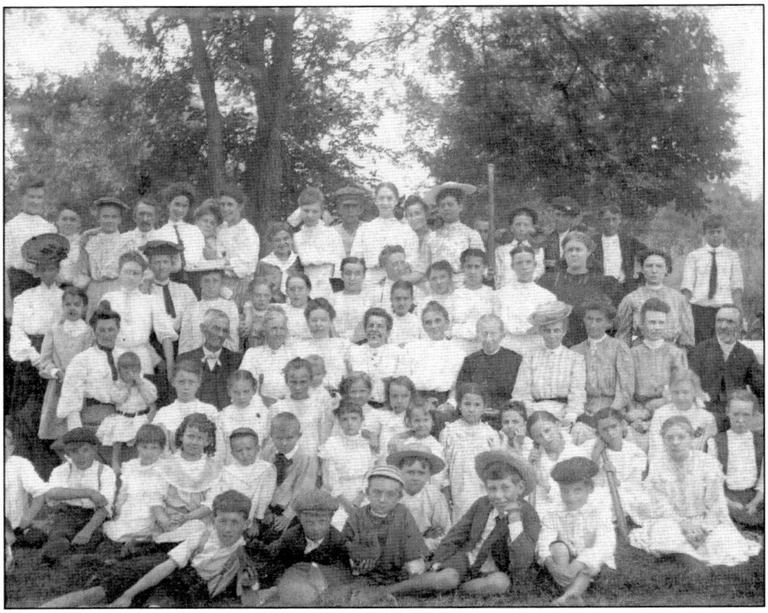

Reformed Church Picnic, 1904. A favorite day in summer is when the whole congregation gets together for an outdoor picnic. This group from the Reformed Church met at Amelia Coffman's home to eat, pray, and play ball together. Some seem unhappy to have the game delayed while the photographer captures the image of all 67 people, young and old alike. None are identified. (SCL.)

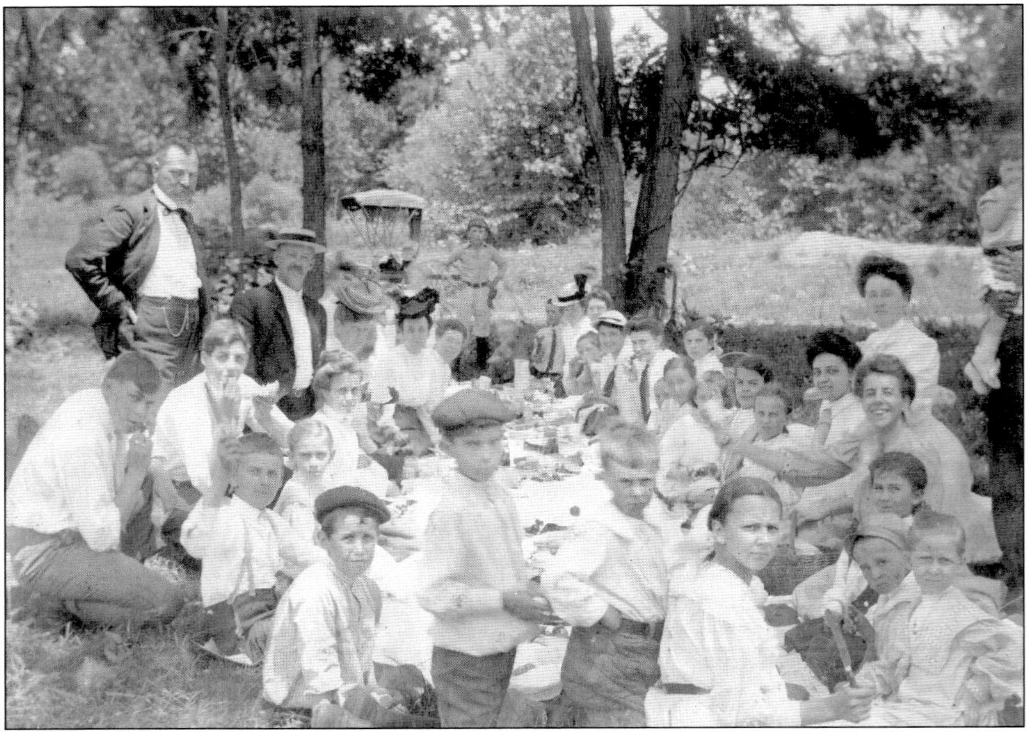

Methodist Church Picnic, 1906. The July 4, 1906, picnic was held on Mrs. Leeding's lot at the ice pond. The photographer is being offered some bread and fried chicken. In 1906, the school year was increased from five to between six and eight months; the opening and closing dates varied from year to year. The baby at top right is labeled "Jeannette"; the others are not identified. (SCL.)

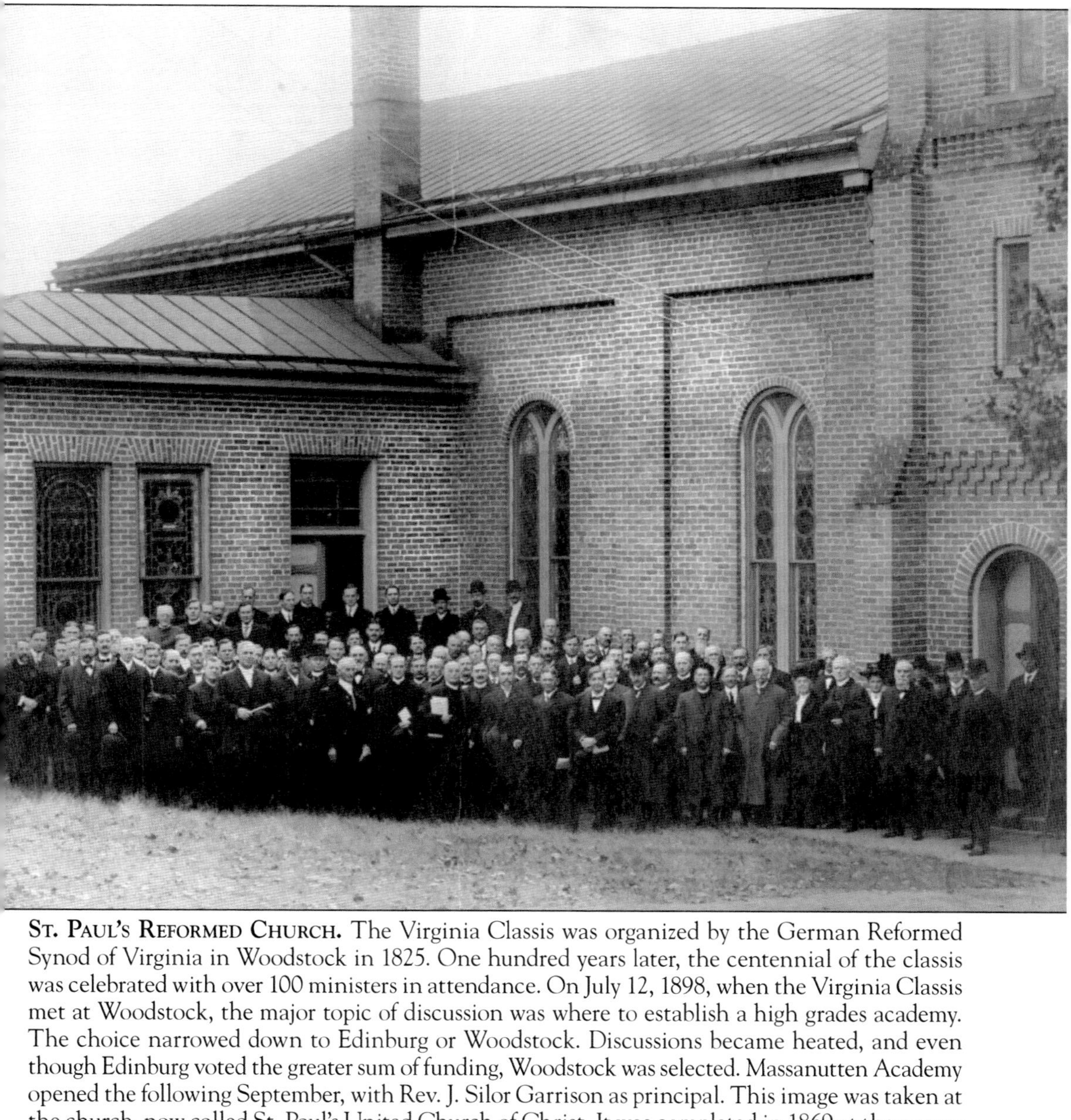

St. Paul's Reformed Church. The Virginia Classis was organized by the German Reformed Synod of Virginia in Woodstock in 1825. One hundred years later, the centennial of the classis was celebrated with over 100 ministers in attendance. On July 12, 1898, when the Virginia Classis met at Woodstock, the major topic of discussion was where to establish a high grades academy. The choice narrowed down to Edinburg or Woodstock. Discussions became heated, and even though Edinburg voted the greater sum of funding, Woodstock was selected. Massanutten Academy opened the following September, with Rev. J. Silor Garrison as principal. This image was taken at the church, now called St. Paul's United Church of Christ. It was completed in 1869 at the corner of South Main and Spring Streets in Woodstock. At the 1925 centennial gathering, tribute was paid to early ministers, including its first, Bernard F. Willy. (SCL.)

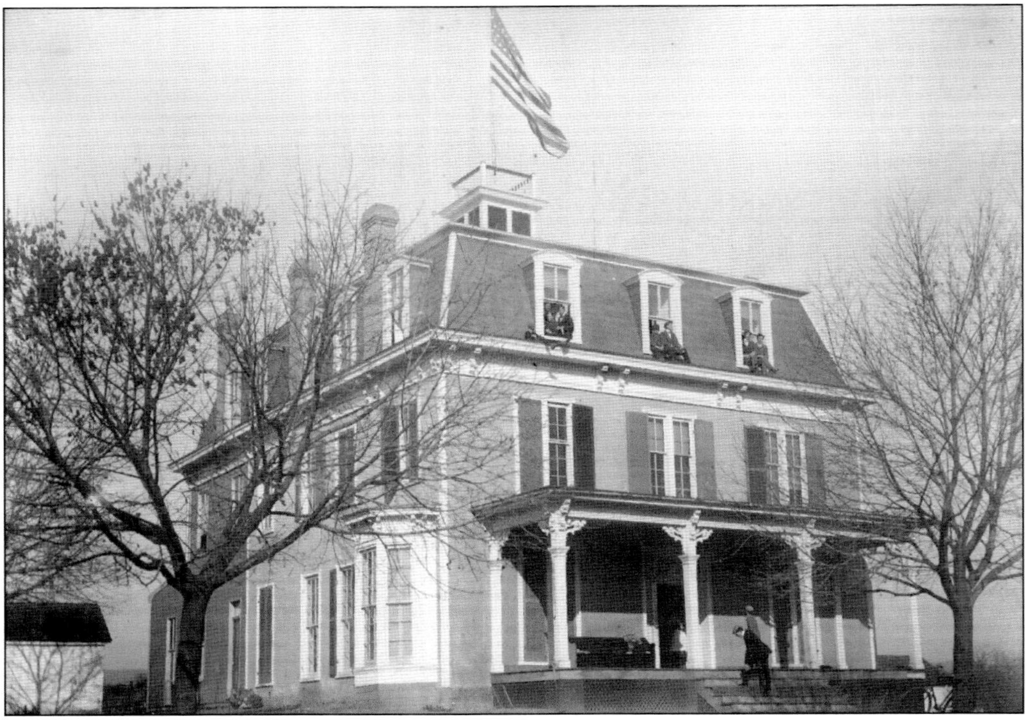

ROY FRAVEL'S SCHOOL AND THE MASSANUTTEN MILITARY ACADEMY. The former home of U.S. senator H. H. Riddleberger sits on a hill on the west side of Main Street in Woodstock. The Reformed Church in America established the academy in 1899 to foster Christian education and prepare boys and girls for college or technical schools. Military training was added during World War I. On the back of the card above, Roy Fravel wrote, "This is the school I go to this season." Printed in July 1899's *Parish Register*, "The addition and third story gives it a more massive and imposing appearance . . . we are greatly encouraged by the present condition on things." The central building in the image below was named in honor of William C. Lantz, a teacher in the Shenandoah County public schools. Riddleberger Hall is on the extreme right. (Above, SCL; below, SCHS.)

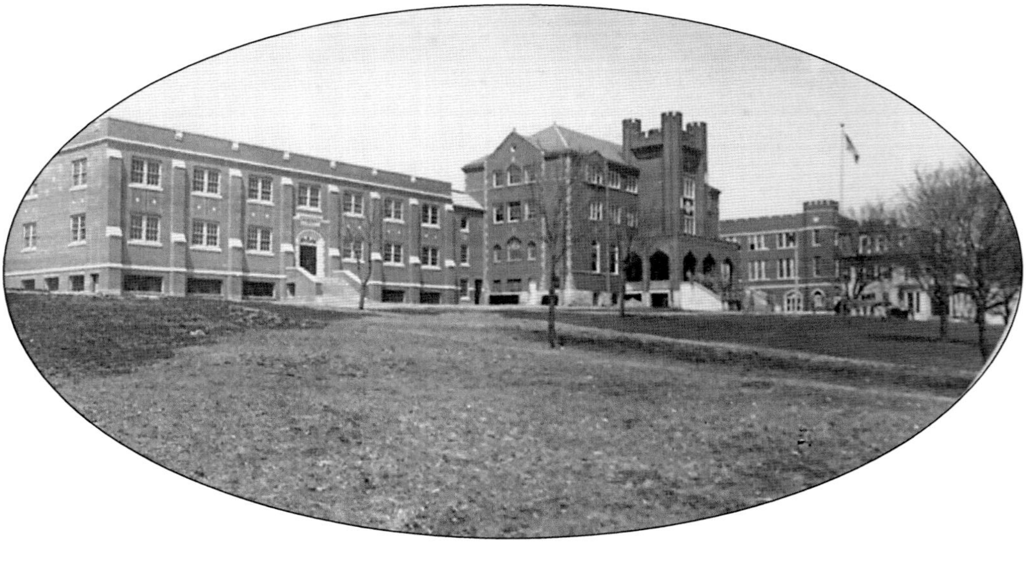

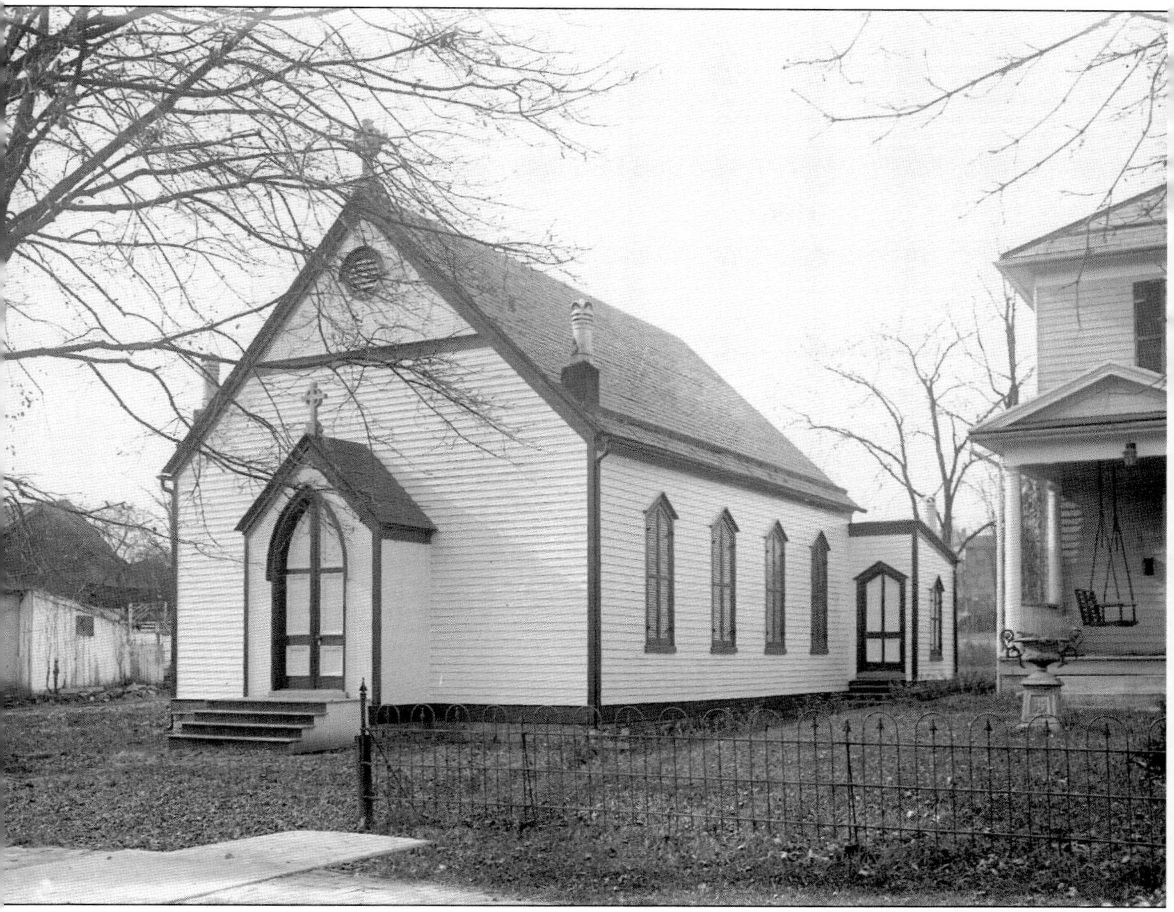

The Only Catholic Church. Built around 1880 in Woodstock, St. John Bosco Church at the corner of Main and Foundry had a cross surmounting its roof peak but no steeple. With its entry of double wooden doors, it made a clear impression of simplicity among the large brick churches built in the county in the second half of the 19th century. On the right is the home of photographer and Mayor Hugh Morrison Jr. and his family. Both the house and church still stand, although they serve different functions for St. John Bosco's parishioners. A new church was built in 1973 on the other side of the mayor's house. Today there are over 500 registered Catholic families in the county, and a mission church at Bryce serves residents of the western part of the county. (SCL.)

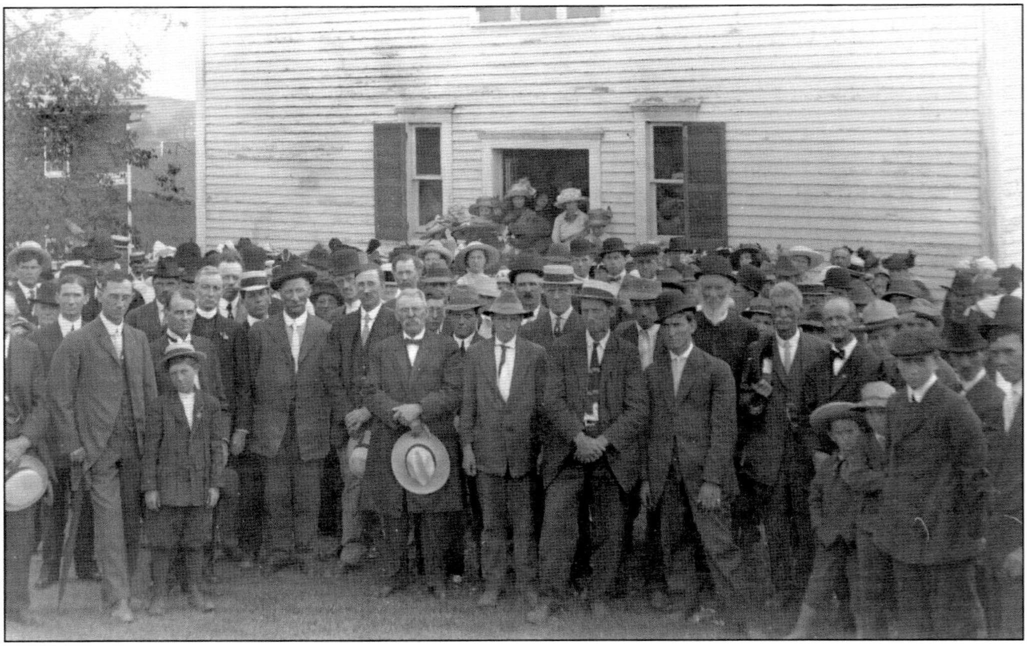

FORESTVILLE LUTHERAN CHURCH AND LADIES. On these postcards from about 1909 are faces of over 200 members of the Lutheran church in Forestville, the social and spiritual center for the town. The church is located at the intersection of South Middle and Quicksburg Roads. In the above image, the ladies are in the back, and most are not visible. They are seen in the image below, taken on the porch at the Nathaniel Samuel Foltz home. The lady with the *x* on her shoulder is Jerelene Estep Foltz. The three ladies in front of her may be her daughters Mollie, Carrie, and Nora, one of whom holds an infant. The other women of the Ladies Aid Society and baby are not identified. These photographs by Mr. Ankrum are from the Estep/Foltz collection. (SCL.)

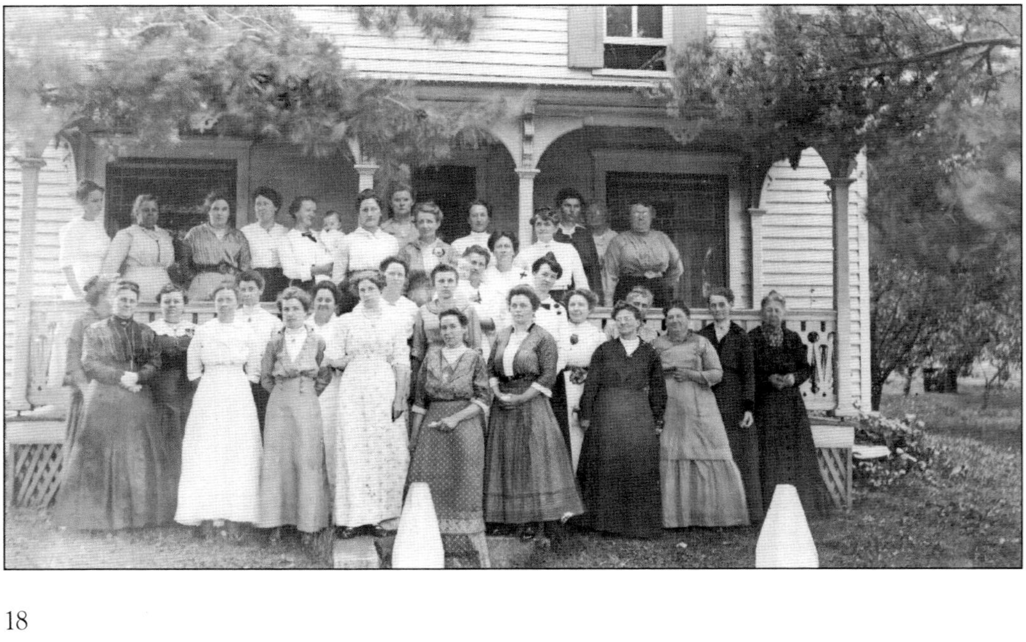

Two

A String of Pearls

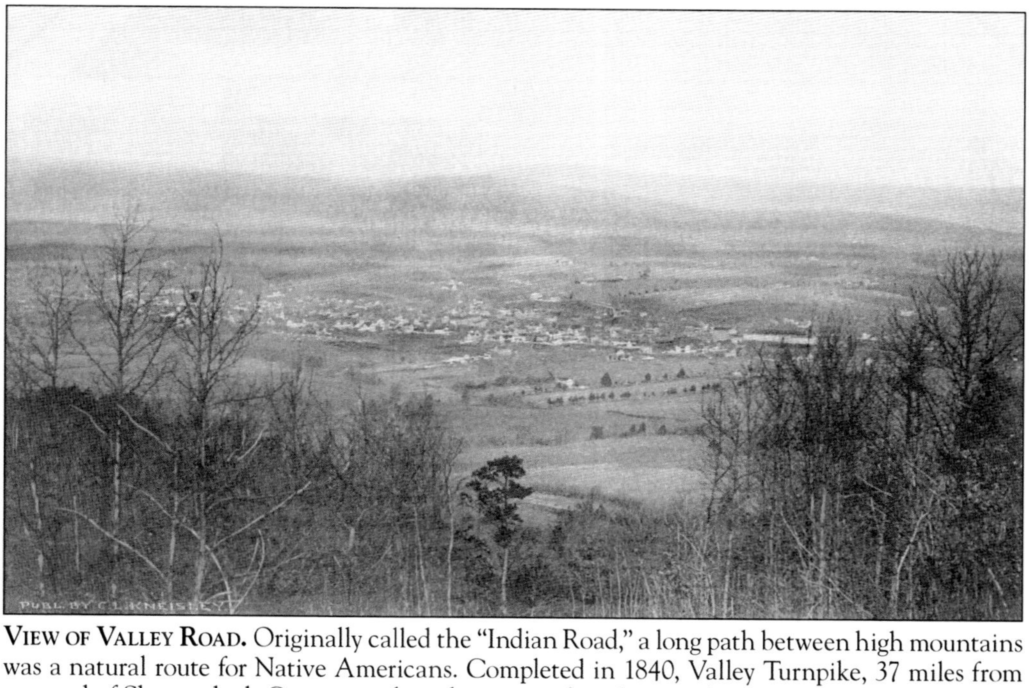

View of Valley Road. Originally called the "Indian Road," a long path between high mountains was a natural route for Native Americans. Completed in 1840, Valley Turnpike, 37 miles from one end of Shenandoah County to the other, was referred to as "the Great Road" by the 1850s. Crossroad towns, places of refreshment every 6 to 8 miles, led to the line of villages being referred to as "a string of pearls." (ML.)

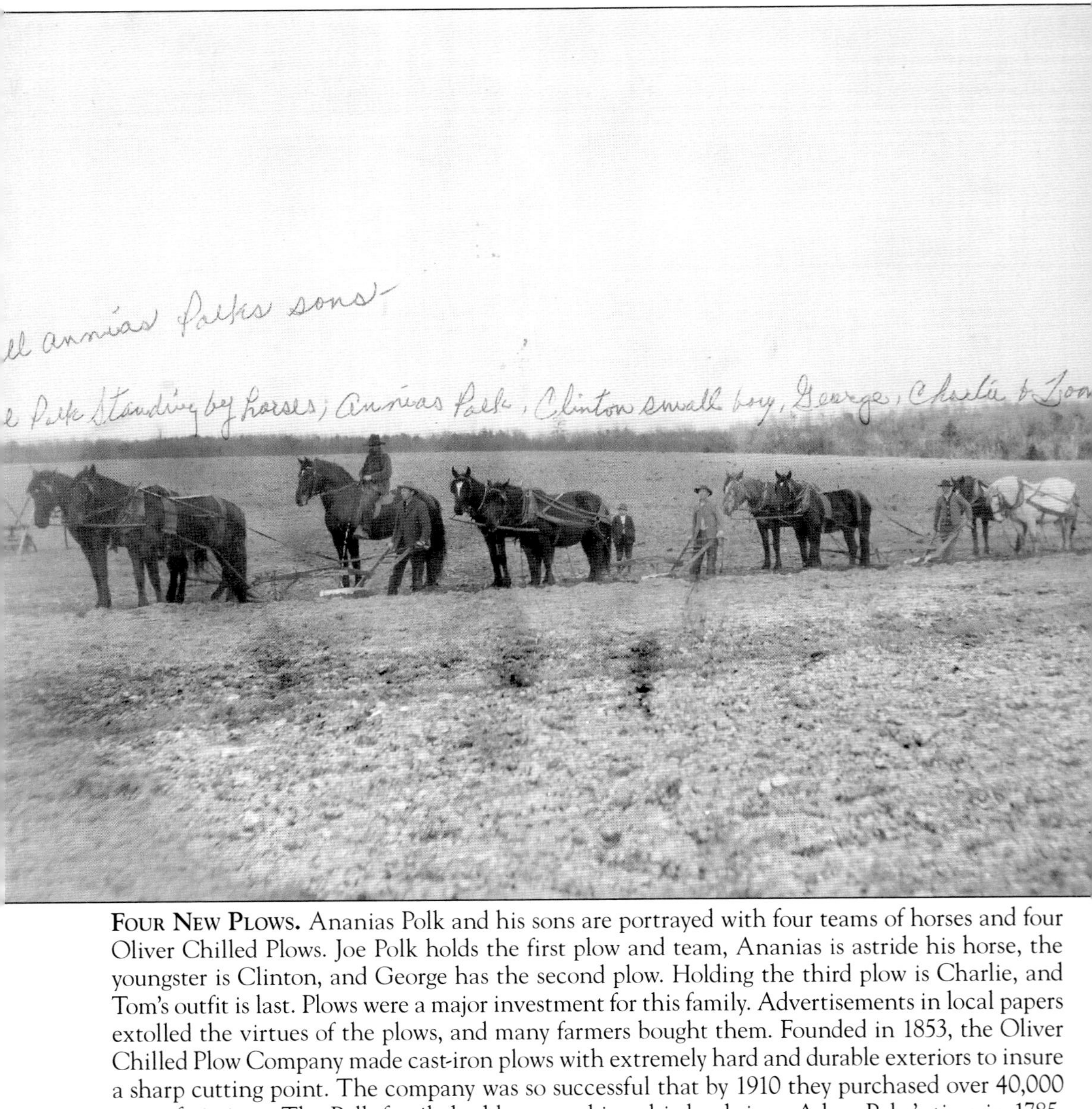

Four New Plows. Ananias Polk and his sons are portrayed with four teams of horses and four Oliver Chilled Plows. Joe Polk holds the first plow and team, Ananias is astride his horse, the youngster is Clinton, and George has the second plow. Holding the third plow is Charlie, and Tom's outfit is last. Plows were a major investment for this family. Advertisements in local papers extolled the virtues of the plows, and many farmers bought them. Founded in 1853, the Oliver Chilled Plow Company made cast-iron plows with extremely hard and durable exteriors to insure a sharp cutting point. The company was so successful that by 1910 they purchased over 40,000 tons of pig iron. The Polk family had been working this land since Adam Poke's time in 1785, when his name was on Jacob Rinker's list. Rinker had helped settlers come to this area, and his list included families who were living in adjacent sections near his home at Cabin Hill (similar to an early census). (MP.)

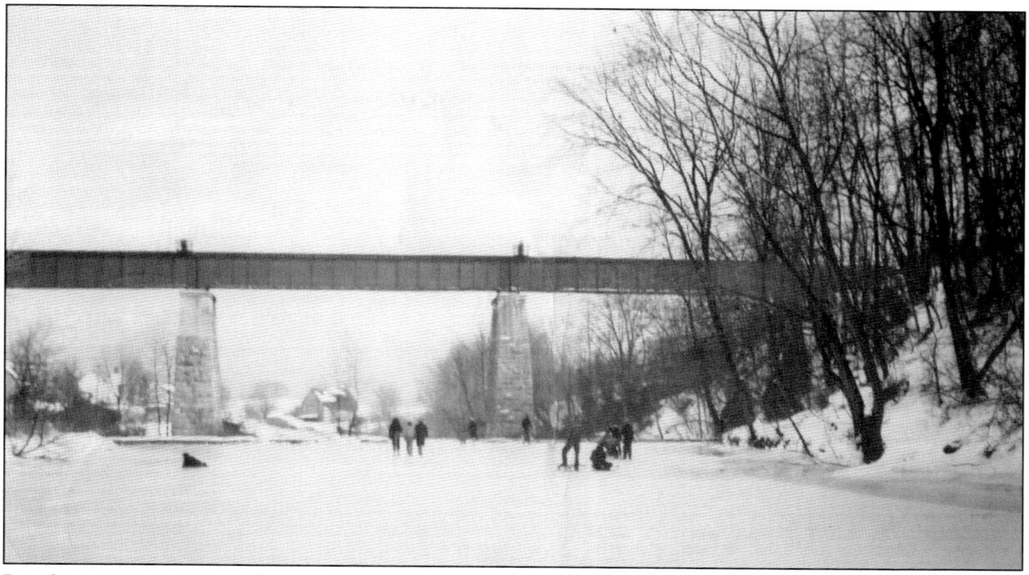

ICE SKATING AT MILL CREEK. The elevated railroad bridge frames Mount Jackson Mill around 1940. Each village along Route 11 had at least one mill on the creek, and this one existed as early as 1746. This village was called Mount Pleasant until 1826. Mount Jackson, terminal point of the railroad during the Civil War, shipped out grain and agricultural products from the surrounding farmlands. In 1922, this railroad bridge burned. (PPS.)

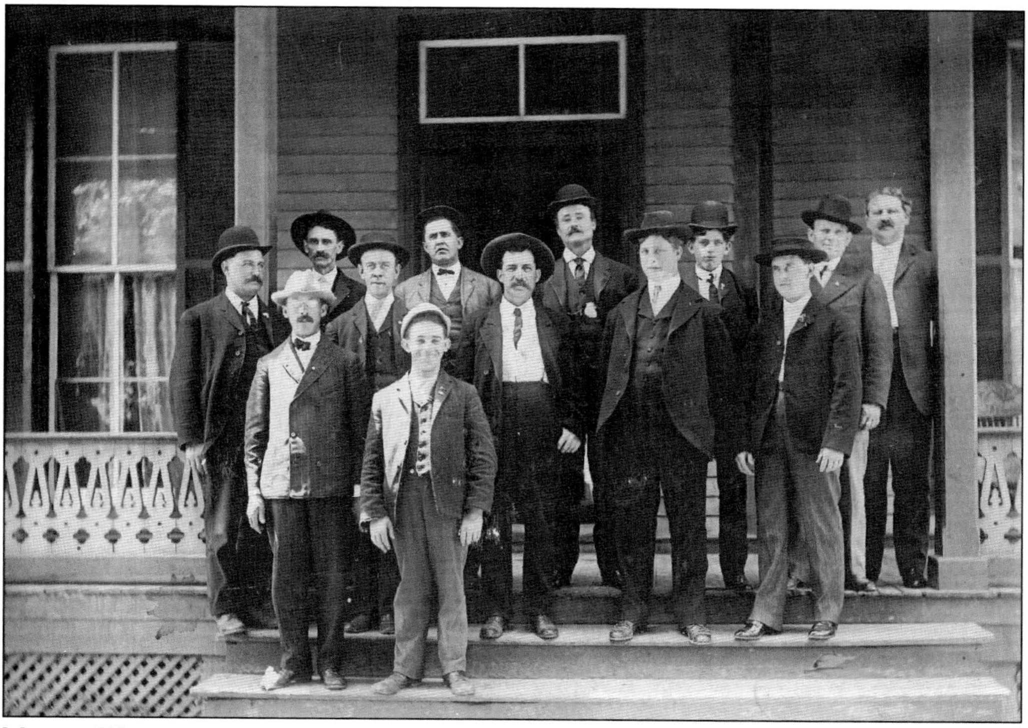

MODERN WOODMEN OF THE WORLD. On the steps of the Mount Jackson Hotel around 1900 from left to right are (first row) O. B. Windle and Harry Ortt; (second row) Jim Hottle, Russell Rosenberger, unidentified, Burt E. Sigler, and Sam Smoot; (third row) Charles E. Phillip, unidentified, C. D. Ward, Charles E. Foltz, Ray Newland, and unidentified. (PPS.)

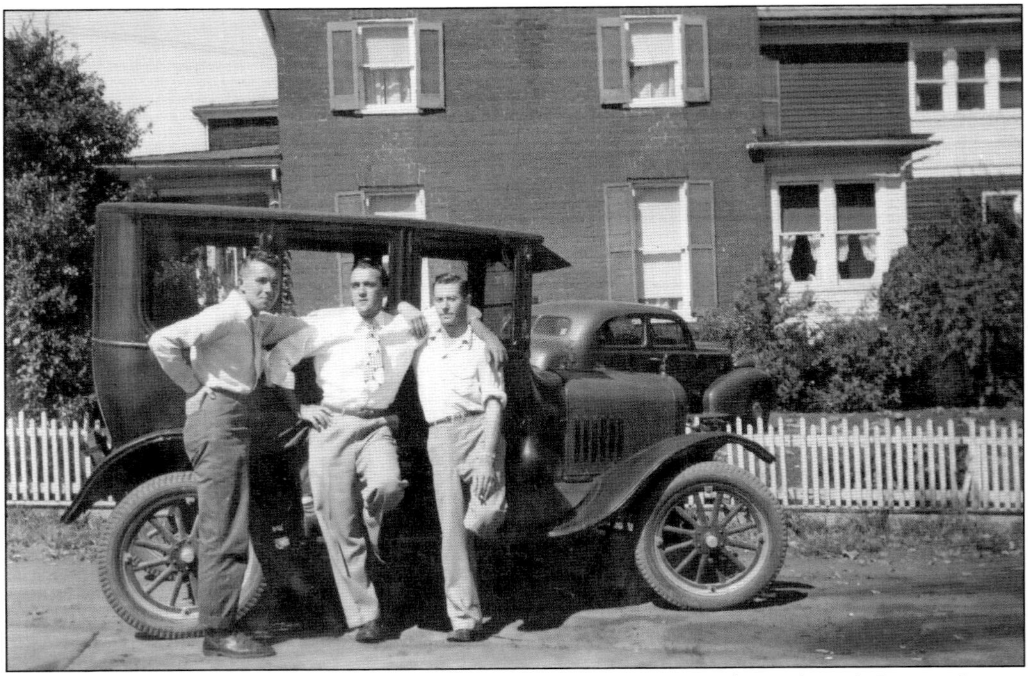

Moore/Hackley House in the Summer. Pictured in Mount Jackson from left to right are Fred O. Middleton, son of William W. Middleton; Elmer "Brownie" Jenkins; and Jesse Smoot Jr. Smoot's car is parked next to the Moore/Hackley house beside Charles H. Phillip's Sunoco station. Large houses like this were used for medical purposes during the Civil War when this town was surrounded with hospital camps. Behind this house were the slave quarters. (PPS.)

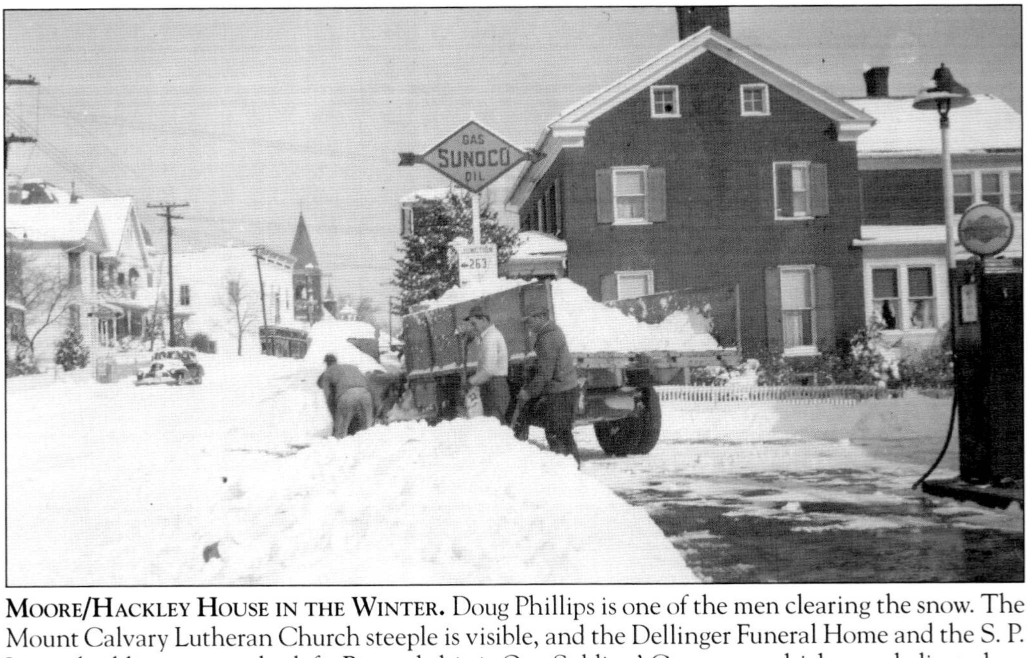

Moore/Hackley House in the Winter. Doug Phillips is one of the men clearing the snow. The Mount Calvary Lutheran Church steeple is visible, and the Dellinger Funeral Home and the S. P. Lonas building are on the left. Beyond this is Our Soldiers' Cemetery, which was dedicated on May 10, 1866. The 1866 Memorial and Decoration Day, arranged by the local ladies, was one of the first such observances in the South. (PPS.)

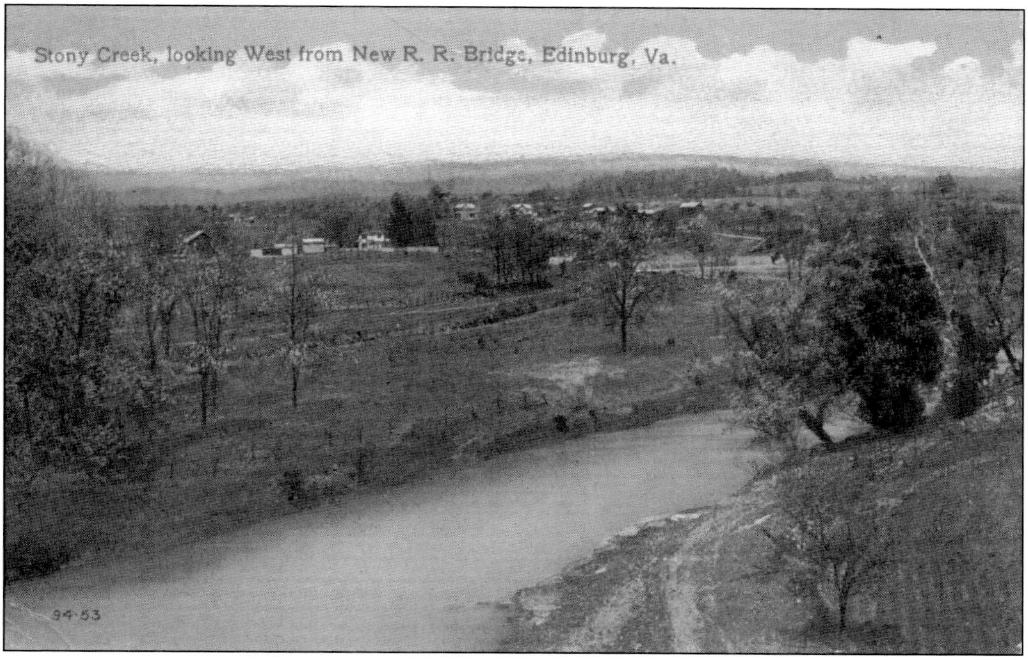

STONY CREEK LOOKING WEST. Shyrock was the early name of the settlement where Stony Creek meets the Shenandoah River. A beautiful garden place, its name changed to Edinburg in 1852. The railroad came through by 1859 after the bridge over Stony Creek was completed. Most of the county's ironworks shipped from Edinburg. The photographer for this image was standing on the railroad bridge, which burned in 1915. (SCL.)

PATSY CLINE'S HOUSE. Virginia "Ginny" Patterson Hensley, later known as Patsy Cline, was born in 1932 and lived here as a teenager. After rheumatic fever at age 13, she had a booming voice. She attended Edinburg High School and sang in the Methodist church choir. The suspension bridge is no longer there. This horse and carriage is crossing Stony Creek before it curves right towards the foundation for the mill. The popular Creekside Campground is here. (SCL.)

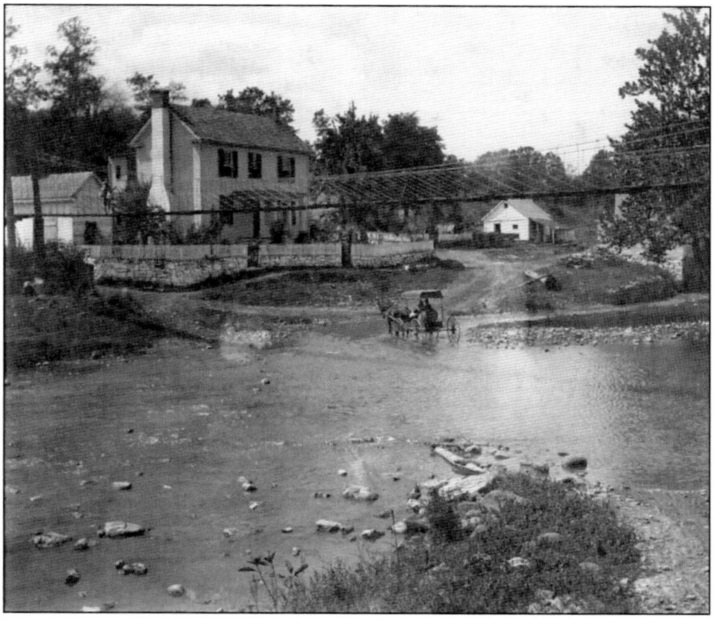

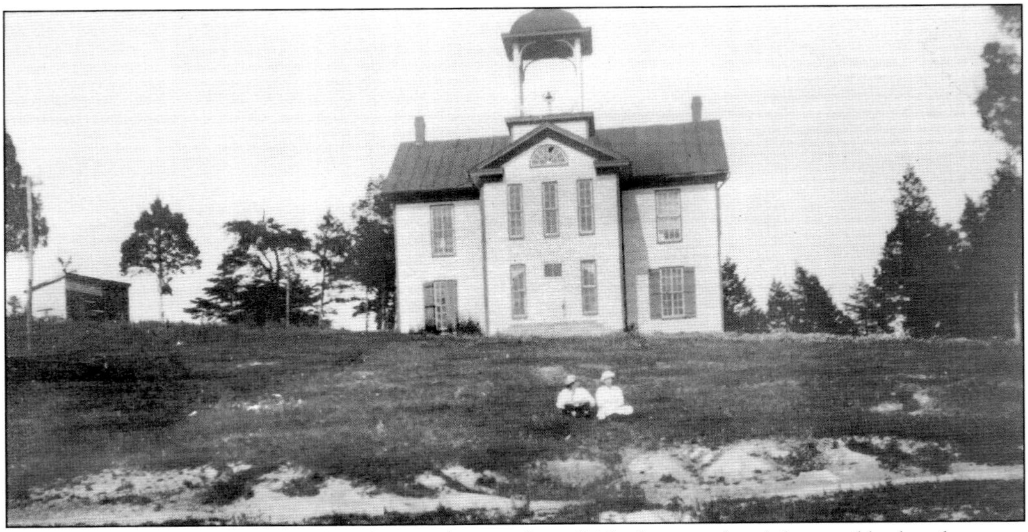

SCHOOL ON THE HILL. Located at the northeast edge of Edinburg on land donated by local tanner Joseph Comer, the Edinburg Graded School, often called Cedar Hill Academy, was built in 1896. One large room, complete with a stage, was on the second floor. The school was at the top of a hill and up a long flight of stairs. To get there on icy days, students would go to the railroad tracks on Stoney Creek Boulevard and walk along the tracks to avoid the steps. The building served for 57 years and was demolished in 1936. (SCL.)

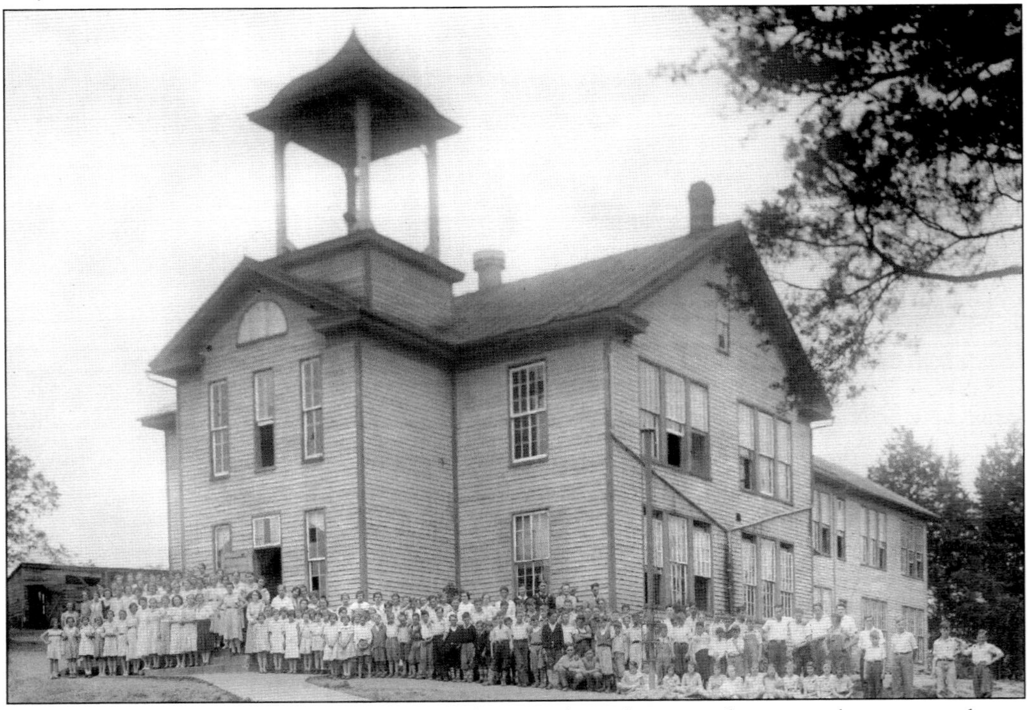

THE LAST DAY OF SCHOOL. All of the students and teachers are shown in the picture above, taken on the last day of school in 1933. To the right is the addition, which accommodated a growing number of students. Classes were also held in other buildings in town. In 1933, teacher salaries were between $25 and $35 a month; principal William Miller, who also taught, was paid $40.28. (SCL.)

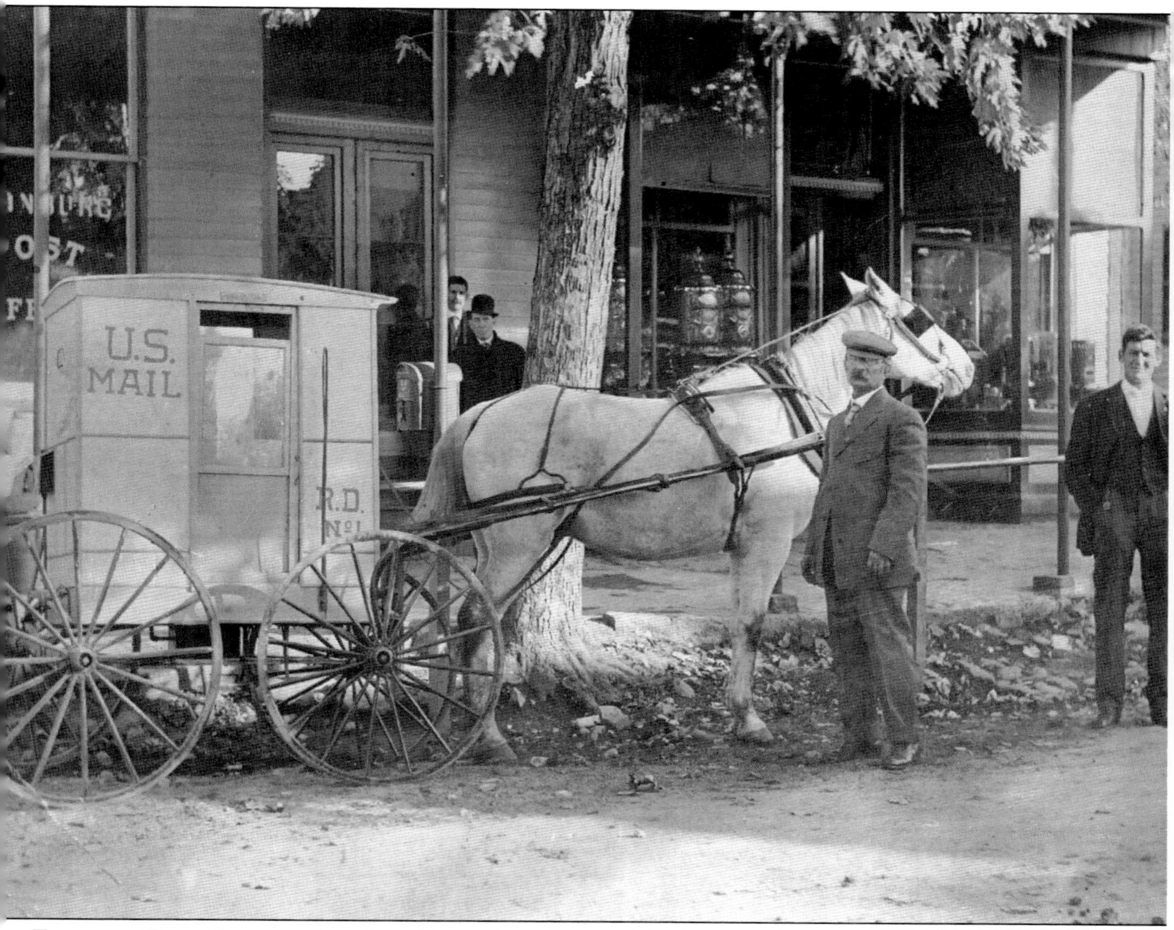

EDINBURG POST OFFICE. All of the villages along Route 11 had a post office at one time. Theodore "Tege" Jennings was the first U.S. postal clerk to deliver mail to the farmers in Edinburg. Until 1902, everyone had to come to the post office to collect or send their mail. John Coffman, in front of the horse, was postmaster. The two men near the doorway are Ottie Race (back) with John "Toad" Painter (front). The rural free delivery route went from Edinburg to Columbia Furnace and came back through Readus and Green Hill. In 1915, Eugene Dellinger purchased a new Ford to enable him to deliver mail in Mount Jackson several hours faster and return in time to meet the Southern Railway and Baltimore and Ohio Railroad westbound train. Edinburg's current post office was dedicated in 1959. (Courtesy of Walter "Butch" Hisey from the Eddie Hisey collection.)

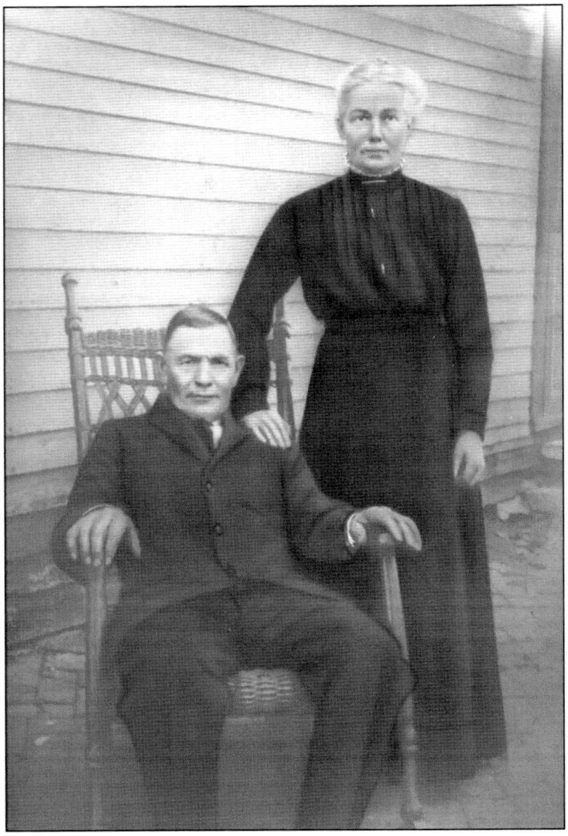

Couple with Rocker at the Grandstaff-Stoneburner House. Charles Lee and Laura Virginia Stoneburner bought the Grandstaff's house after they had been married many years. It is possibly the oldest house in town and is log under the clapboards. George Grandstaff built this house sometime after 1765, when he married Magdalina Hough. The year "1783" is carved into a log beam in the dining room. The Stoneburners raised here three daughters, Laura, Ada, and Alma, and four sons, Ed, Will, Russell, and Lee, who all became millers. Charles and Laura and one daughter are seen in the front yard of this house. As a young man, Charles helped build the railroad through the valley and became a master mason. Gary and Ann Laing bought the house and began restoration work in 1988. Gary passed away in 2007, but Ann continues to spend time here with family members. (AL.)

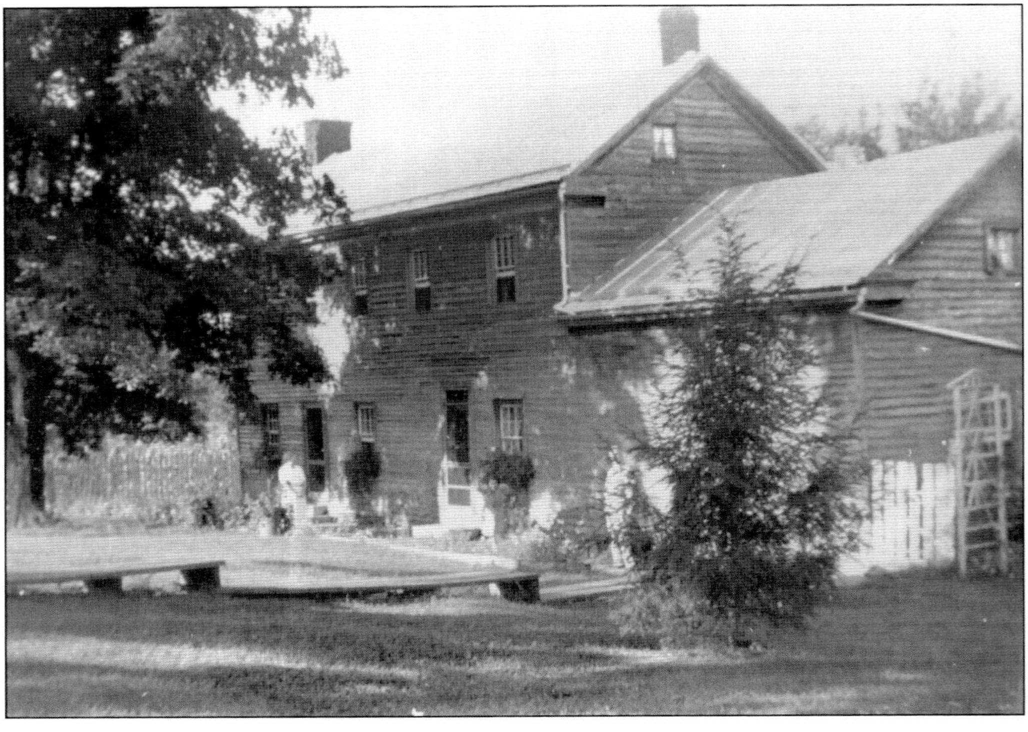

Lois Evans with Doll and Teddy. Lois Evans was born in 1897, the only child of Lemuel Clifton and Laura Grabill Evans. The only barber in town, Lemuel built his family "Westover," a beautiful home in Edinburg. Charles Lee Stoneburner did the work here.

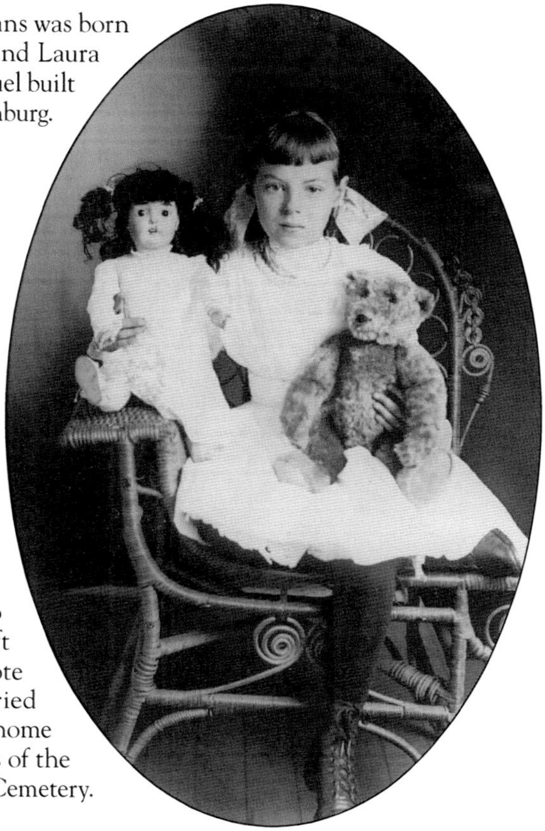

Camp Fire Girls. Laura Grabill Evans was the organizer and sponsor of the Edinburg Camp Fire Girls, a group in which Lois Evans and her friends participated. Known as Li-Su-Lo Camp Fire Girls, it stood for "life, sunshine and love." The girls camped out, hiked, and learned nature lore and handcrafts. They also did service projects and raised funds for thrift stamps and liberty bonds. Lois's mother wrote a campfire song for her 22 girls. Lois married William Ebberly Marks, and they made their home at Westover. They were both active members of the Union Church and are buried in Cedarwood Cemetery. (Both SCL.)

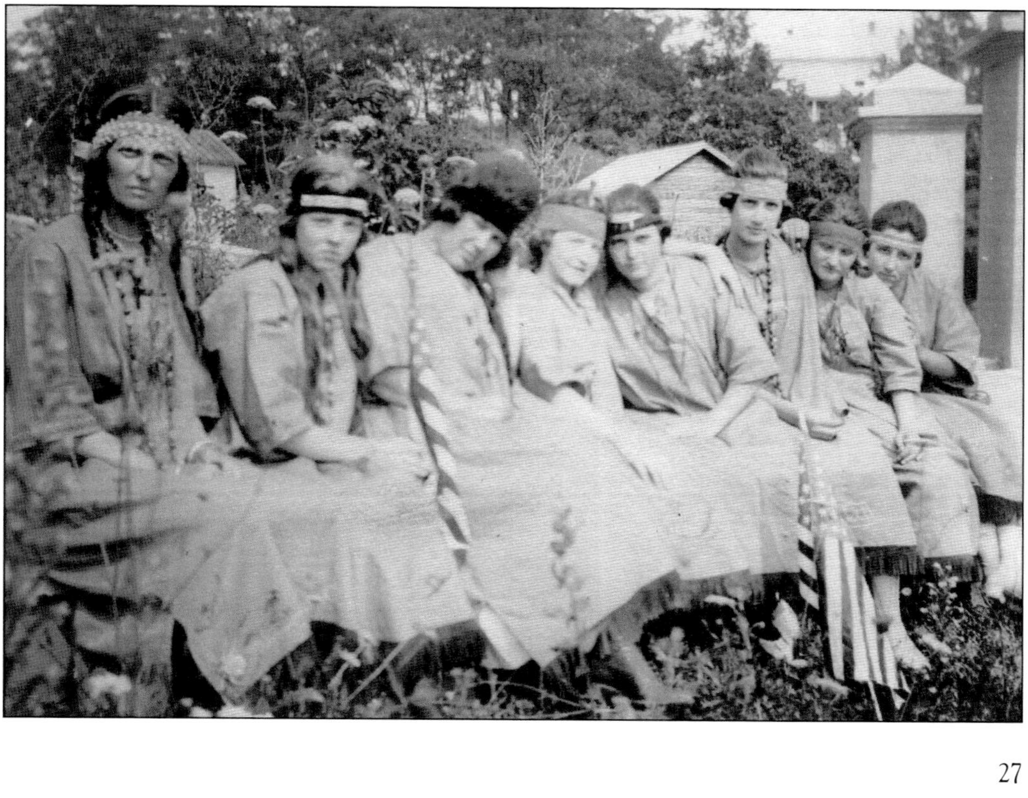

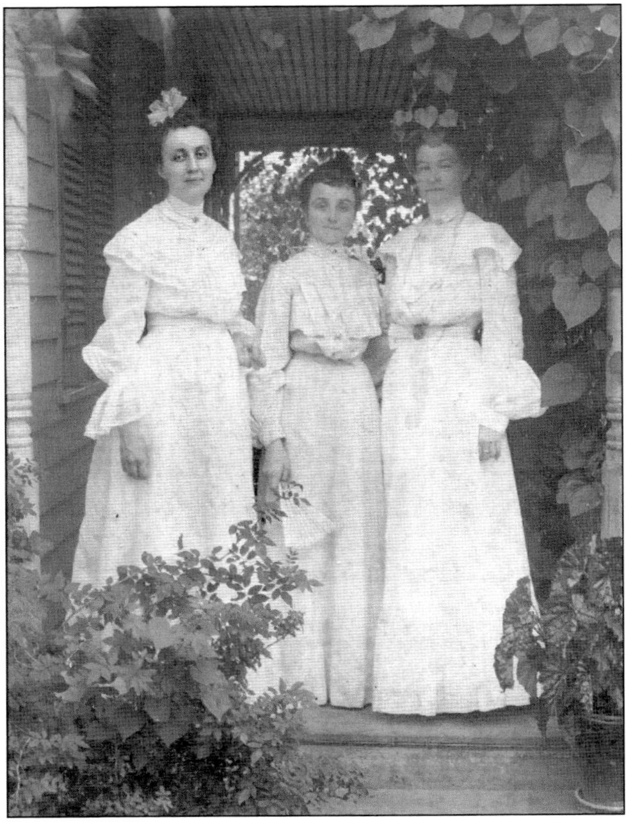

Edith Miller. With two friends on her Main Street front porch, Edith Miller (on the left and below) could keep an eye on everyone who went by. Lot number one in Edinburg, now 207 South Main Street, is next to the bridge. The Vincent family built the house around 1835. Edith, the daughter of George M. and Fannee Vincent Miller, may have been born here. She never married and was a very successful mantua maker in Maggie Hisey's shop. Edith opened her own shop on Picadilly Street, where she sold ladies' wear and fashion hats and hair ornaments. She also taught Sunday school classes at St. John's Methodist Church for more than 60 years. The small yard seen in front of the foundation of her vine-covered porch was lost in 1933 when sidewalks were put in and the Valley Turnpike was widened. (SCL.)

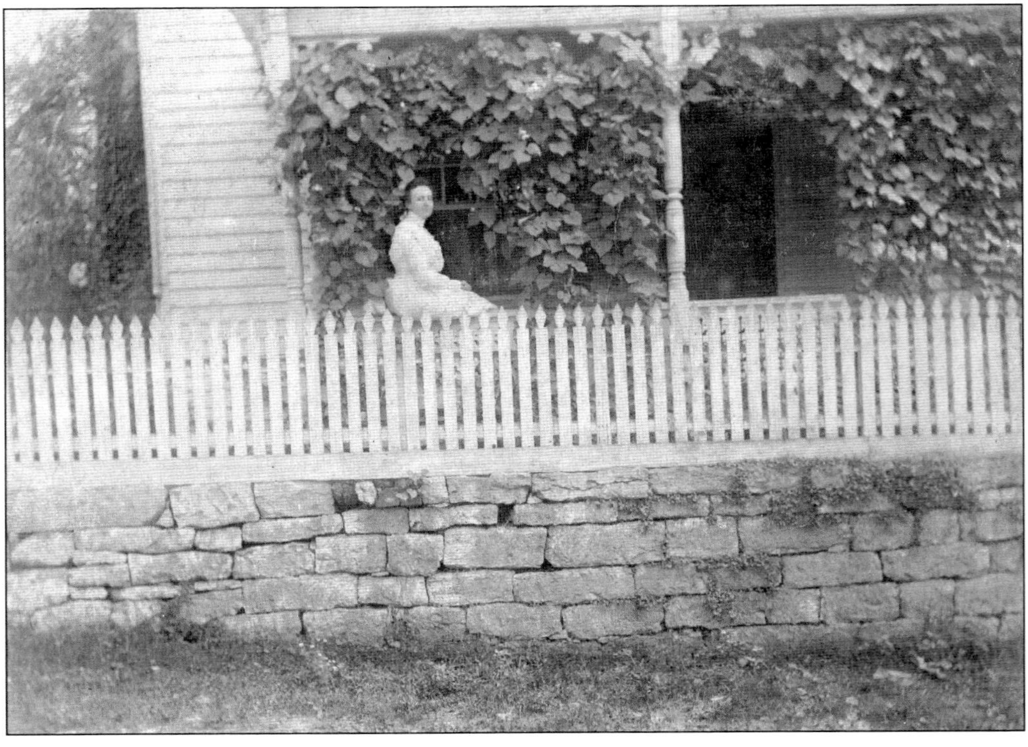

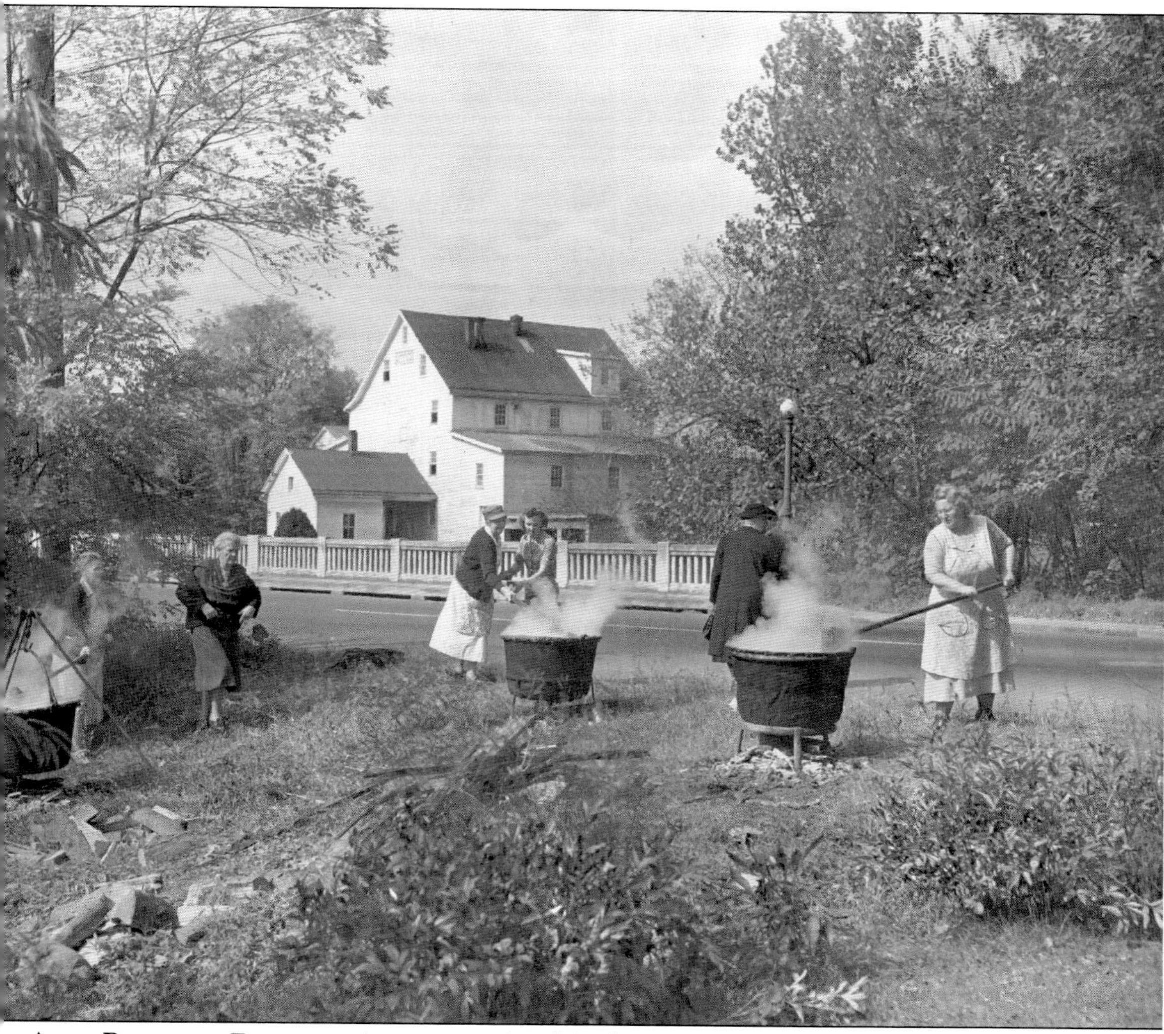

Apple Boiling in Edinburg. A major social and fund-raising event of the fall in Shenandoah County is apple boiling. Each church or family has their own recipe. Apple butter is made from apples, sugar, and spices. The hard work begins in the weeks and days before boiling. In this photograph, three copper kettles have boiling snitzed apples being stirred with paddles. Most of the women have on aprons to cover their dresses and protect them from the hot, sticky mush and the soot and ashes from the wood fire. The kettles each have three or four copper pennies at the bottom. This photograph was taken in Edinburg in Edith Miller's side yard on Stony Creek in 1940. She is the one wearing the long coat and hat with her back to the camera. The other ladies from left to right are unidentified, Alma Stoneburner Lamp, unidentified, Arline Davis, and Ada Stoneburner McNeer. The Edinburg Mill, seen here, escaped burning during the Civil War. The concrete bridge, built in 1933, washed away and was rebuilt in 1944. (AL.)

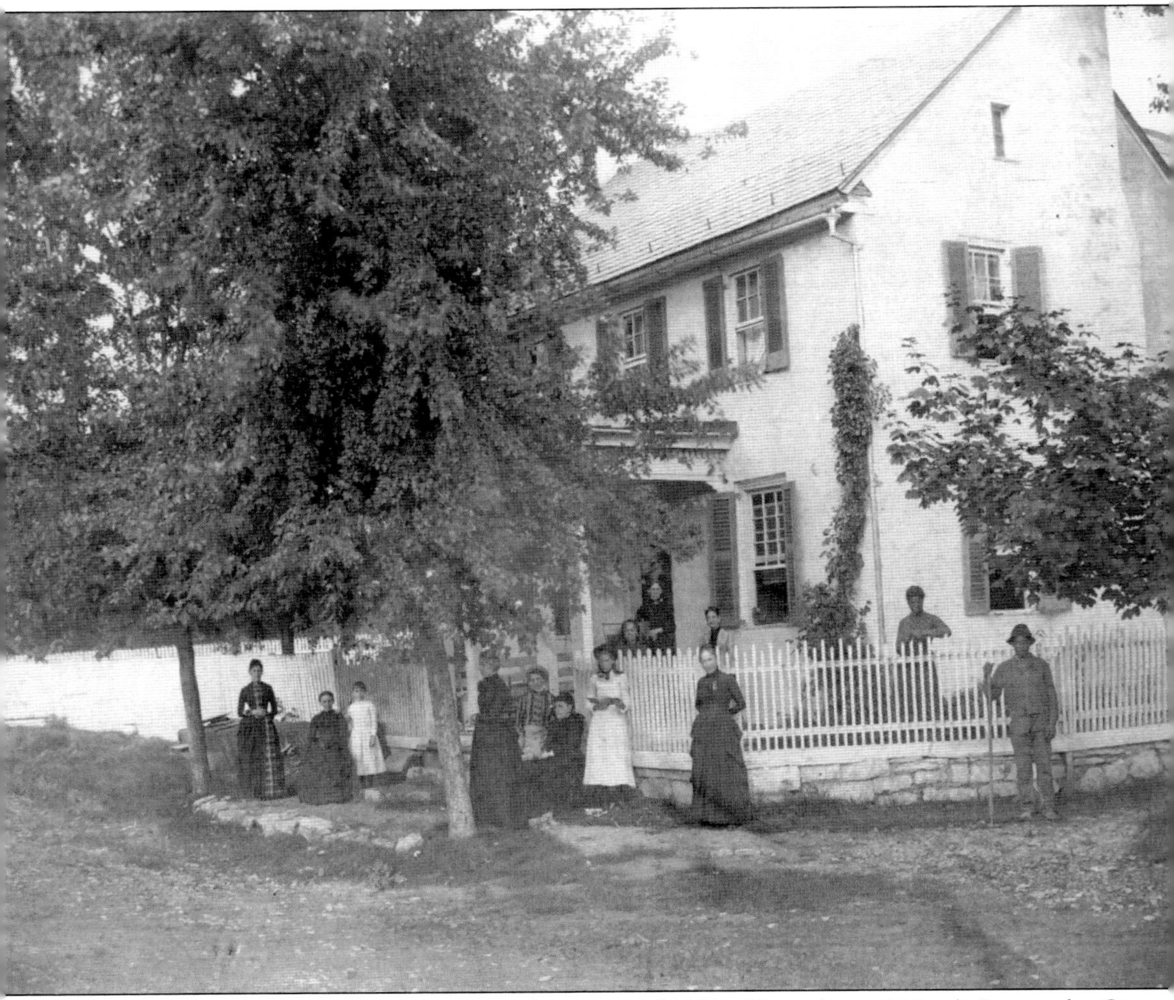

Ott House at North Street. On the corner of Valley Turnpike and North Street, the Ott family is assembled in front of their home. In 1750, Jacob Ott Sr. built the house of trees cleared from the adjacent lot. Ott and other members of the church applied to the Virginia General Assembly in 1803 to hold a lottery for the Lutheran church in Woodstock. In 1822, Ott's son was appointed to accept proposals to do the joinery work at the church. In 1817, Ott obtained a charter to establish the Woodstock Academy. In 1847, William and Jacob Ott Jr. were trustees of the Woodstock Female Seminary. Pictured here are Susan and Em Ott on the porch and Lyde Paull in the yard near the porch. Identified outside the fence in an unknown order are Sidney Lauchlin, Sidney Ott, Maggie Ott, and Annie McGruder (on the chair). Lucy Ott and Lizzie Paull are on the stone steps. Inside the fence on the right is Betty, and uncle Sam is outside the fence. The photograph was taken on November 18, 1921. (JH.)

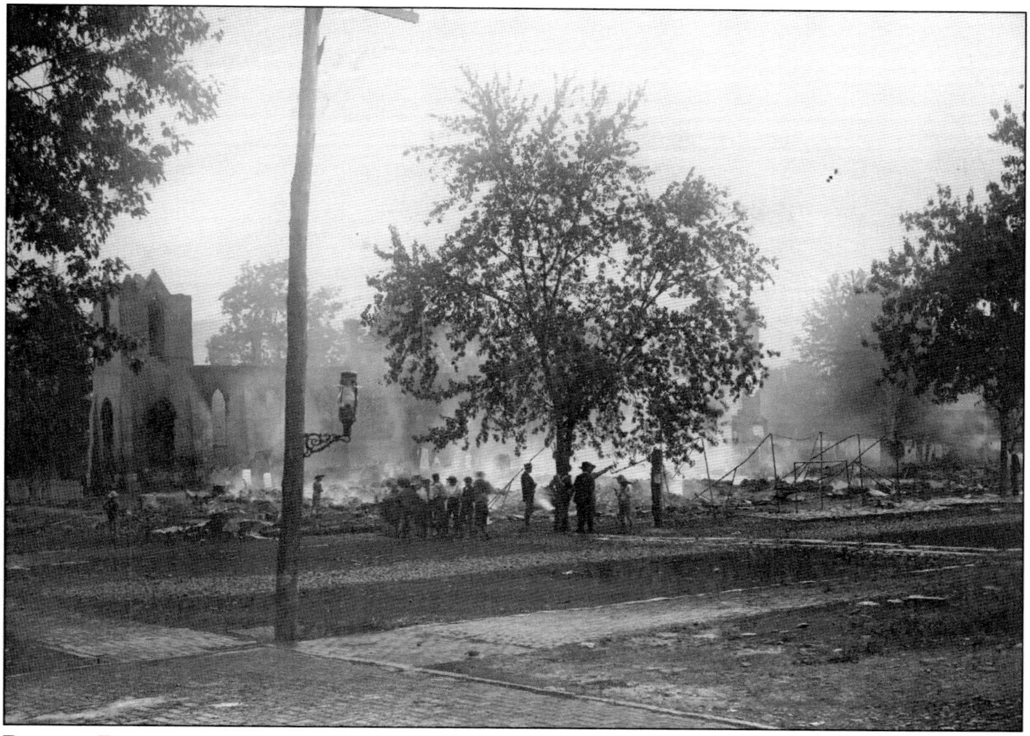

Burner Block Fire and New Burner Block. Diagonally across from the old courthouse, the Burner Block in Woodstock caught fire on August 14, 1900. The lampposts and brick sidewalks show what was there for a streetscape before the fire. The entire block had to be cleared. The Stickley-Boyer building on the corner of Main and Court Streets was totally destroyed, as was the Geary Hotel and everything in between, including Horsey and Atwell, Mauck and Young, Bargelt's Jewelry, Ramey's Meat Store, Boyer's Restaurant, and the offices of W. H. Martin and Lemuel Borden. The brick outer walls of Emmanuel Episcopal Church were the only part of the block that survived. The rebuilt block was constructed of brick instead of wood and housed Gibbs Hardware and a grocery store until it was remodeled about 1937 for Wender's Department Store. (SCL.)

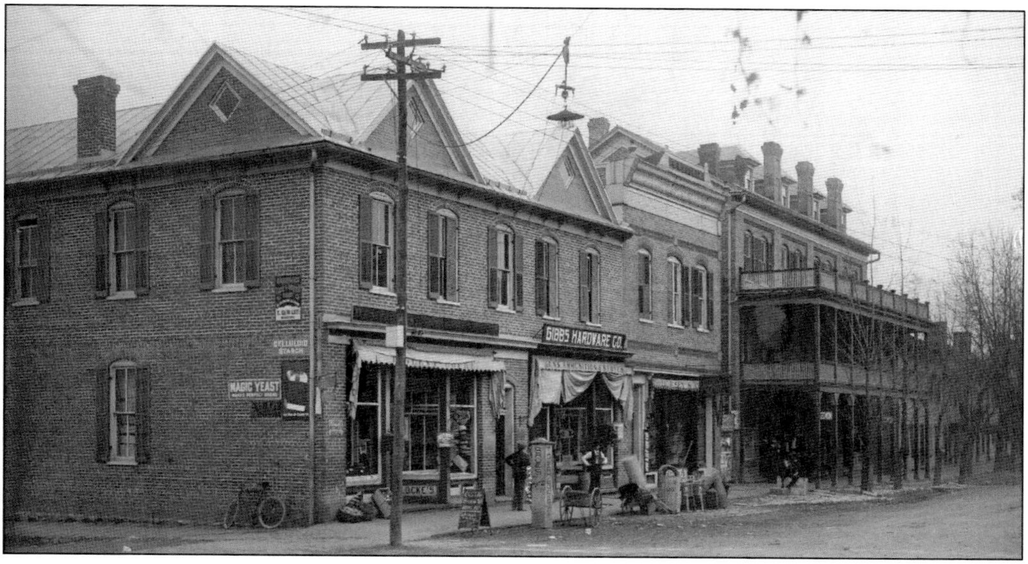

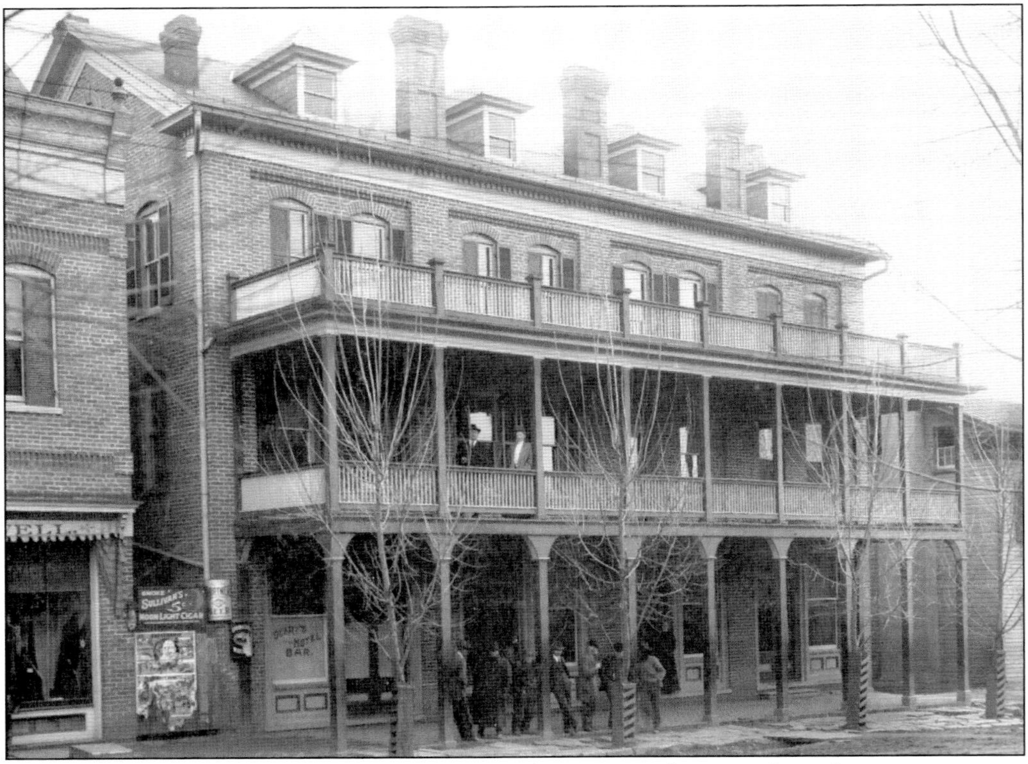

GEARY HOTEL. Rebuilt after the fire, Geary Hotel was across the street from the present county jail and new courthouse. This local lodging house provided a view of everything happening along Main Street from the early 1900s. Massanutten Academy operated this as the Woodstock Hotel in the 1930s. When fire damaged the third and fourth floors in 1975, they were removed. Walton and Smoot Drug Store is there in 2009. (SCL.)

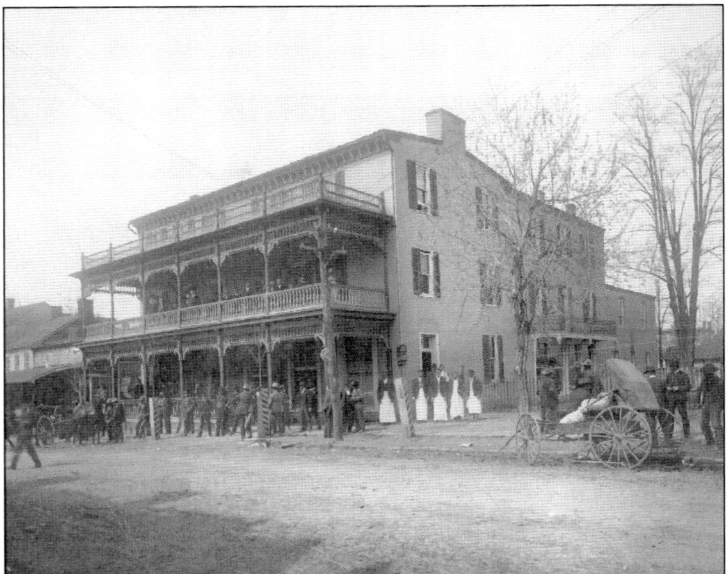

THE HOTEL HOLTZMAN. On opening day, the hotel's kitchen staff lined up wearing white aprons. The carriages and crowd attest to the excitement of the day. Electricity had been installed for the businesses in town. By the 1920s, the building's first floor included a movie theater, a barbershop, and a restaurant. Apartments were on the upper floors. The building burned down in 1949. In 1974, the new courthouse was constructed here. (SCL.)

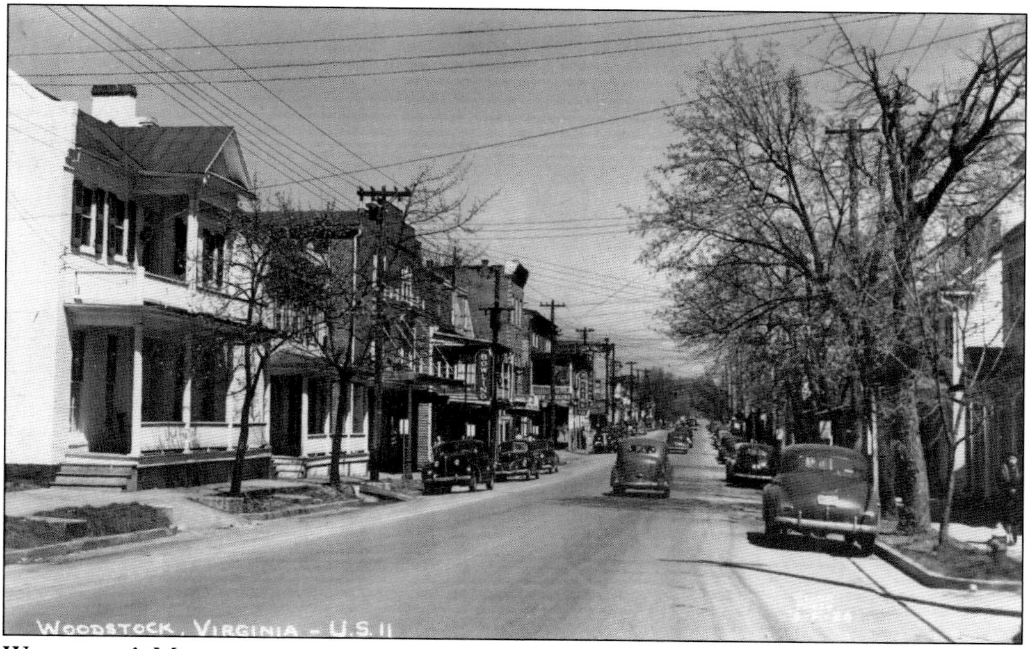

WOODSTOCK'S MAIN STREET. Seen in this view looking north on Route 11 in Woodstock is a nicely paved street with electrical street lamps, which were installed in 1904. On the west side is a bowling alley and signs for the theater. Two blocks farther north is the courthouse. The buildings in this image escaped fires and continue to show their early mantles and woodwork while being used as shops and offices. (SCL.)

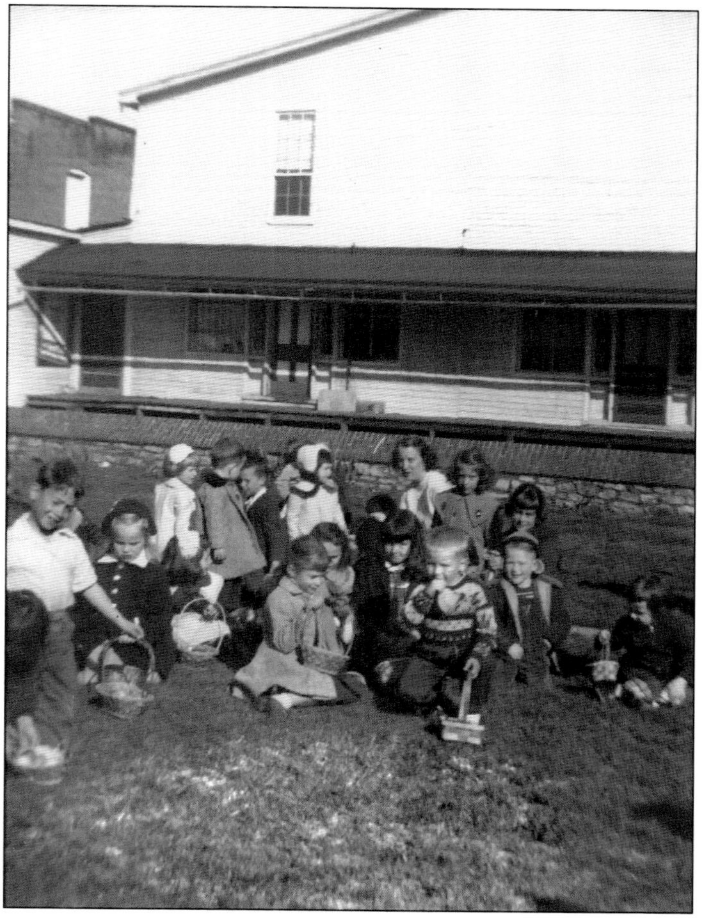

EASTER EGG HUNT. This 1950 photograph shows the annual Woodstock Easter Egg Hunt with many happy children, as they show Beulah Wever their baskets. Behind the little ones is a nearby shopping center, known as Bowman's Store from 1896 until 1964. In 1972, the building was demolished to make way for the parking lot on the corner of Muhlenberg and Court Streets. (SCL.)

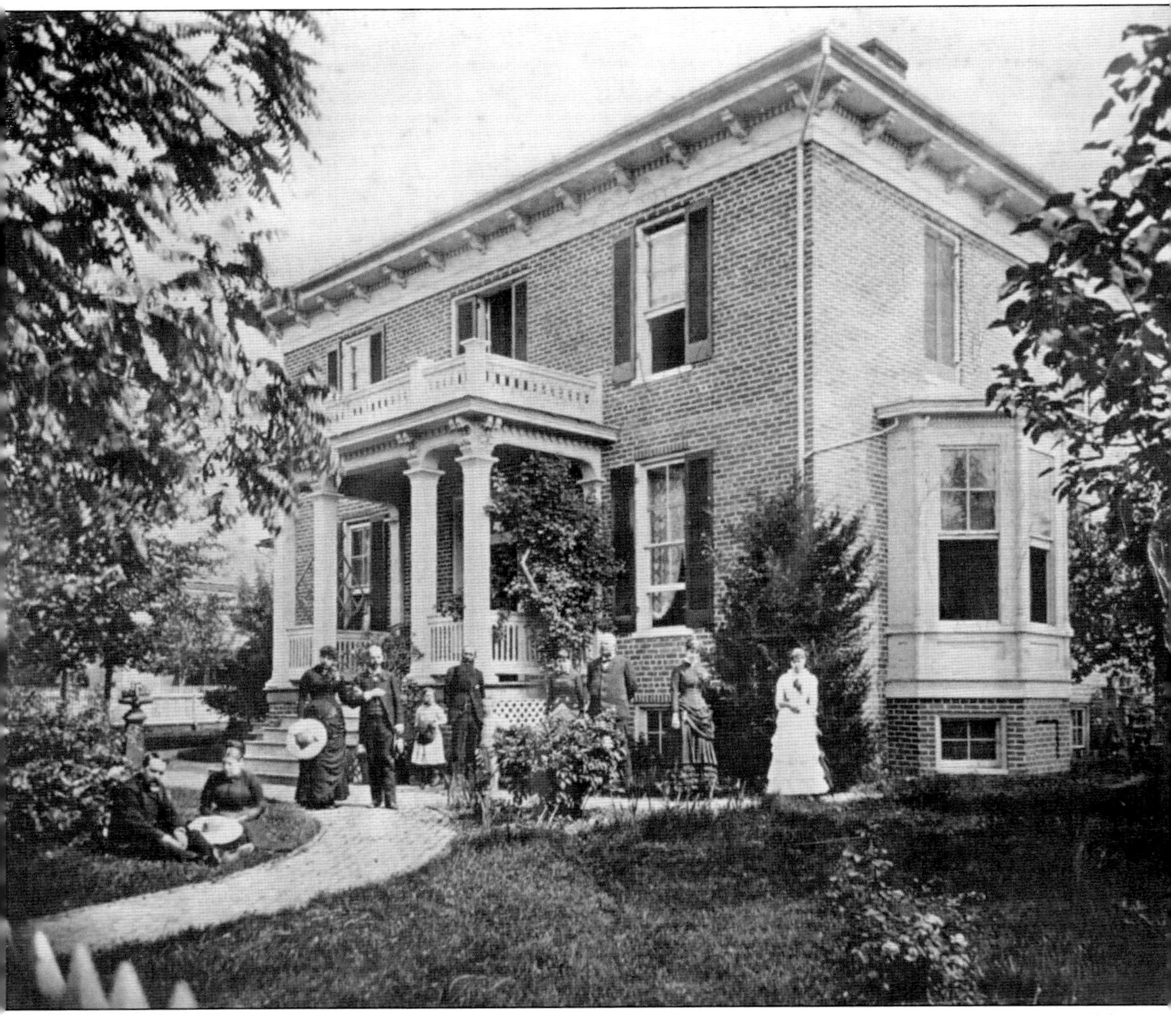

STICKLEY FAMILY. Born in 1839 near Strasburg, the son of prominent farmer Levi Stickley interrupted his law studies to join with the other brave men of the county in the 5th Virginia Infantry. Col. Ezra Eugenius Stickley served in the Stonewall brigade and fought in many battles, including Antietam, where he lost his right arm. In 1868, the colonel built this large brick mansion on the corner of Muhlenberg and Spring Streets. Members of his family are in the front and side yards of their home in this 1884 Morrison photograph. The bearded colonel stands at the corner of the porch. In 1883, he represented the 5th Virginia Infantry and was the first to return to the North a captured flag after the Civil War. Meredith, his oldest son, followed in his father's footsteps and became an attorney; when his father died he inherited his law library and desk. Stickley Hall has been well cared for by its successive owners and today serves once again as a residence and offices for a lawyer. (Courtesy of Jeremy D. McCleary.)

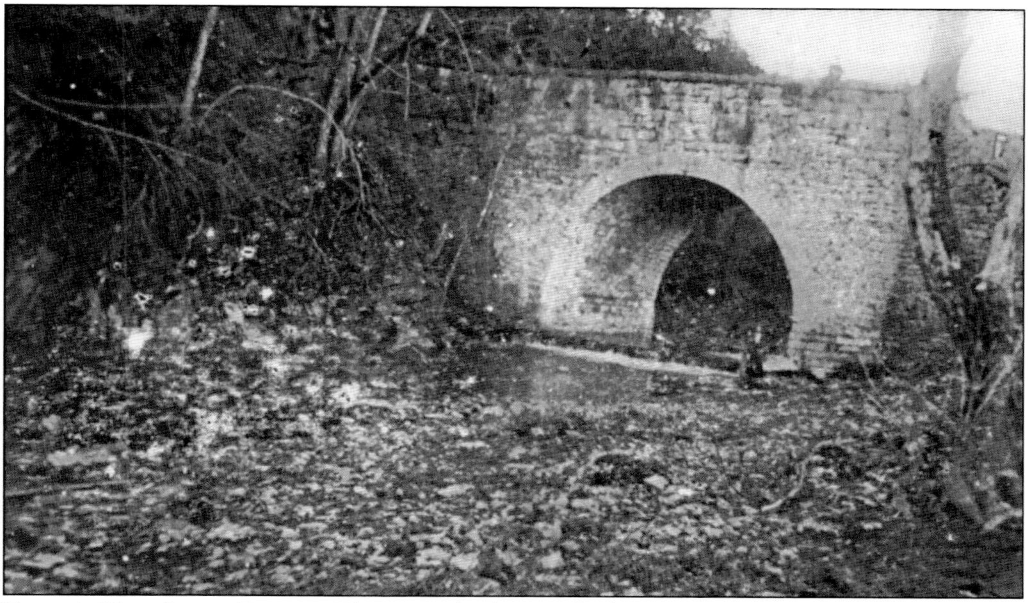

FISHER'S HILL STONE BRIDGE. This stone bridge was built over Tumbling Run 2 miles south of Strasburg. The limestone bridge was probably built in the 1840s. On September 19, 1864, Union general Philip Sheridan dislodged Confederate general Jubal Early. Scouts are said to have changed uniforms here while the enemy crossed above. Only the abutments are visible today. This photograph by Parker and Stickley was taken in 1908. (ML.)

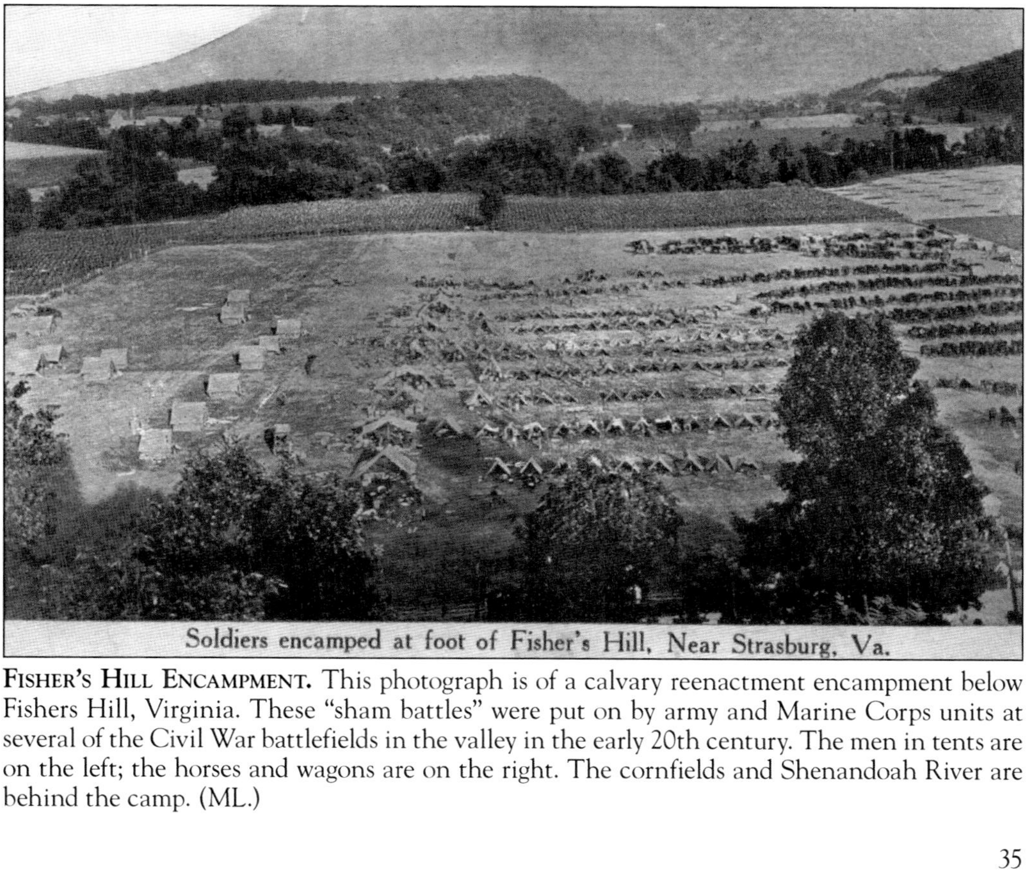

FISHER'S HILL ENCAMPMENT. This photograph is of a calvary reenactment encampment below Fishers Hill, Virginia. These "sham battles" were put on by army and Marine Corps units at several of the Civil War battlefields in the valley in the early 20th century. The men in tents are on the left; the horses and wagons are on the right. The cornfields and Shenandoah River are behind the camp. (ML.)

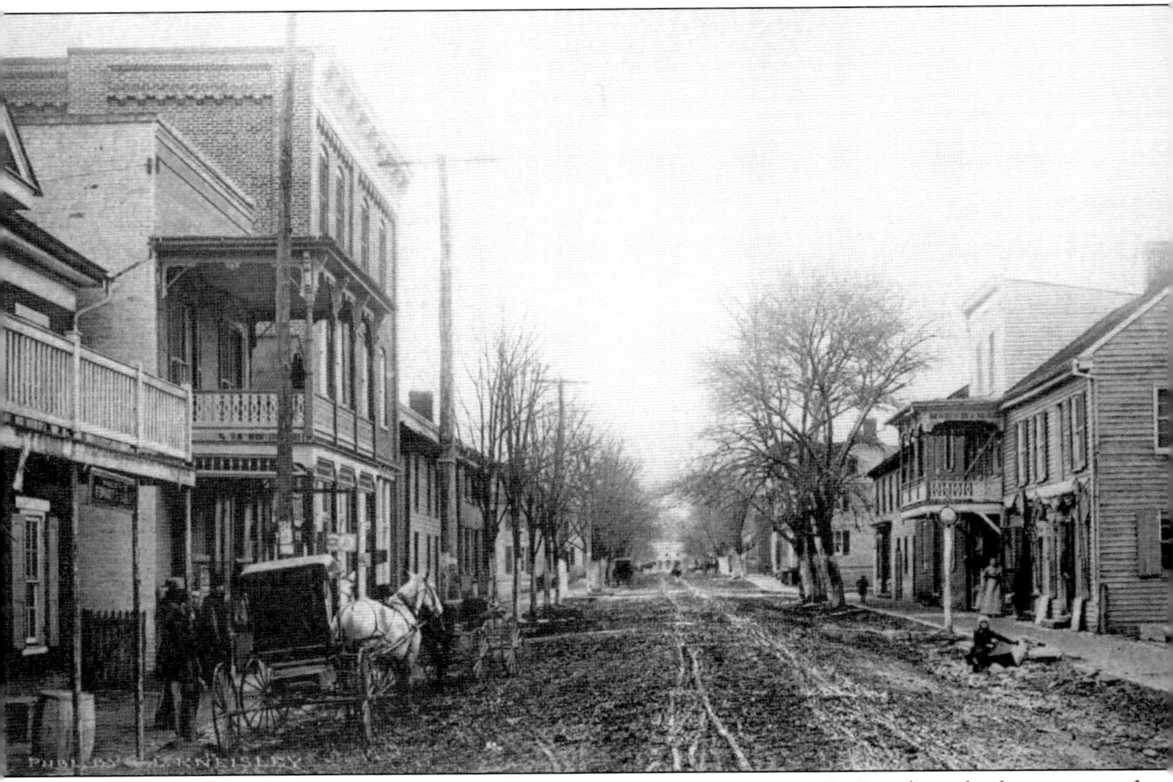

Strasburg's Main Street. In the early period from 1747 to 1753, Strasburg had a variety of names, including Funkstown, Funk Mill, and Staufferstadt (a German word meaning Stovertown). Peter Stover laid out the town in 1761 as Strasburg. Some of the early settlers were probably from Strasburg in Alsace, Germany, and adopted the name of the old home city for their new town in the Shenandoah Valley. According to *Martin's Gazetteer of Virginia*, in 1835, Strasburg contained 78 dwelling houses; three churches; three schools, including an academy; three mercantile stores; two taverns; an apothecary shop; four tan yards; two gunsmiths; five cabinetmakers; four blacksmith shops; a tinner; a factory making stoneware and earthenware; a plasterer; three bricklayers; five tailors; four cooper shops; six boot and shoe factories; and six regular physicians. It had a population of 470. The view of Strasburg's unpaved main street shows horses and carriages, as well as pedestrians. On the pole at right is a jeweler's sign in the shape of a clock. Barrels and sacks are used to display and contain the merchandise. (ML.)

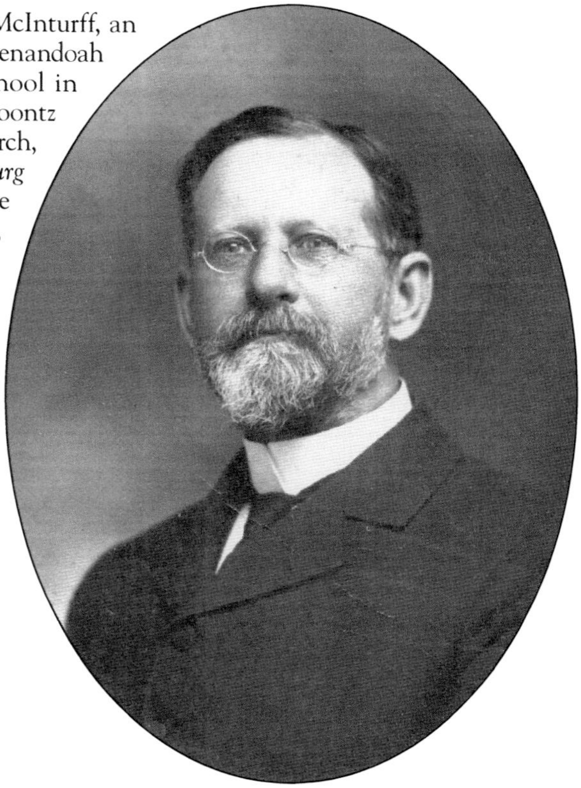

Rev. Joseph B. McInturff. Joseph B. McInturff, an only child, was born on May 4, 1845, in Shenandoah County. While a teacher at Stover School in Woodstock, he met and married Ellen Koontz in 1867. He was an elder of the Baptist Church, a Civil War veteran, the founder of *Strasburg News*, editor of the church newspaper the *Old Paths*, principal of Woodstock School, and superintendent of Shenandoah Public Schools from 1886 to 1909. (JMC.)

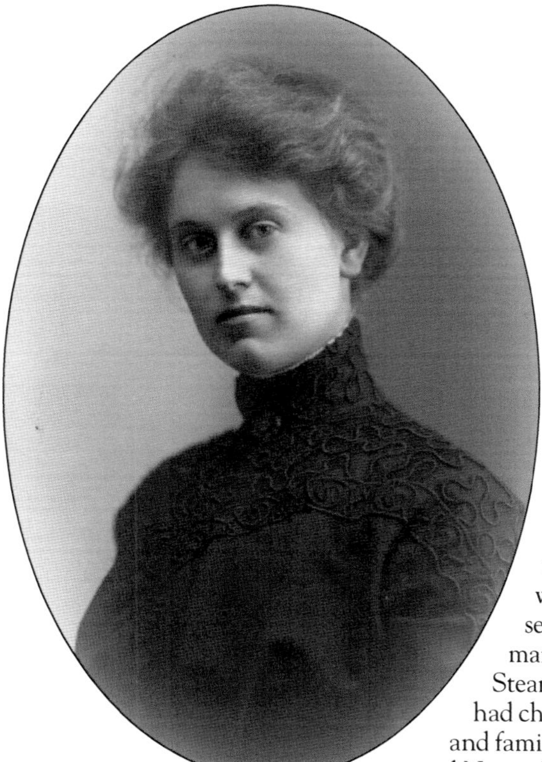

Ruth McInturff. Ruth McInturff, one of two daughters of Rev. Joseph B. McInturff, was a very photogenic young woman, as can be seen in this Hugh Morrison studio portrait. She married Charles D. Smith, who ran the Strasburg Steam Flouring Mills from 1908 to 1938. After they had children, Ruth dedicated her time to her church and family. Her children were Charles Gardner Smith and Nancy Ellen Smith. (JMC.)

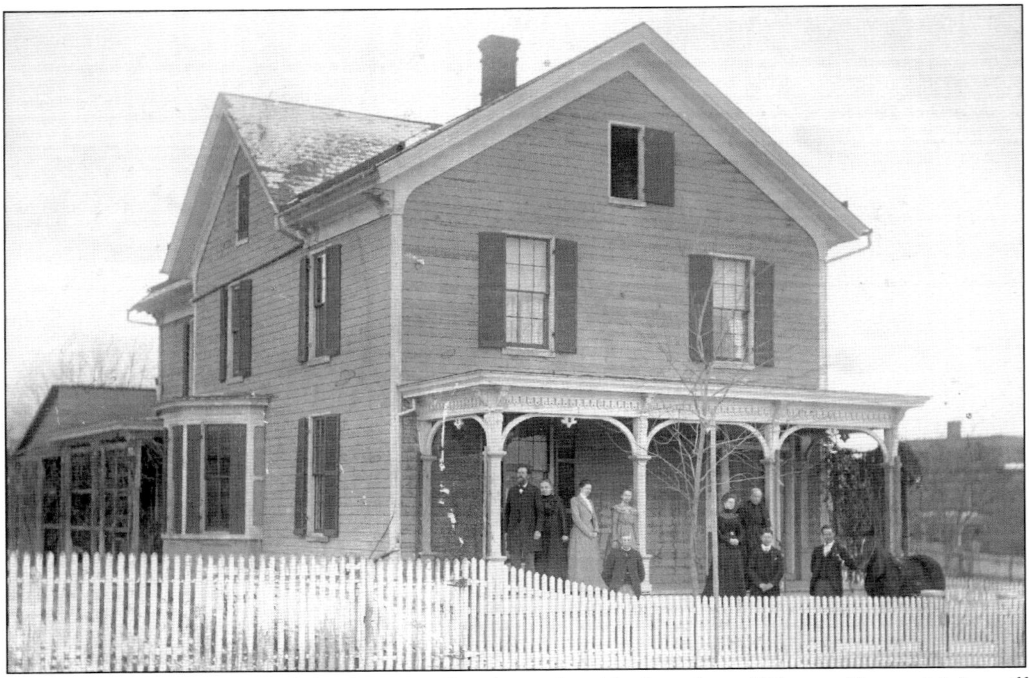

McInturff House. On Holiday Street in Strasburg, the elder Joseph and Eleanor Koontz McInturff are seen with their family and his mother. Sisters Ruth and Rose McInturff left scrapbooks and the pictures in this section are from those black pages. Rose married Dr. Harold T. Hopewell, a physician for the Southern Railroad Company. They built a big home next door to her parents, where they lived with their three children. (JMC.)

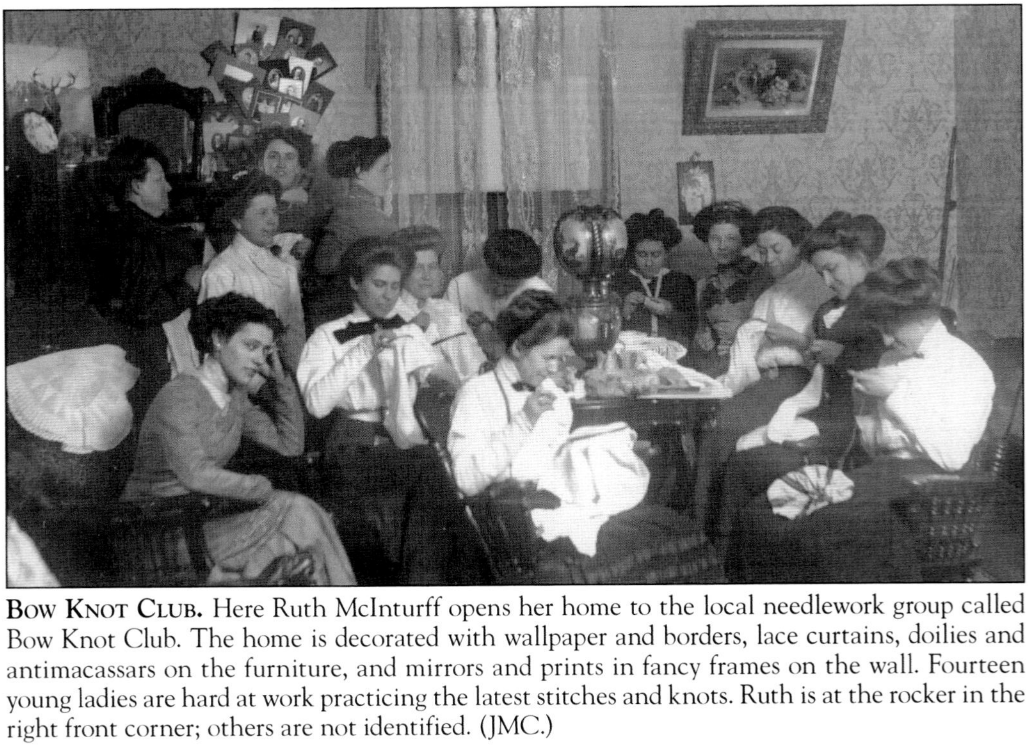

Bow Knot Club. Here Ruth McInturff opens her home to the local needlework group called Bow Knot Club. The home is decorated with wallpaper and borders, lace curtains, doilies and antimacassars on the furniture, and mirrors and prints in fancy frames on the wall. Fourteen young ladies are hard at work practicing the latest stitches and knots. Ruth is at the rocker in the right front corner; others are not identified. (JMC.)

Charles Gardner Smith. At right, Charles Gardner Smith, still wearing a dress, is shown with his grandmother in the yard. The photograph below, where he leans on the birdbath, shows the dapper young man in his teen years. Smith was born in 1912, and his sister Nancy was born in 1915. Smith and his wife, Connie, lived on Massanutten Street in Strasburg. Nancy graduated in 1933 from Strasburg High School. She taught home economics at Handley High School in Winchester, where she met her future husband, Charles P. McVicker. Her aunt Ruth Hopewell sang at the wedding ceremony, and her brother gave her in marriage. Charles P. McVicker attended Handley High School and graduated from Randolph Macon Academy in Front Royal. The McVicker's daughter Judith McVicker Copenhaver cares for the scrapbooks that provided these family photographs. (JMC.)

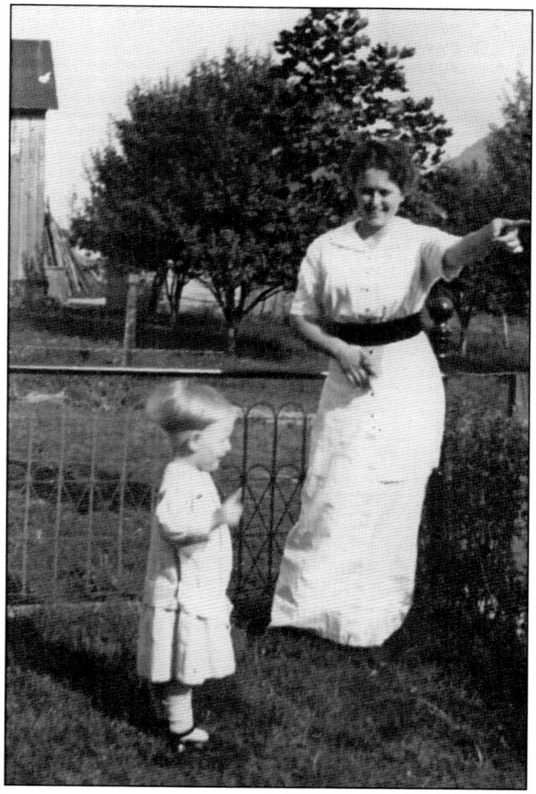

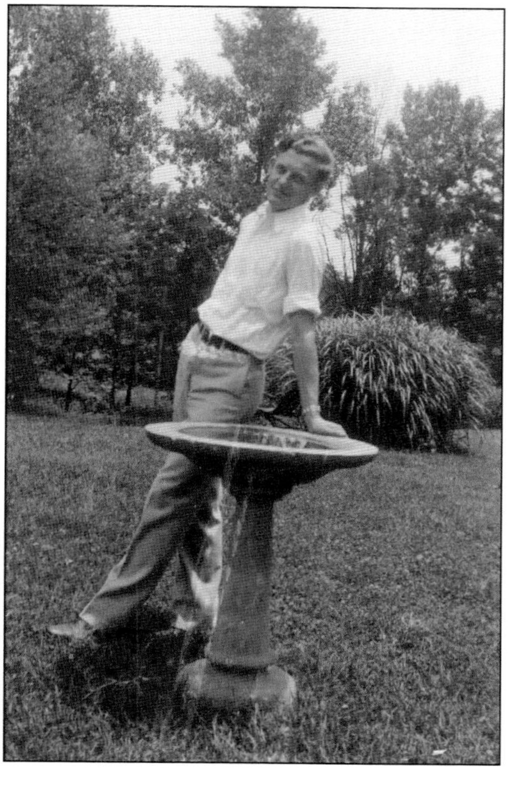

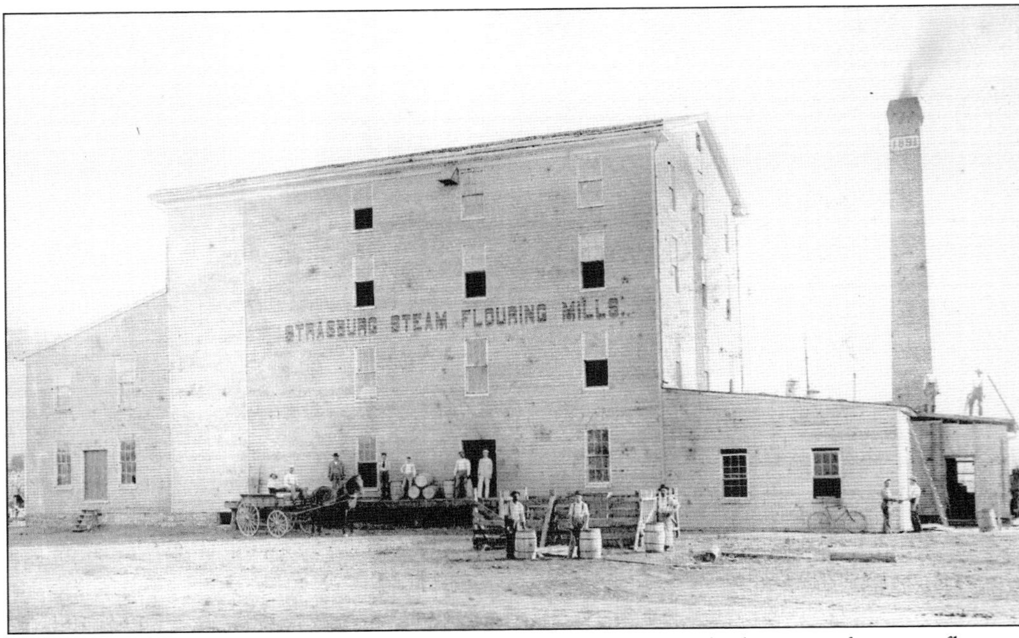

STRASBURG STEAM FLOURING MILLS. In 1834, Shenandoah County had 34 manufacturing flouring mills, two furnaces, and four forges. William H. Smith started this mill in 1891. He was followed by his son Charles D. and his grandson Charles Gardner. Smith's granddaughter Nancy's uncle Clifford Grim later became president of the mills. The smokestack was a landmark until the mill was taken down about 1950. (JMC.)

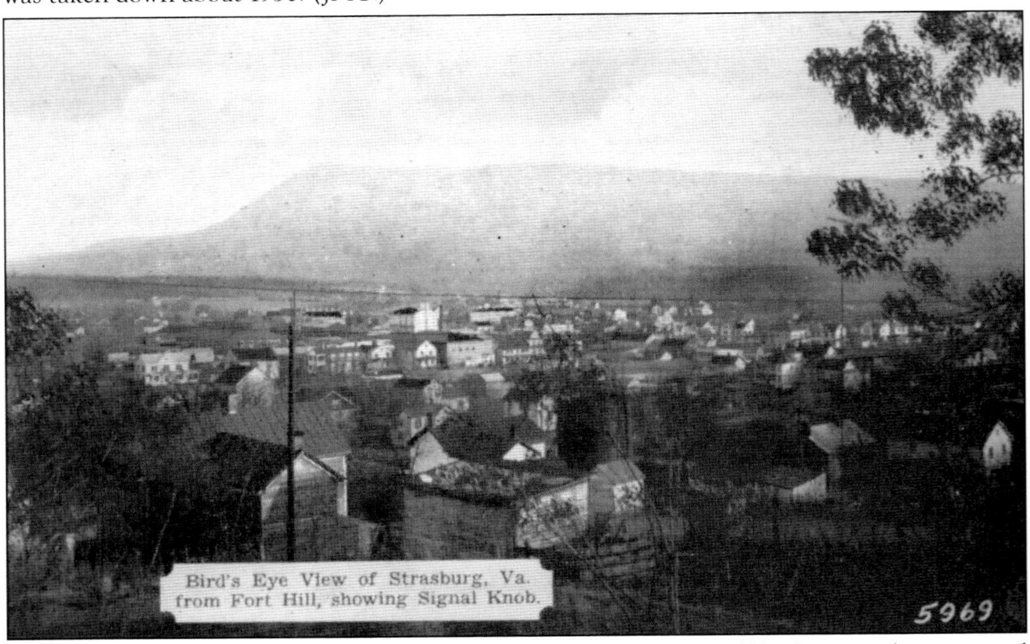

VIEW OF STRASBURG, 1907. This photograph was taken from Fort Hill looking southeast toward Signal Knob and Massanutten Mountain. Queen Street used to be the main street of the town, and some of the oldest houses were built there. Often called "Pot Town," Strasburg's chief industry was manufacturing redware and stoneware pottery. Using the native clay, some of the well-known potters were the Bells, the Keisters, the Eberlys, and the Hickersons. (ML.)

Three

Scattered Jewels

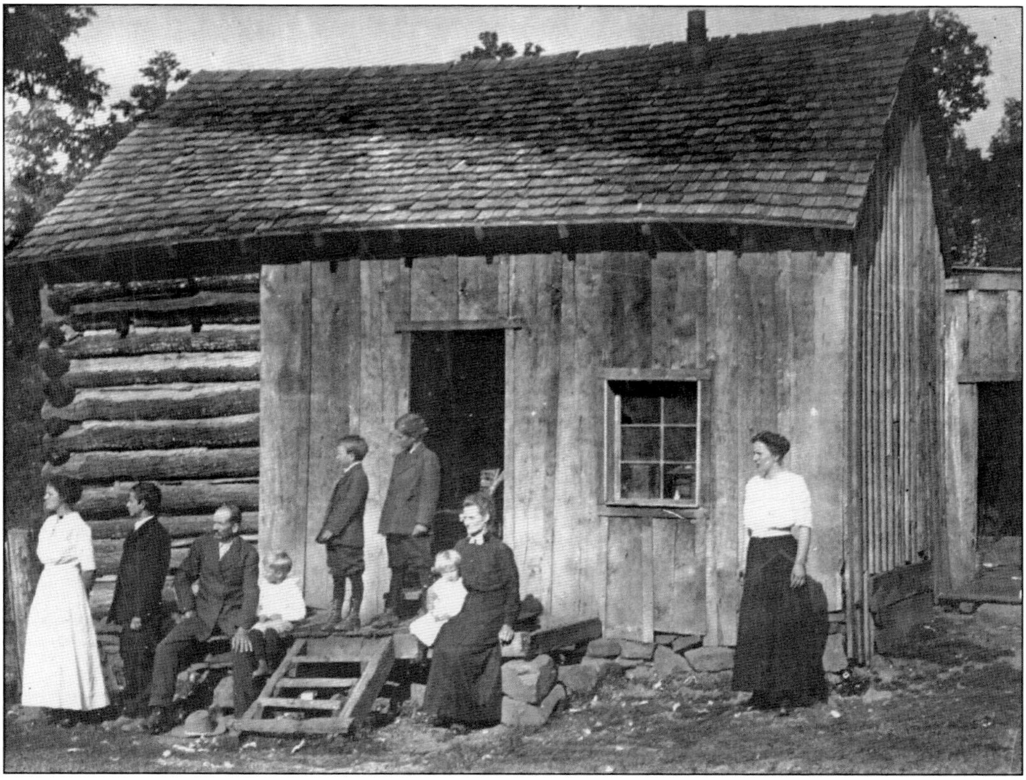

Log and Frame Home. Scattered like gems at the crossroads about the county are little towns and clusters of buildings with one or more churches. This photograph comes from a Hugh Morrison negative, but the exact location is unknown. It is a good example of houses in the county built in stages. The homes continued to be occupied and modified as circumstances improved and the size of families increased. (SCHS.)

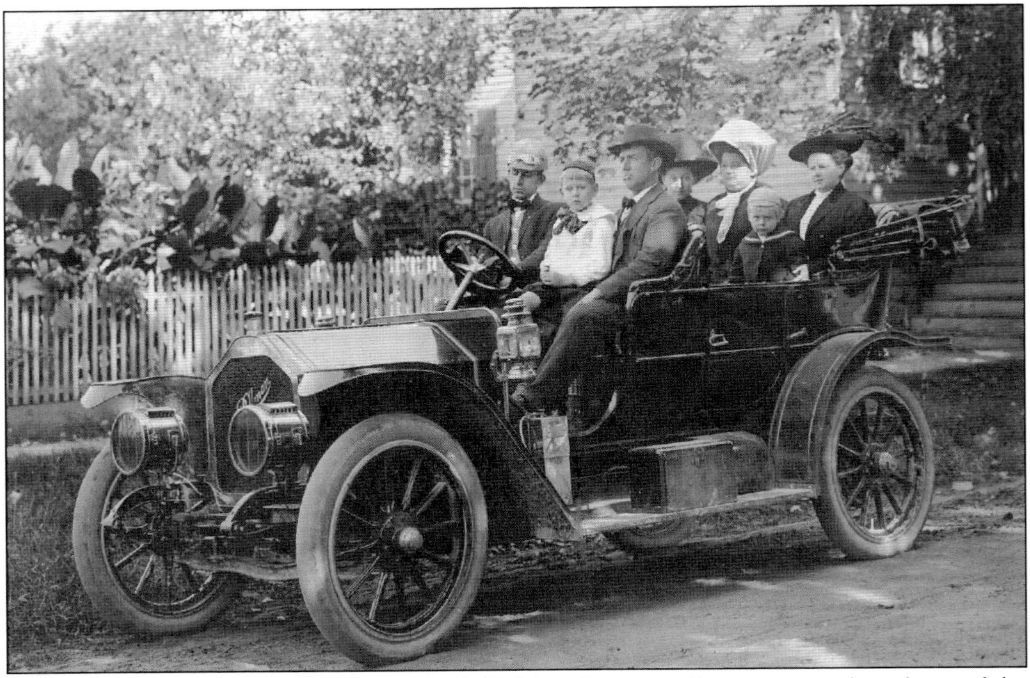

Pullman Car. Don Crabill, owner of Crabill's Manufacturing Company, purchased one of the first cars in Shenandoah County. It is seen here parked in front of their home in Woodstock. Frank Fravel is behind the wheel next to his oldest son, Frank Fravel Jr. The three sisters in the back are Flota Grandstaff Fravel, Lute Grandstaff Bird, and Maude Grandstaff Crabill. Landon Fravel is the little boy. (MFC.)

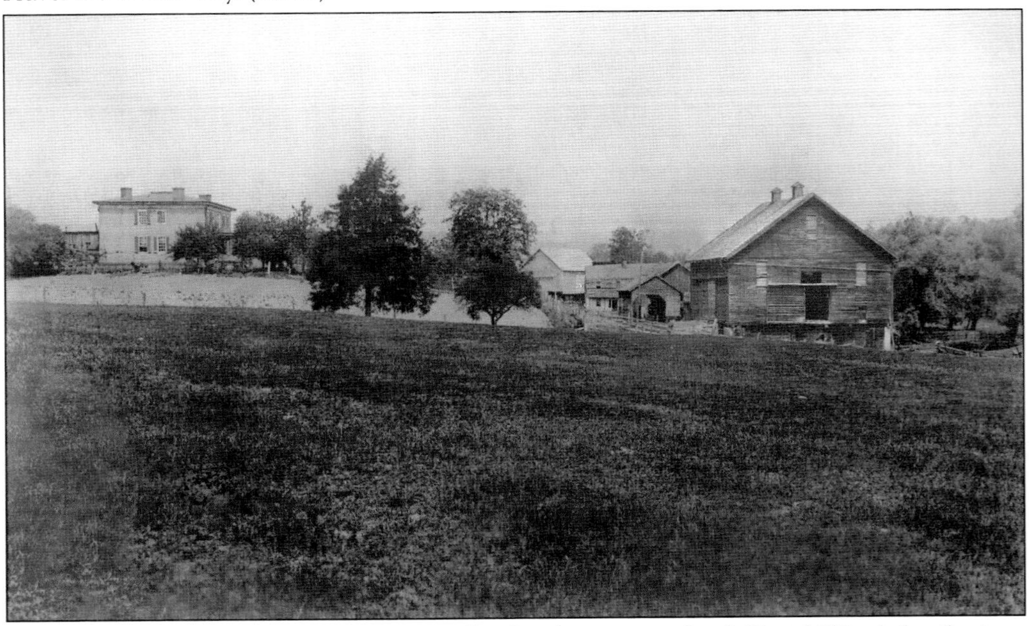

Wine Family Farm. Located near Forestville, this farm was in Jacob David Wine's family since 1906. This view shows all the necessary outbuildings for a dairy and fruit farm. To the left are the large foursquare house and garden plot. The dairy barns for hay storage and sheds for tractors and machines are in the center. Pasturelands, sheds, and fruit trees are to the right. (JCW.)

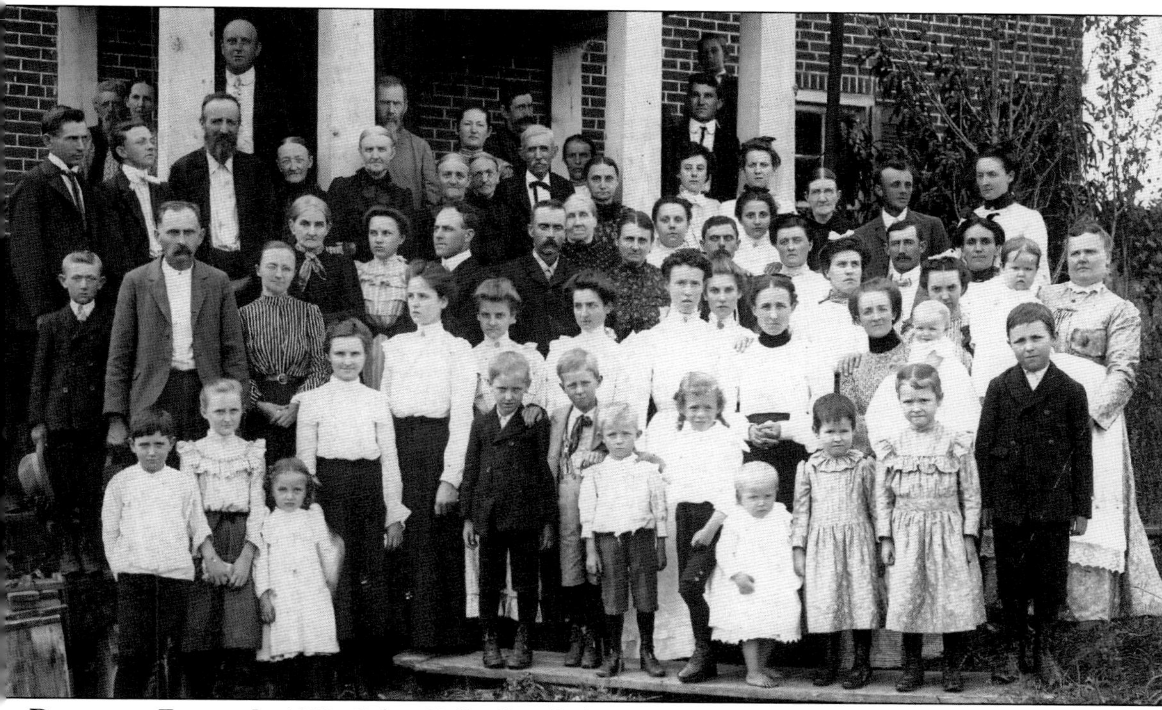

DELLINGER FAMILY. In 1892, Cabin Hill officially became Conicville. This solid brick home complete with a rectangular pillared porch is where the Dellinger family lined up to have the photographer capture this image. Each of the 63 people in the photograph has been identified. They are Peter D.; Dora D.; Clara D. Mumaw (Dupie); Bessie (or Laura) D. Polk; Martha D., daughter of George and Mary V. D.; Dycie (or Dysie) D., daughter of George and Mary V. D.; Russell D, son of George and Mary V. D.; Annie D. Fadley, daughter of George and Mary V. D.; Samuel Polk and Clearence Polk, sons of Mary Elizabeth Helsley Polk; Cletus Helsley, son of Alice Helsley; Alice Helsley, mother of Cletus; Esther D. Andrick, daughter of George and Mary V. D.; Mary Long; Bessie Wilkins; Mary Ryman, daughter of Mary and Peter Ryman; Beulah Ryman, daughter of Mary and Peter Ryman; William, son of Mary and Peter Ryman; Emeline Tersie Helsley Wilkins, wife of Rufus; baby of Rufus and Emeline Wilkins (no name given); Fannie Ryman, baby of Lucy and Peter Jacob; Sarah Wilkins George; Mary (Lucy) Ryman, wife of Peter Ryman; Jane Trumbo, wife of Phil; Annie Helsley, wife of Robert; Philip Trumbo, son of Emeline and George Trumbo of Upper Track, West Virginia; Myrtie Helsley, daughter of Jess (Jeptha) and Mary Helsley; Robert Helsley, husband of Annie, son of Sarah and Jacob (Josh) Helsley; Ciry Fadely; Tirzah Tersie Helsley, daughter of Sarah and Jacob (Josh) Helsley; Fannie D. Good, daughter of Noah, married Warren Good; Charles M. D., son of Noah; Dillie Miller; Sarah D., daughter of Noah and Betty D., later married Charles Vetter; unidentified friend of the Trumbos; Will Fadely, husband of Annie D.; Samuel Dellinger; Mary V. Dellinger, wife of George; George Dellinger, son of Mordacia and Eliza D.; William (Will) Helsley; Laura Helsley; Lydia Alice D., wife of Philip; Philip D., brother of George and son of Mordacia and Eliza D.; Stanley D., son of Caleb; Lester D., son of Caleb; Caleb D., son of William and Eliza D.; Charles D., son of Phil; Josh Helsley; Sarah D. Helsley, daughter of Phillip C. D.; Dliza Ann S. D., wife of Mordacia and after his death married his brother William, mother of Phil, George, Paul, Caleb, and Lucy; Lydia D. Wilkins, daughter of Phillip C. Dellinger; Dilman D.; Mary R. D. Helsley (Beck), daughter of Phillip C. D. and wife of Jess (Jeptha); Fannie D.; Emeline D. Trumbo, daughter of Phillip C. D.; Noah D., son of Phillip C. D.; Mantonie D.; Frances Helsley; Mrs. Weatherholtz; Elizabeth (Betty) D., Noah's wife; James Wilkins, son of Lydia and Jacob; Rachael Wilkins; and Kane (Cain) Miller. (Courtesy of Cheryl Dellinger.)

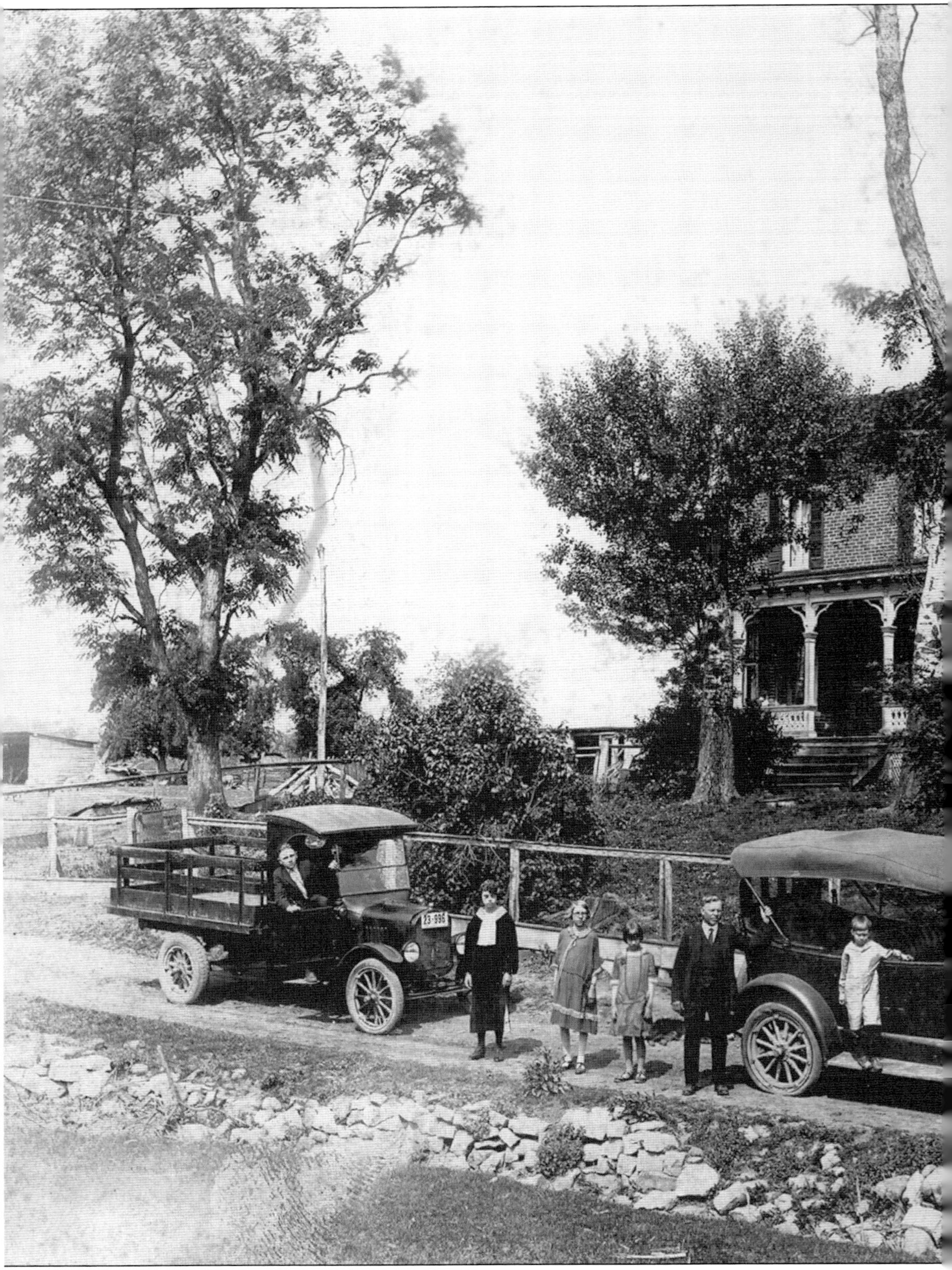

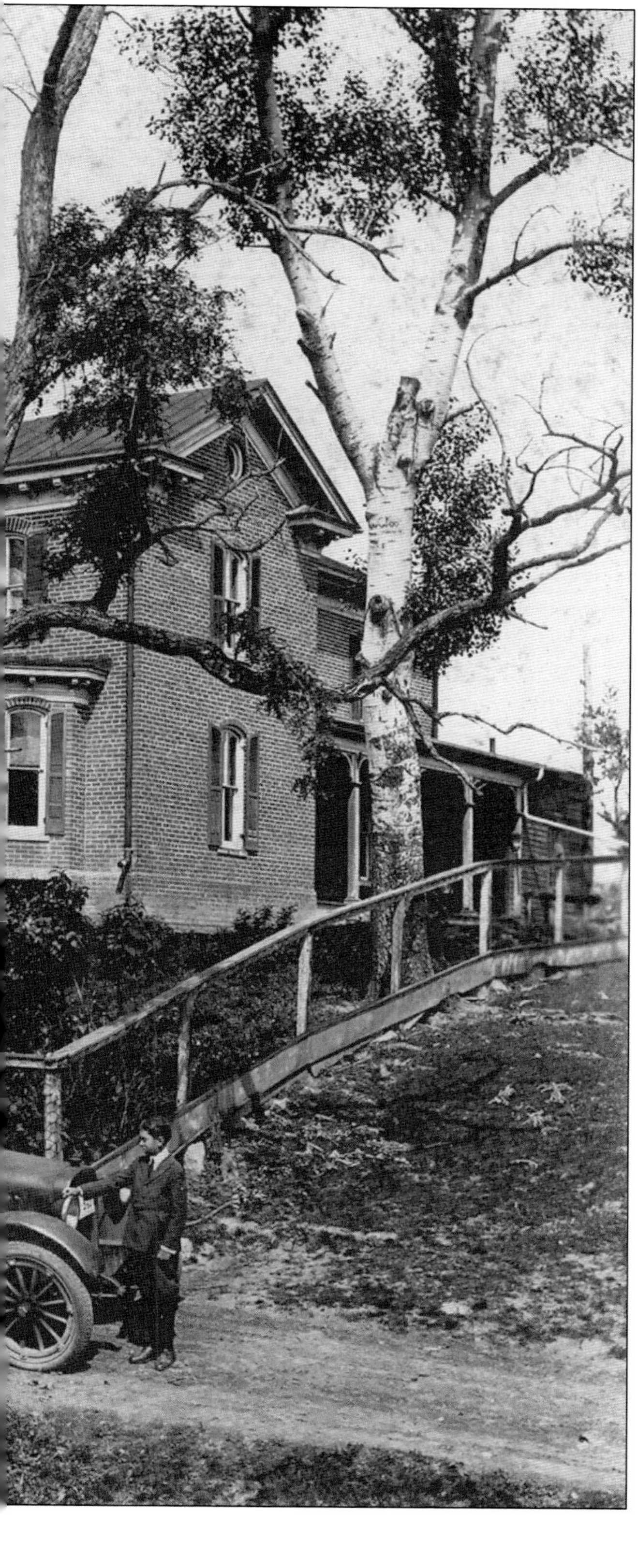

WILKINS FAMILY OF CEDAR GROVE. Three miles north of New Market near the summit of Rude's Hill is the Brethren's Cedar Grove Church, built in 1857. John Paul Wilkins operated a large river bottom farm nearby. In this portrait, taken about 1925, Wilkins success is seen. His mother, Elizabeth Frances "Franny," was a Bowman before her marriage to George L. Wilkins. John Paul's family included two sons and three daughters when this picture was taken. Daughters Beulah May and Annie Elizabeth were both born in 1910, and Frances was born in 1915. First son, George Paul, died at two years old in 1909, Gilbert Franklin was born in 1913, and Earl Kline was born in 1919. Earl Kline continued to live and work on this family farm until 1985. His two sons, Joseph and Wayne, inherited the farm and still run the Wilkins Brothers Repair Shop there. (SCL.)

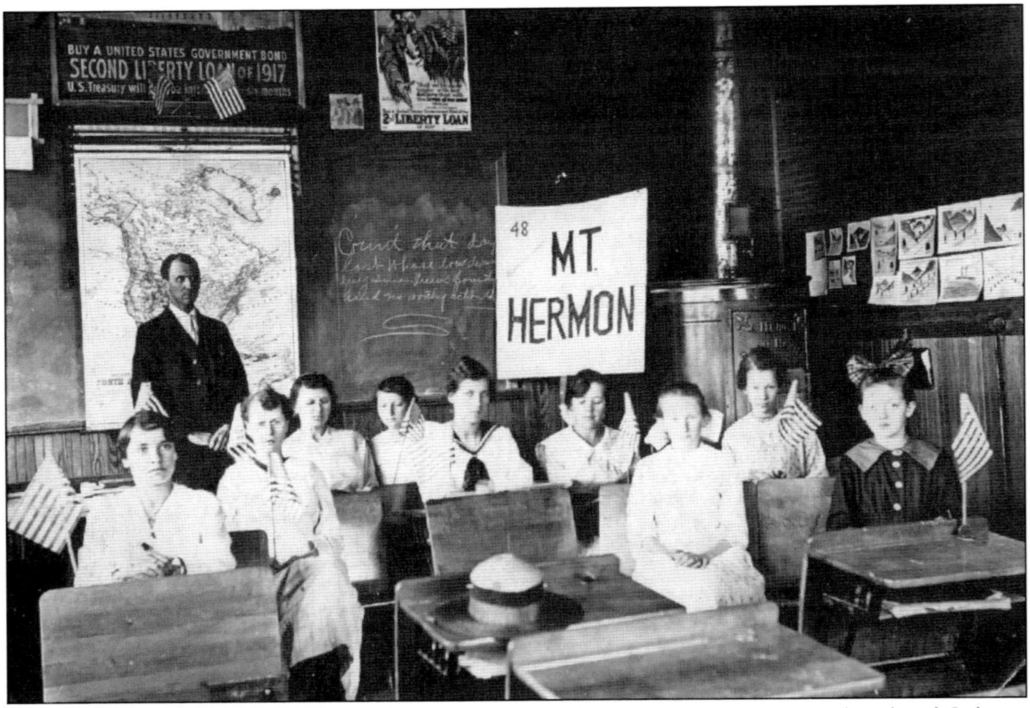

MOUNT HERMON SCHOOL. Mount Hermon School, No. 16, was on the north side of Orkney Grade and predates 1855. The United Brethren of Christ used it for worship. This photograph from about 1917 shows the teacher and nine students. Florence Mumaw is the only student without a flag; the others are unidentified. The board's motto reads, "Count that day lost whose setting sun views from thy hand no worthy action." (PPS.)

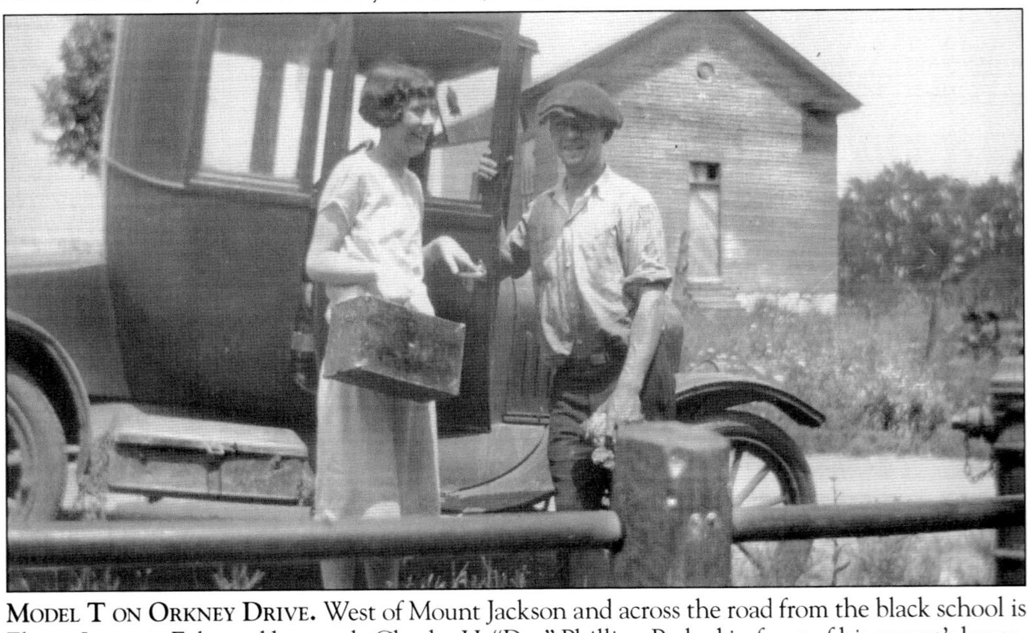

MODEL T ON ORKNEY DRIVE. West of Mount Jackson and across the road from the black school is Elnora Lavania Foltz and her uncle Charles H. "Dee" Phillips. Parked in front of his parent's home, working on his Model T Ford, Philips's 18-year-old niece Foltz holds the toolbox. It looks as though he has been working on this problem for a while. The photograph was taken about 1927. (PPS.)

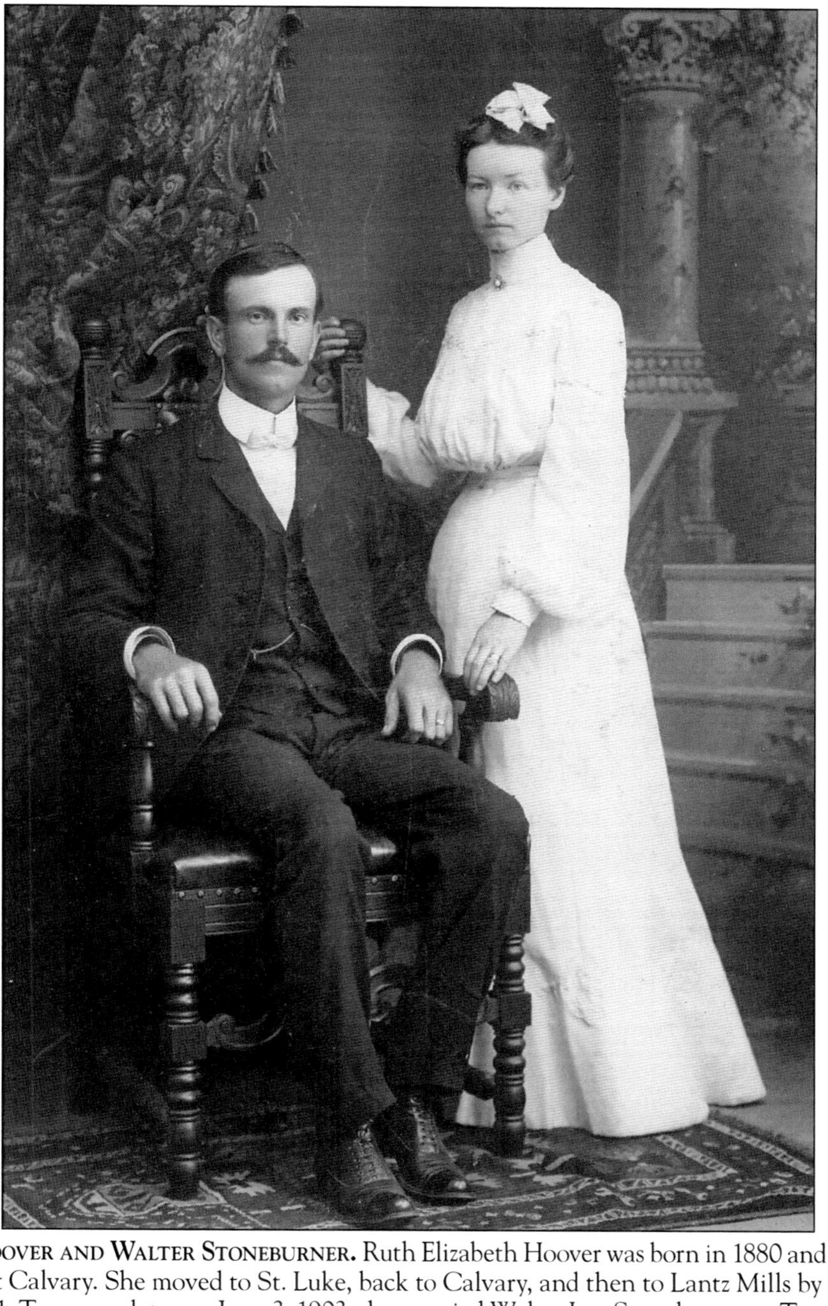

Ruth Hoover and Walter Stoneburner. Ruth Elizabeth Hoover was born in 1880 and baptized in 1881 at Calvary. She moved to St. Luke, back to Calvary, and then to Lantz Mills by the time she was 21. Two years later on June 3, 1903, she married Walter Lee Stoneburner at Tom's Brook. In 1905, they had their only son, Carl Francis. The Lantz Mill that Carl knew was typical of the many mills built in Shenandoah County. Constructed before 1813, possibly by Peter Holler, the mill was burned by General Sheridan and reconstructed in 1867. It is timber framed, three full stories high, and sits on the edge of the fast-running Stony Creek. It was one of 34 flouring mills in Shenandoah County, according to the 1843 *Martin's Gazetteer of Virginia*. Walter, Carl, and Ruth lived at Lantz Mills near the swinging footbridge. A miller, farmer, and barber, Walter died in 1923. On Christmas Day in 1934, Ruth married William Isaac Wilkins. They continued to live in Ruth's house until her death in 1967. She is buried in Union Forge Cemetery. (SCHS.)

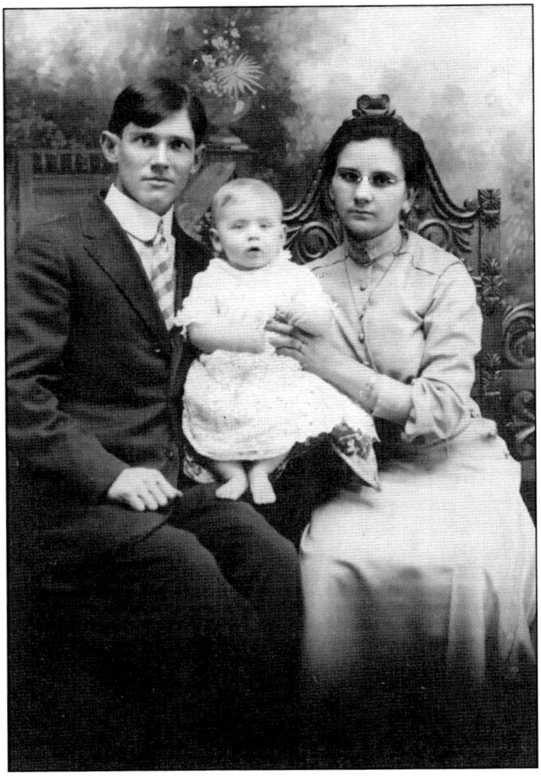

Lantz Family. Edward Lee and Della Eva Pence Lantz were married on Christmas Day in 1913. They are seen in this Hugh Morrison portrait with William Edward, the first of their six children. West of Edinburg and along Stony Creek, Lantz Mill is at the site of the old Union Forge. On top of the hill is Union Forge Church, the first image in this book. (SCL.)

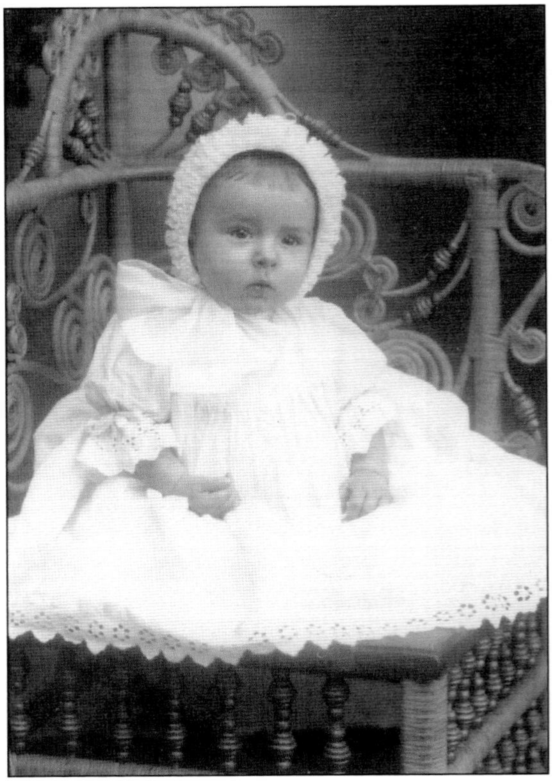

James Raymond Foster. Nannie Irene Sheetz Foster married James Edward Foster in 1908. They are the parents of James Raymond Foster, seen in this 1909 Morrison photograph. He is the first of three children who grew up in the Sheetz Mill area of Calvary. James is descended from Mathias Sheetz and lived near the mill that bears his ancestors' name. (Courtesy of Beverly Ward.)

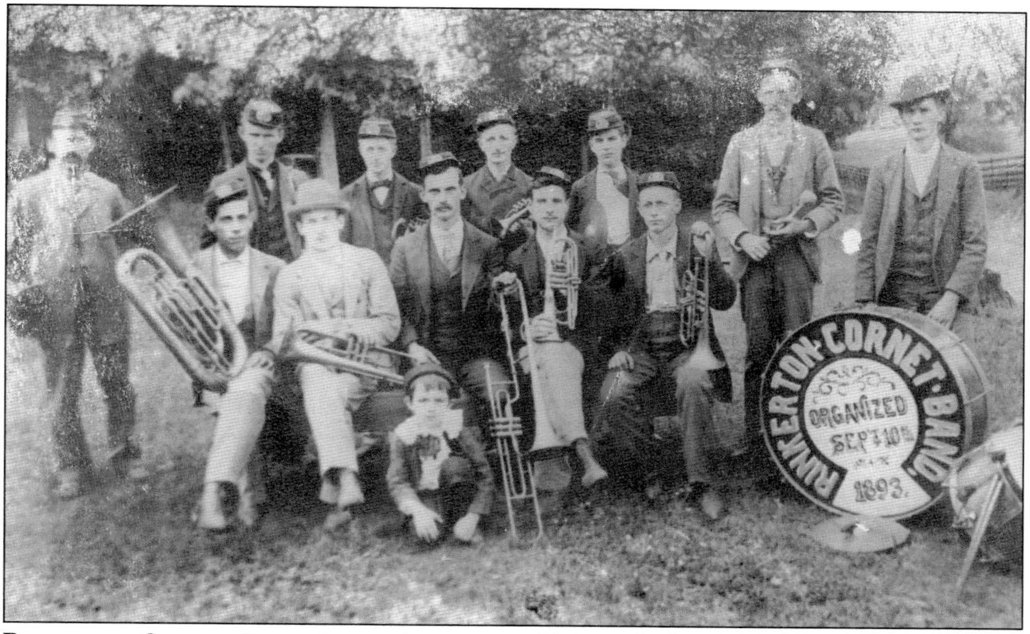

Rinkerton Cornet Band. Located just west of Mount Jackson on the Orkney Grade and originally called Mill Creek, the name changed to Rinkerton before 1790. One store, a flouring mill, a sawmill, a chopping mill, a shoemaker shop, and a blacksmith shop were found at the crossing with Middle Road. The band was organized in 1893. Peter Snyder Ursinus Rinker, with the child sitting at his feet, is the only member identified. (SCL.)

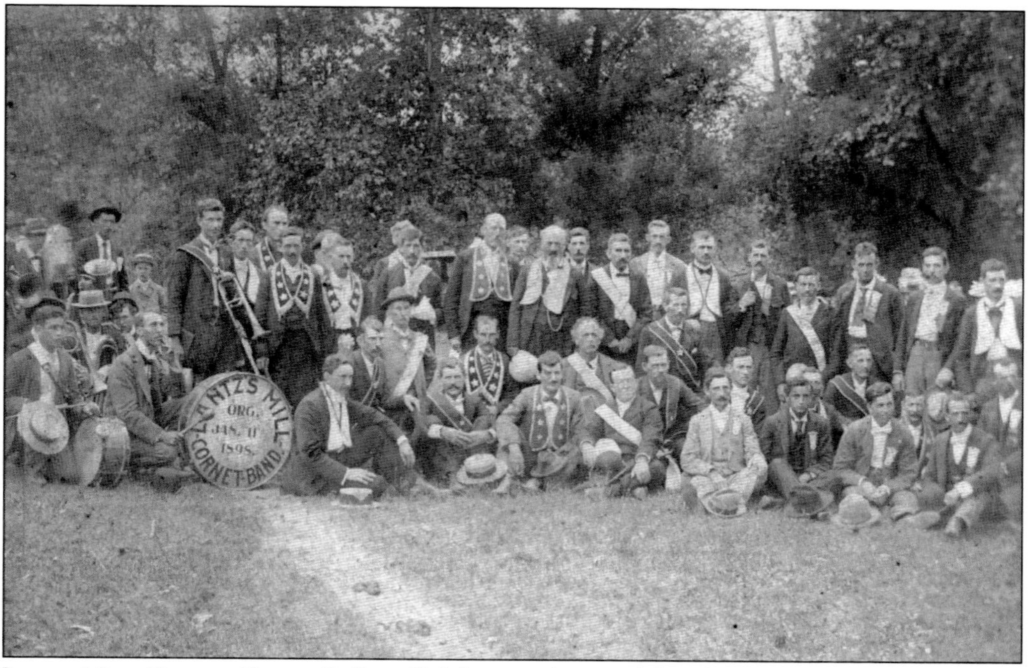

Lantz Mill Cornet Band. Delbert Fadely owned part of the island in Stony Creek at Lantz Mill that had a bandstand. Organized on January 11, 1898, with Dexter Fadely as the leader, the band was a social and musical outlet for the community. Many musical groups, including cornet bands, played on the island for the Saturday night festival. (WF.)

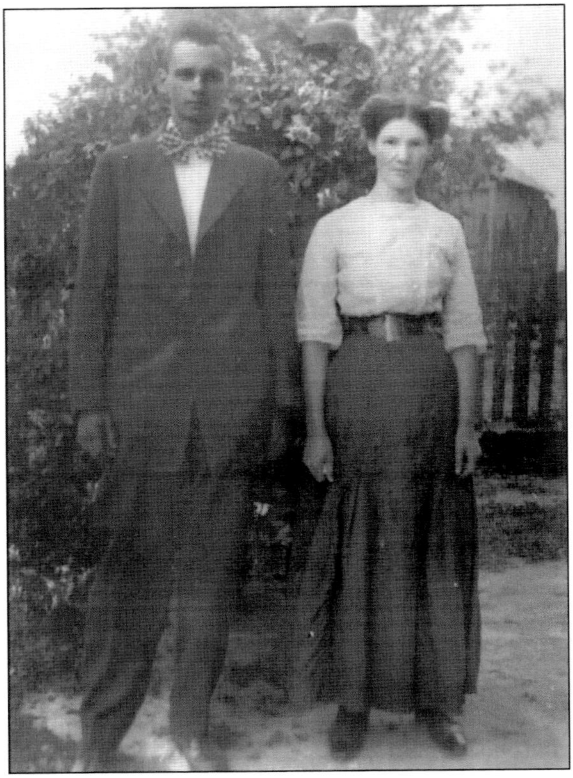

Emma and Emery Helsley. Emery Lorenza Helsley and Emma Florence Combs were married at Zion Church on June 11, 1913. In celebration of the day, he tossed his hat on the mock orange bush, which is still living on their farm. He was a farmer in Ridge Hollow near Columbia Furnace, where they lived the rest of their lives. They had nine children. (FHK.)

Oak Ridge School, 1905. Located between Jacob's Church and Columbia Furnace, this school also served students from Liberty Furnace. In 1879, Captain Grabill visited 38 students and their teacher Mr. Keller at the school. The family names of some of the students in 1905 included Barricks, Dellinger, Hottle, Johnson, Lear, Mumaw, Polk, Shipplett, and Helsley. Pictured sixth from the left in the back row is teacher Walter Hockman. (FHK.)

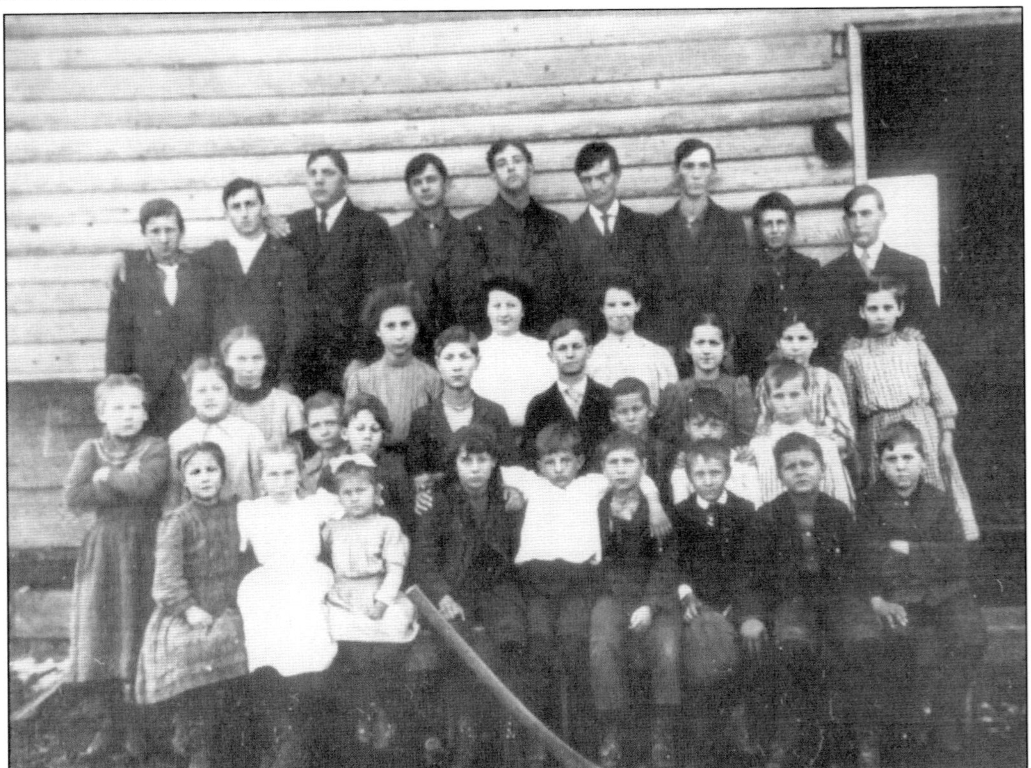

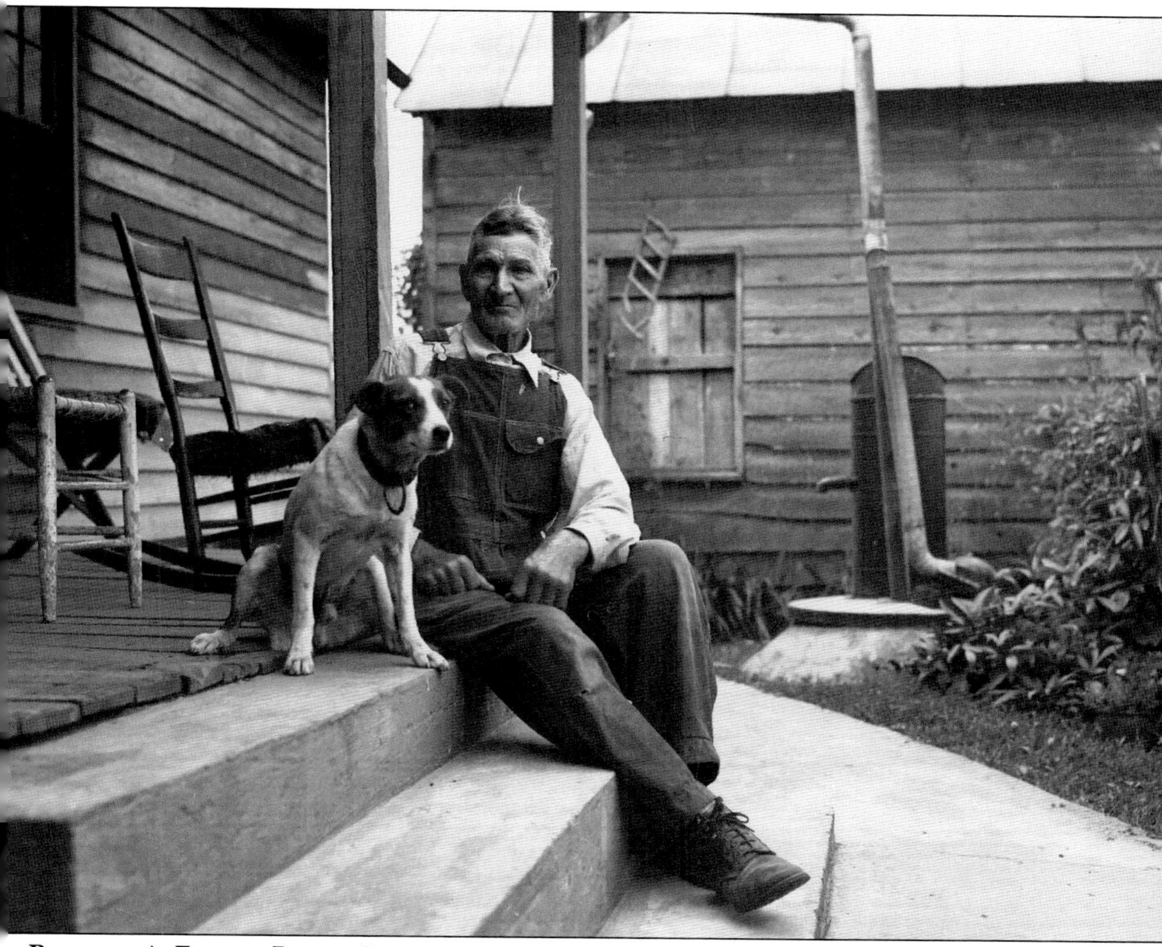

Benjamin A. Fry and Butch. Benjamin A. Fry was born in 1871. He worked on Ripley Walker's farm in Hawkinstown as a laborer and lived in this tenant house. The following are reminiscences by his great-granddaughter, who supplied this photograph. He is sitting on the steps with his dog Butch. Behind them on the porch are several chairs; the padded one belonged to his wife, and after her death, he kept it there in her memory. On the right is a cistern pump. The cistern is an underground tank for storing water. Visible are the pipes that catch the water off the building roof and channel it into the cistern. In 1932, when he was let go from his job on the farm, Fry bought the tenant house. After that, every fall he shucked corn for other farmers. On Ascension Day, he never worked and instead went fishing, and every Easter morning it was his tradition to eat 13 fried eggs. Fry was a fine man who never spoke a harsh word. Lawrence Lucas took this photograph in 1946. (PPS.)

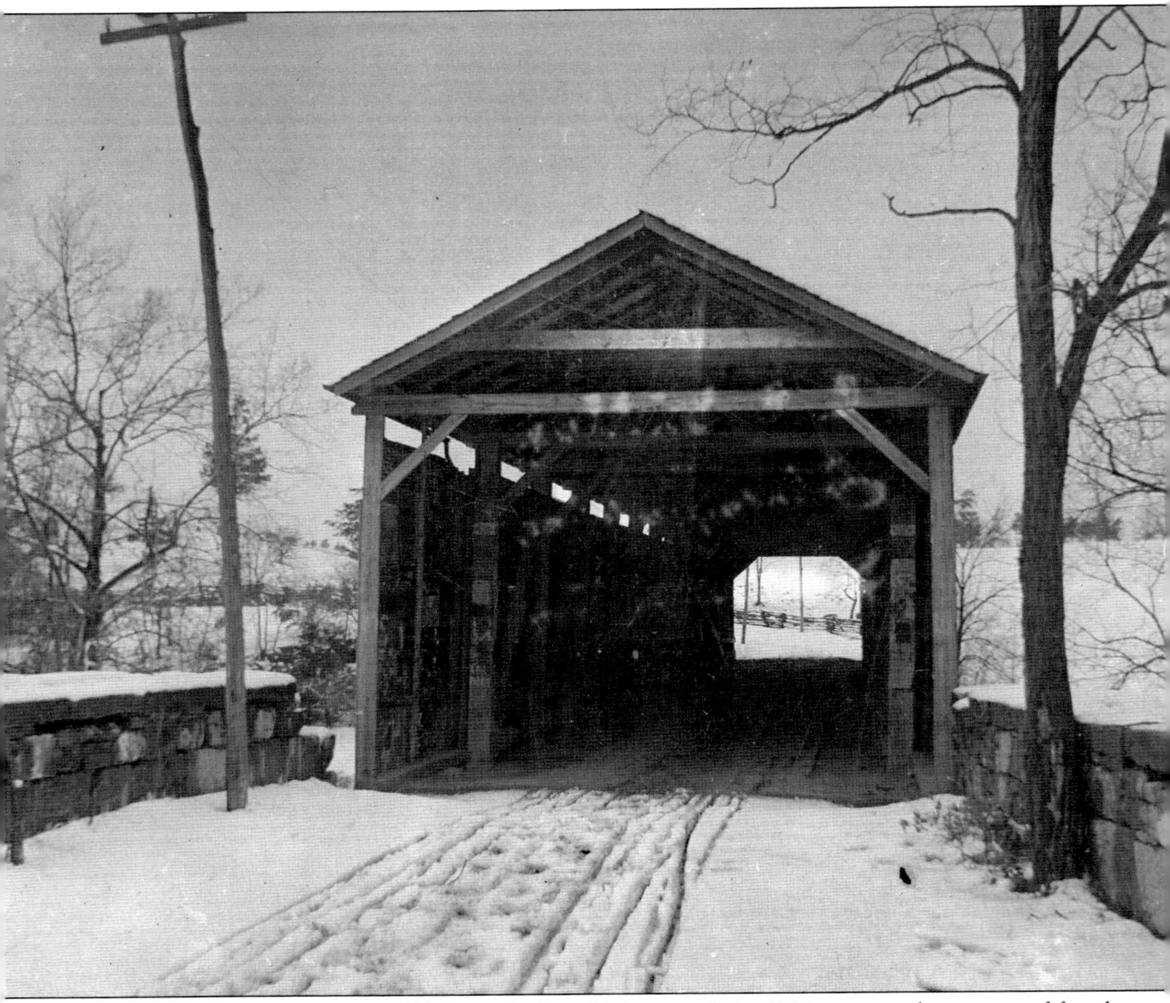

CEDAR CREEK BRIDGE. In William A. Booth's list, made in 1785, appear the names of families who lived in the northern part of Davis Magisterial District. It also included names for Lebanon Church, Wheatfield, Top Not, and the area north of Cedar Creek. Jacob Stickley, with seven "white souls," one dwelling house, and one other home is listed as well. The Stickley family still owns farmland near this creek. This wooden bridge was destroyed several times during the Civil War and was repeatedly rebuilt using stonework still in place. Gen. Turner Ashby burned this bridge after falling back from the battle of Kernstown on March 23, 1862. The wooden structure was replaced by a steel frame truss bridge. It was abandoned in the 1940s when Route 11 was moved and a new bridge built downstream. The tracks in the snow made by the horses and buggy wheels suggest the image was taken before the 1920s. Local stories say the gypsies slept in the covered bridges and made money walking travelers' horses across the bridge. (GRS.)

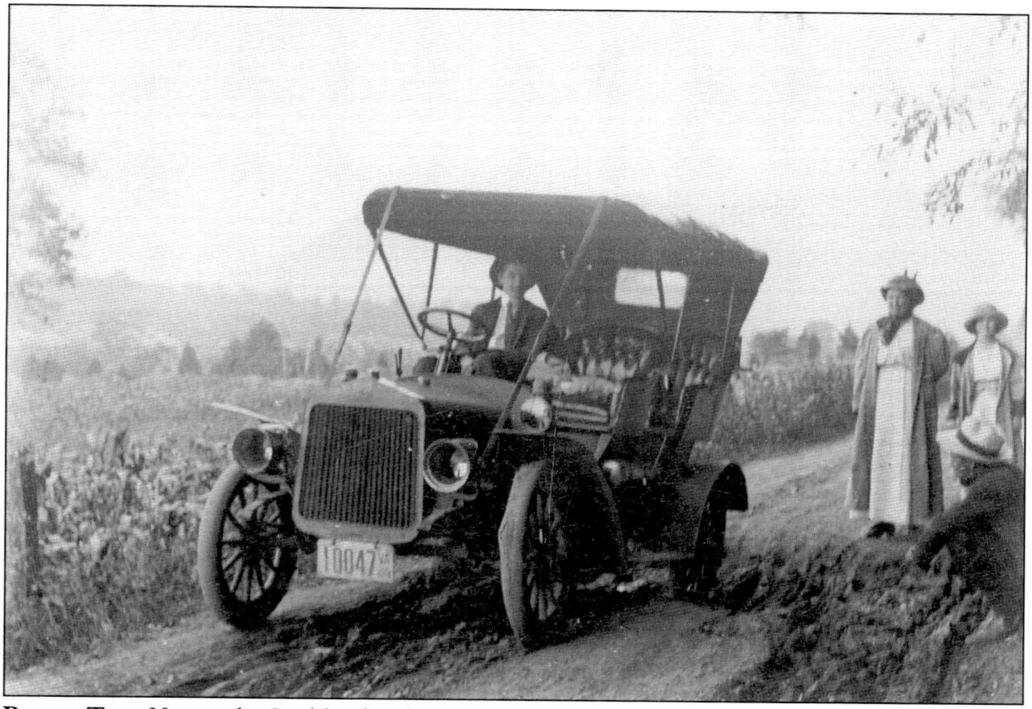

Blown Tire. Here is the Stickley family on the way from Cedar Creek to their home in Strasburg. They are stranded on this narrow, rutted dirt road because the front left tire of their fancy vehicle is no longer inflated. Walter Stickley is pondering how to fix the tire, and in the background are his wife and daughter. (GRS.)

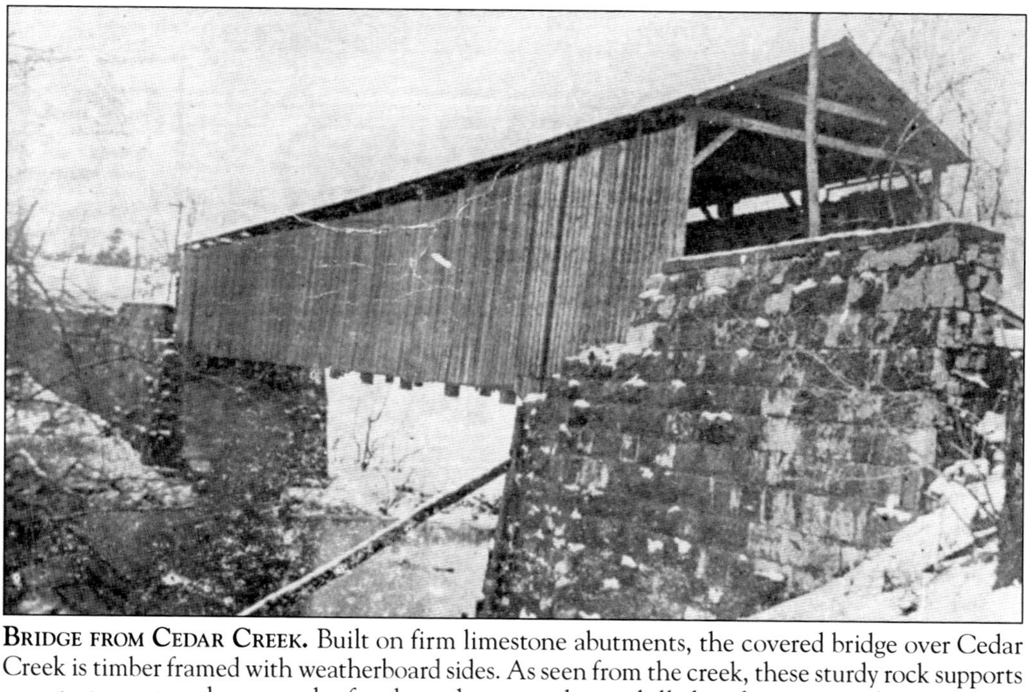

Bridge from Cedar Creek. Built on firm limestone abutments, the covered bridge over Cedar Creek is timber framed with weatherboard sides. As seen from the creek, these sturdy rock supports are a testament to the strength of rocks and mortar when a skilled craftsman puts them together. John Woods and Robert Jones were master bridge builders in Shenandoah County. (ML.)

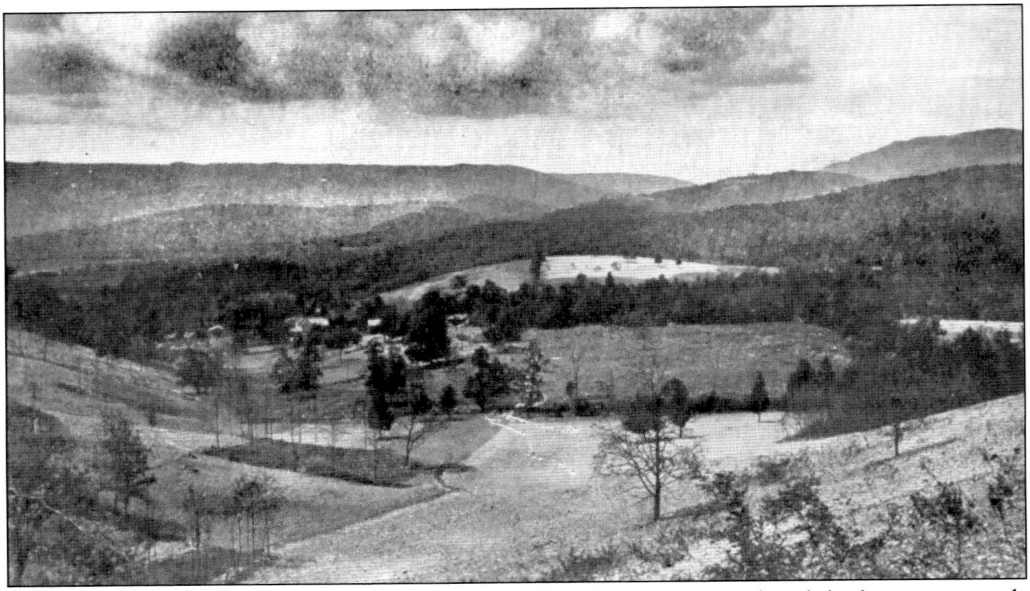

ZEPP. This view of Zepp north of the Mountain View Inn, a summer hotel, looks west towards Vance's Cove and Paddy Mountain from the foothills of Little North Mountain. Several small masonry limekilns have been identified in the coves near Cedar Creek in the Zepp area. Manganese and coal were also mined here as early as 1830. These were some of the earliest manganese mines in the nation. (WMSC.)

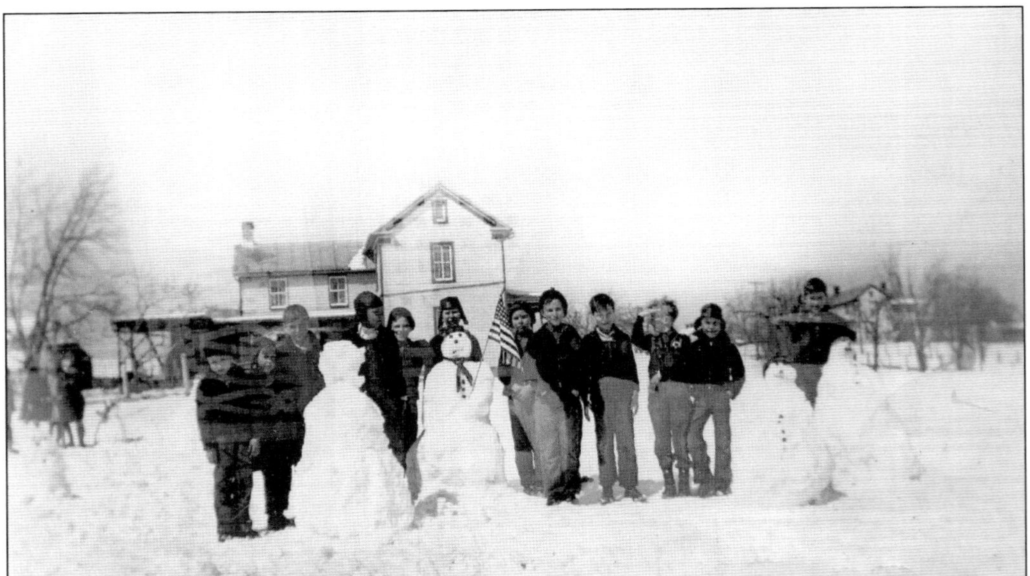

ORANDA. This tiny village is about 2 miles northwest of Strasburg. In this lime-making district in the 1940s, children had long distances to walk to school. Alice Loving made lunch for her own children, and for 20¢ the other children could get a hot lunch. Unidentified children are pictured here in the Oranda schoolyard in front of Henry and Alice Loving's home. (ML.)

Four

SHIMMERING RIBBONS

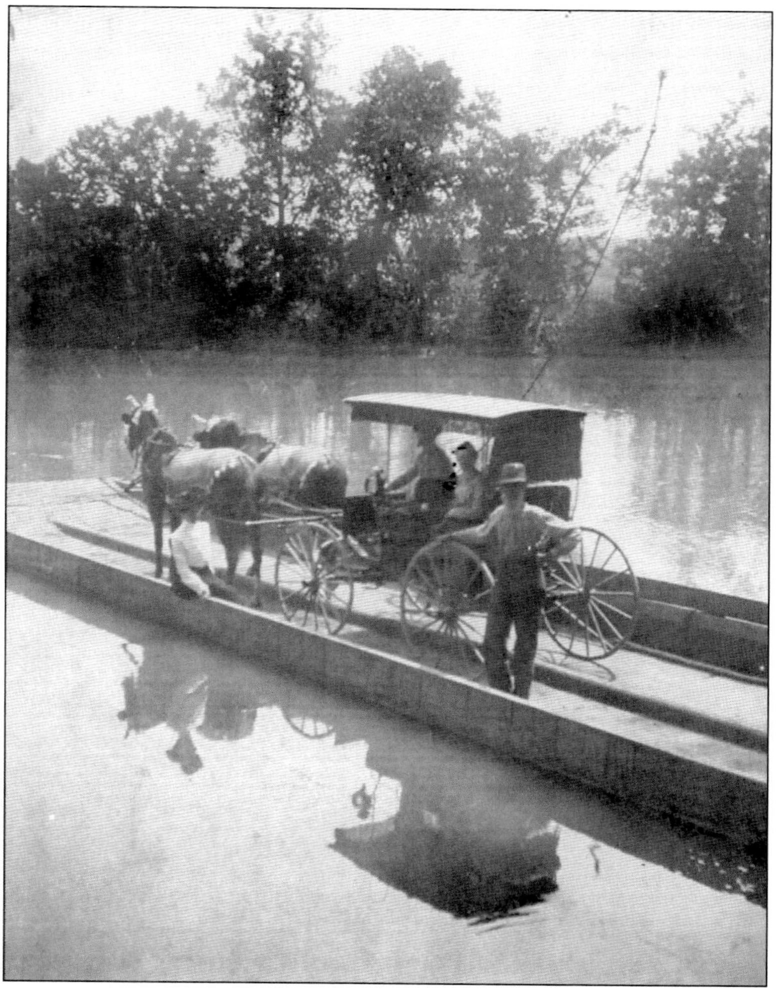

FERRY CROSSING THE NORTH FORK RIVER, 1902. If one flies over Shenandoah County on a bright day, reflections in many runs, creeks, ponds, lakes, and the river are visible. As the water tumbles over the rocks, it creates a soothing sound. Floods on this river have washed away ferries and bridges. This carriage and team look completely safe, and the rope on the wire is seen in the river. (SCL.)

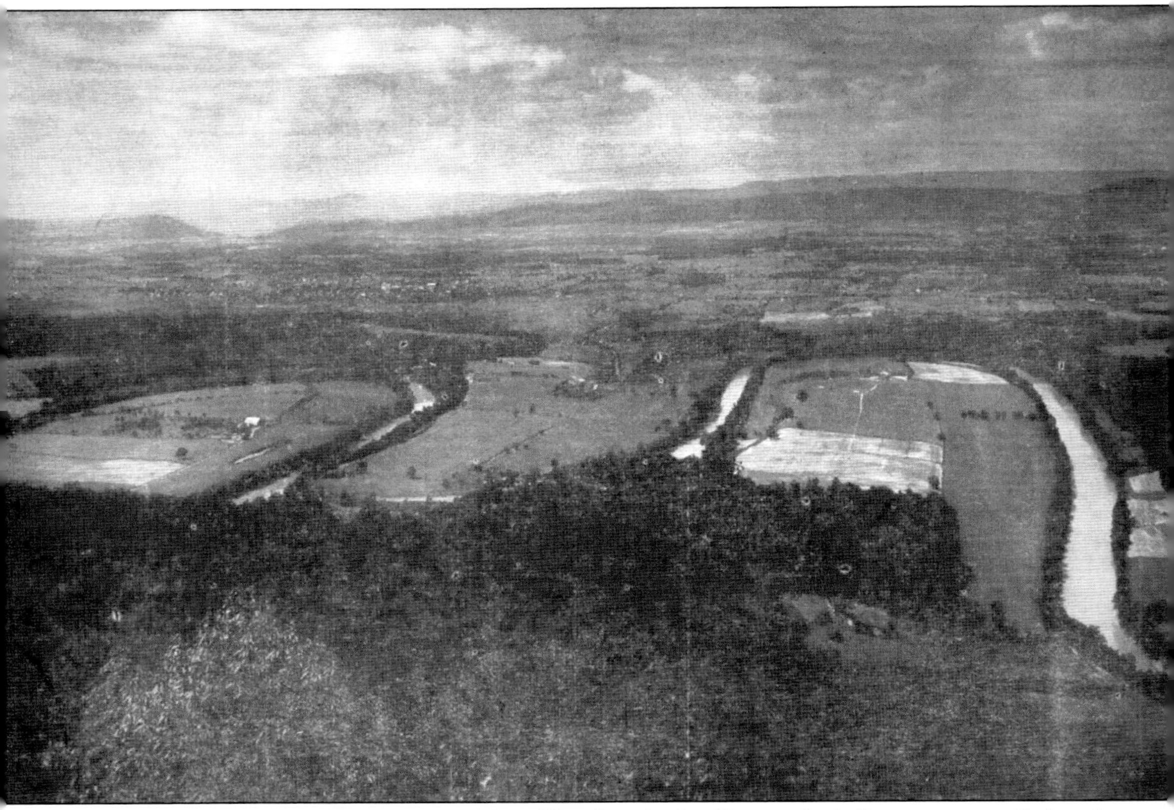

NORTH FORK NEAR WOODSTOCK. Near Woodstock, the Shenandoah River continually bends at this low elevation, creating a wide swath of water at flood times. As it recedes, the river leaves the silt from higher elevations, making fertile fields along the river. Shenandoah County has been flooded many times, notably in 1870, 1924, 1936, and 1942. In the 1870 flood, over 8 inches of rain fell within 48 hours, and the river reached 30 feet above its previous level. It was a half-mile wide in some places, and the railroad bridge at Strasburg was destroyed. The bridge at Red Banks was washed away, according to the May 13, 1924, *Daily News Record*, and "a family driving a Buick automobile became stranded, escaped before the car was swept away by the raging floodwaters." In this photograph, the river is within its normal banks, and fields are planted. The occasional cluster of farm buildings is seen within the bends. Farther back on the left is Woodstock, with fields and mountains beyond. The photograph was taken from the tower east of Woodstock. (SCL.)

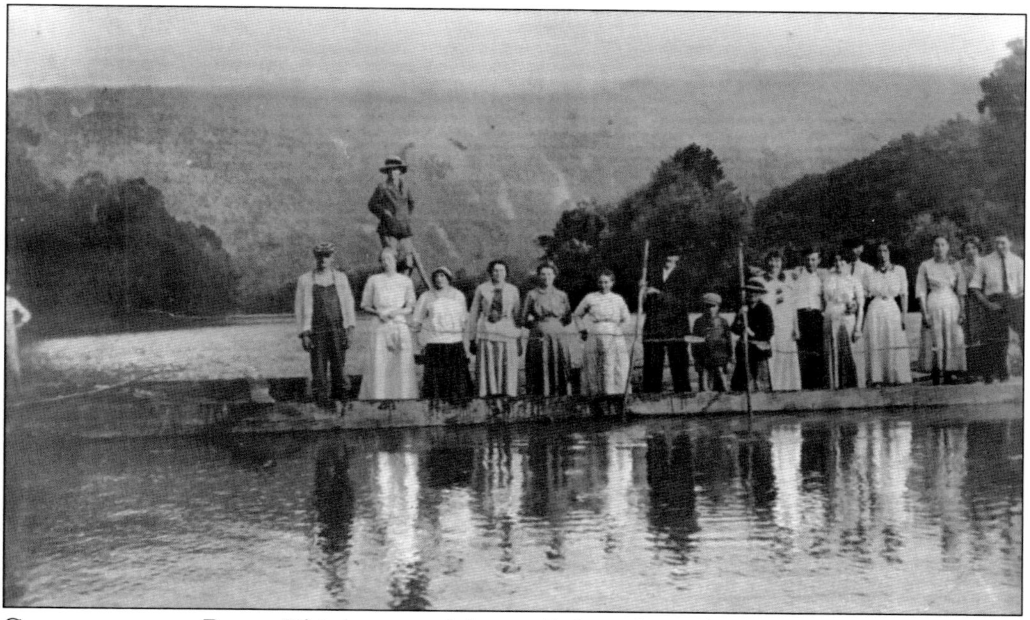

Gondola on the River. This large gondola is pulled up alongside the mill on the North Fork of the Shenandoah River. Dr. James and Patricia Miller now own the mill. The people on the flatboat are on an excursion. The larger ones were used to transport grain, produce, and pig iron. Often they were taken as far north as Harper's Ferry, West Virginia, where the boats would be sold for scrap lumber. (Courtesy of Dr. James and Patricia Kiser.)

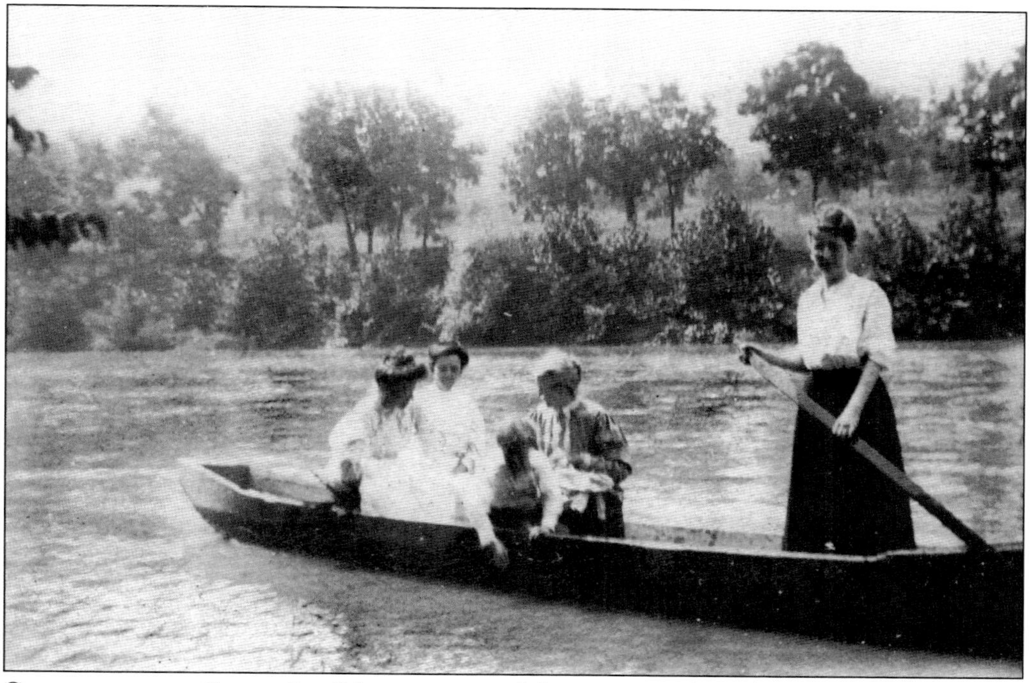

Company on the River. Small boats were used for outings such as this one, showing the five ladies from the Stickley farm near Tumbling Run. Lucille Stickley, standing in the boat with the pole, enjoyed entertaining her family and friends with a leisurely ride on the placid river. (Courtesy of Gloria and Ralph Stickley.)

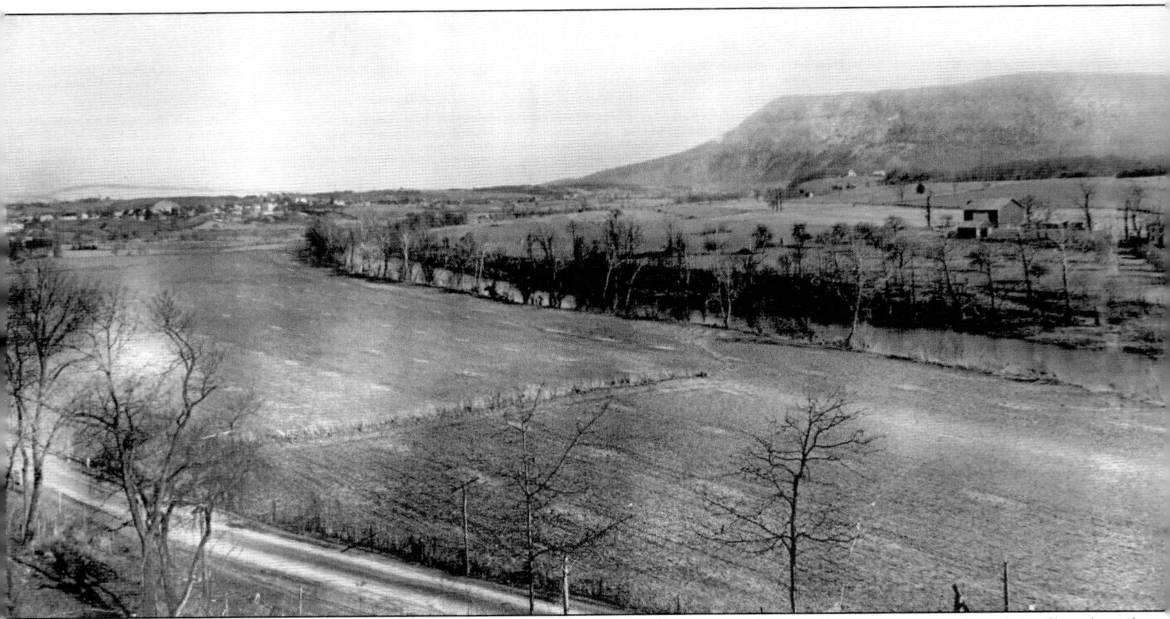

River near Tumbling Run. Corn seems to be the crop planted most often in this flat land between Route 11 and the river because the river often floods and the soil is fertile. Strasburg is farther north along the turnpike on the left side. Josiah Stickley's farm is seen on the extreme right. To the right of the farm is where Tumbling Run flows down from Fishers Hill and enters the North Fork of the Shenandoah River. Signal Knob is in the background, and between that and the farm is a high place with trees behind it. It is there that the current Stickley family built their ranch home. They have sold some of this high ground to the Shenandoah County Schools, and athletic fields are being installed there. (GRS.)

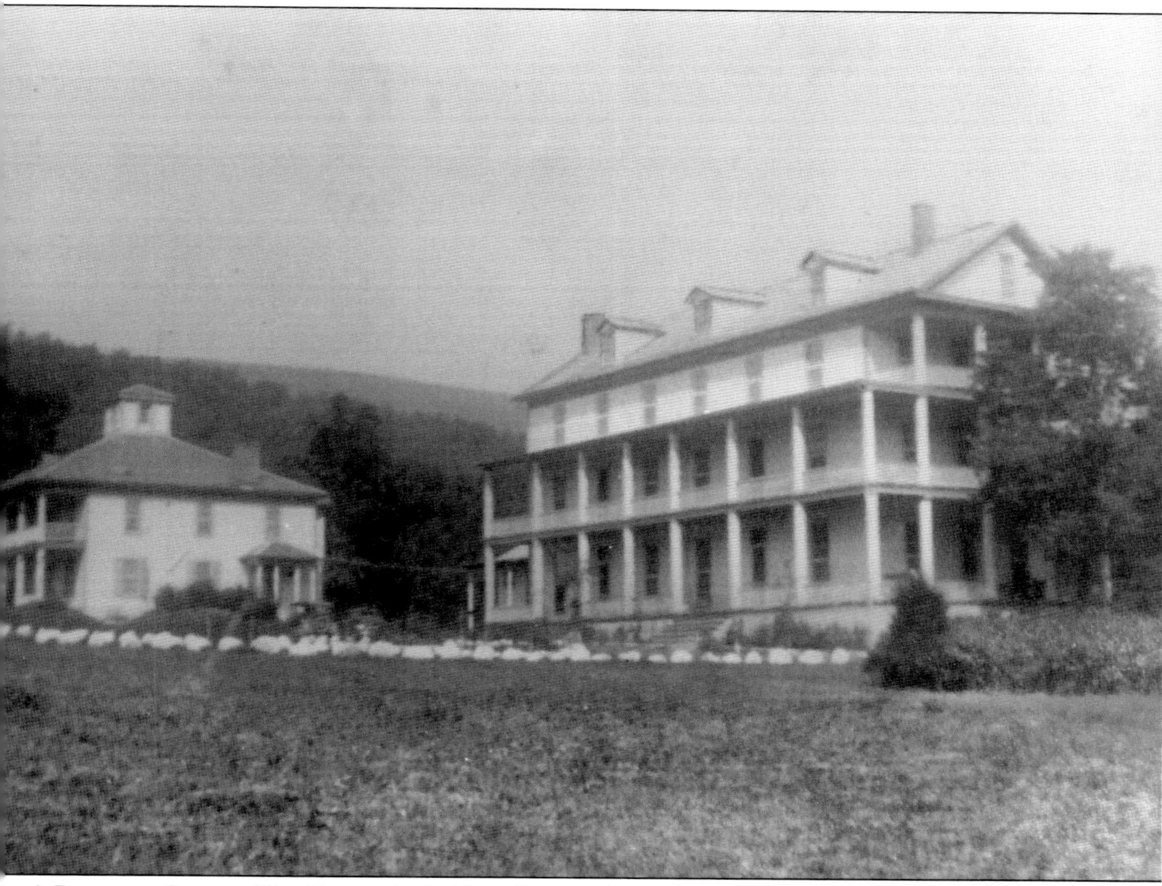

A Place of Charm. The Shenandoah Alum Springs, located on the headwaters of Stony Creek close to its sources, are in the southwest corner of the county. The Alum Springs Hotel opened in 1870 and operated until the early 1900s. A gap in nearby North Mountain created a constant flow of air about all sides of the hotel. The post office was here for many years. The Shenandoah Woodworkers was a community of craftsmen and their families. They located here at Bird Haven in the 1920s after needing to find a way to provide employment during the Depression years. They combined and organized their skills and used creative ways of advertising. They carved bowls and birds of wood; made birdhouses, puzzles, and games; and printed books. The items were made in these buildings after they no longer served as home to the ironmaster or as a fancy resort. The buildings began to decline, but the community of Bird Haven thrived in them for many years. The simple pieces they made are considered collectible today. (OBG.)

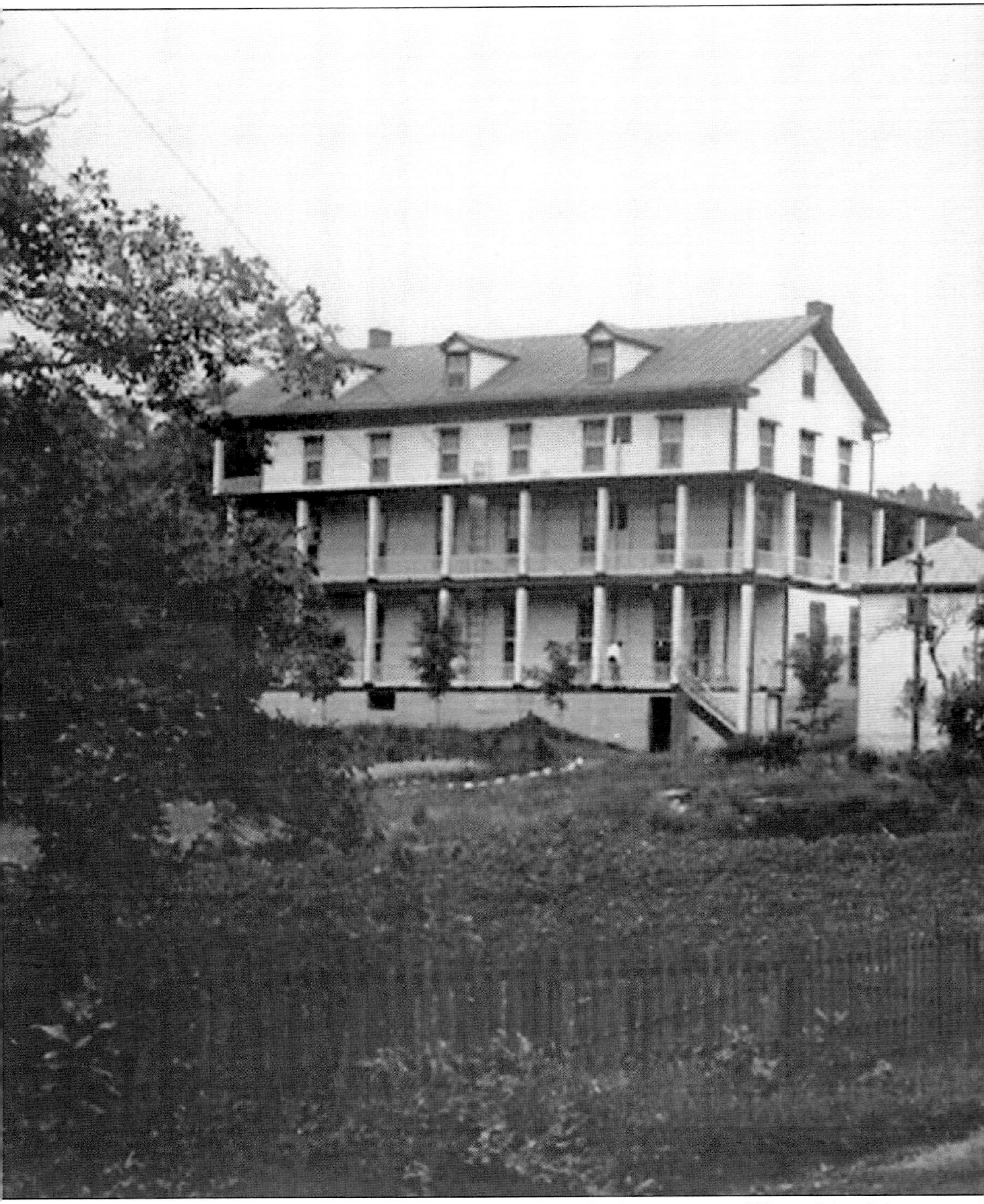

VIRGINIA'S POPULAR RESORT. Yellow Spring Mountain, the former name of Shrine Mont Mountain, is located 12 miles southwest of Mount Jackson. At 2,300 feet above sea level, the natural formations and scenery brought visitors to partake of the medicinal mineral waters. Three alum springs near the house held a solution of sulphate, aluminum, and iron. One had a pleasant astringent taste, another was stronger, and the third puckered the lips. Five other springs held chalybeate, healing,

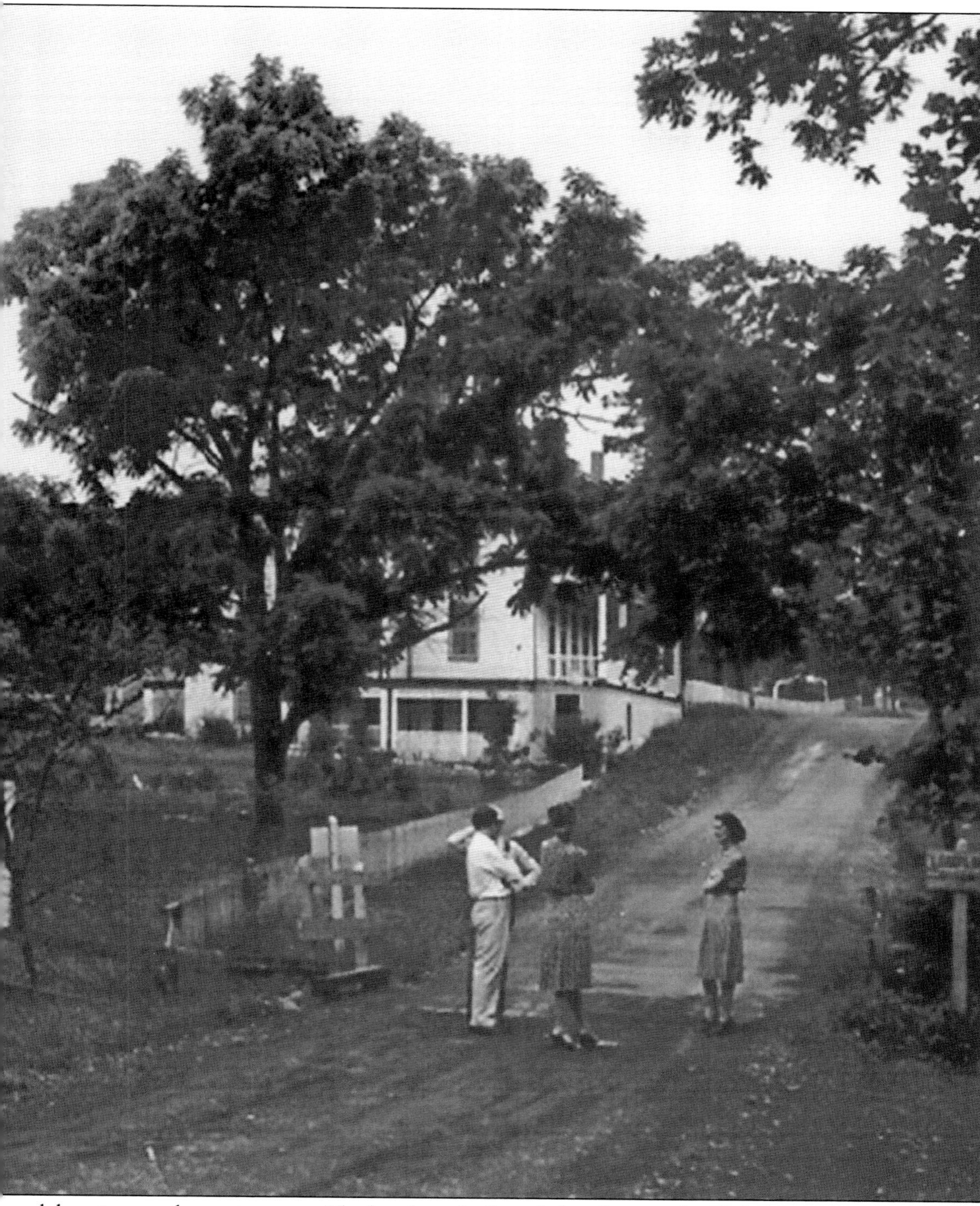

sulphur, iron, and arsenic waters. The hotel was built with four floors, a double balcony, and 26 sleeping rooms. A small group is seen on the road entering the grounds, and ahead of them is the house built in the early 1830s for the ironmaster of Henrietta Furnace. The Alum Springs Hotel operated until the early 1900s. (OBG.)

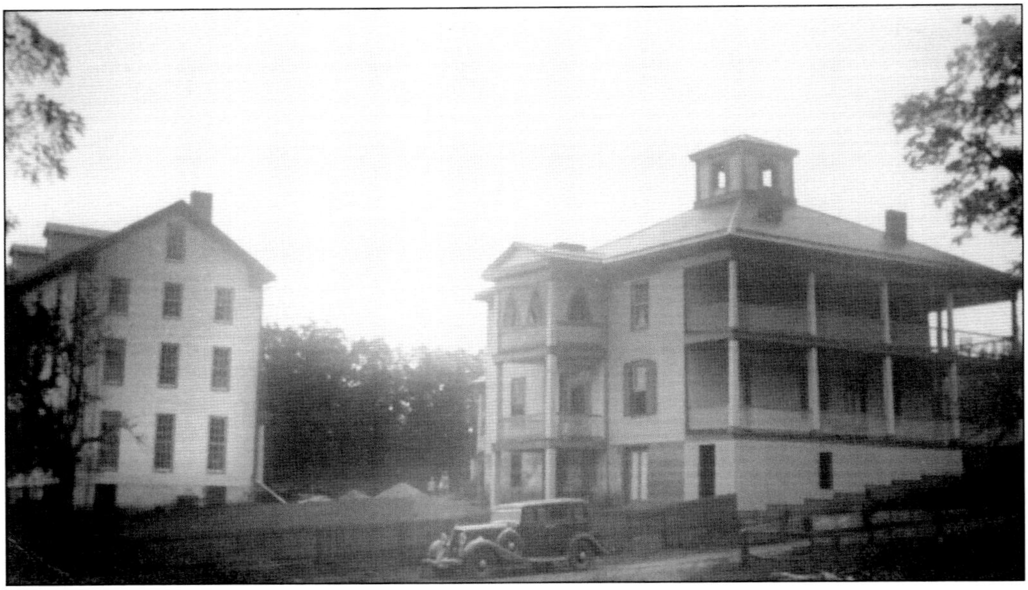

IRONMASTER'S HOUSE AND FAMILY SUMMER RETREAT. Henrietta Furnace ironmaster A. J. Myers, from Pennsylvania, built this home and these offices for the furnace in the late 1830s. The Myers family owned the furnace until it burned in 1864. In 1934, John Ross, a lawyer from Mount Jackson, purchased and modernized the hotel. He added a swimming pool and tennis courts, and during World War II, diplomats visiting Washington, D.C., were brought here to enjoy the mountains and mineral springs. A lightening strike and declining business motivated Ross to convert the hotel into a poultry house. Shortly after his death in 1950, the building was destroyed by fire. Ross's daughter and her friends bought and used the old mansion as a summer retreat. The donor of these photographs, Olivia Bland Gentile, granddaughter of John Ross, remembers those 20 years joyfully. (OBG.)

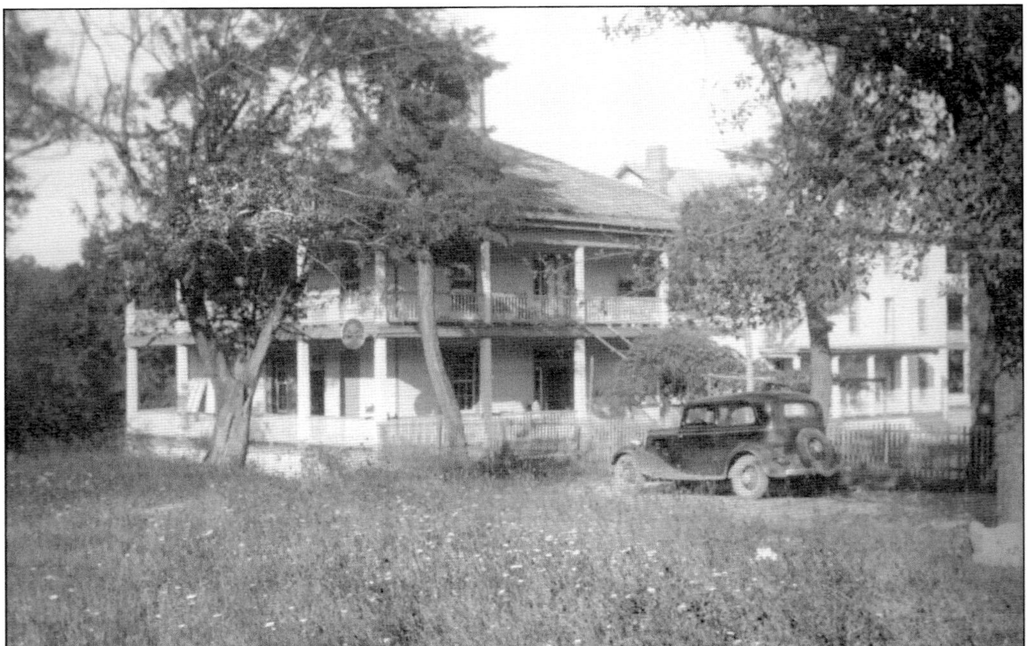

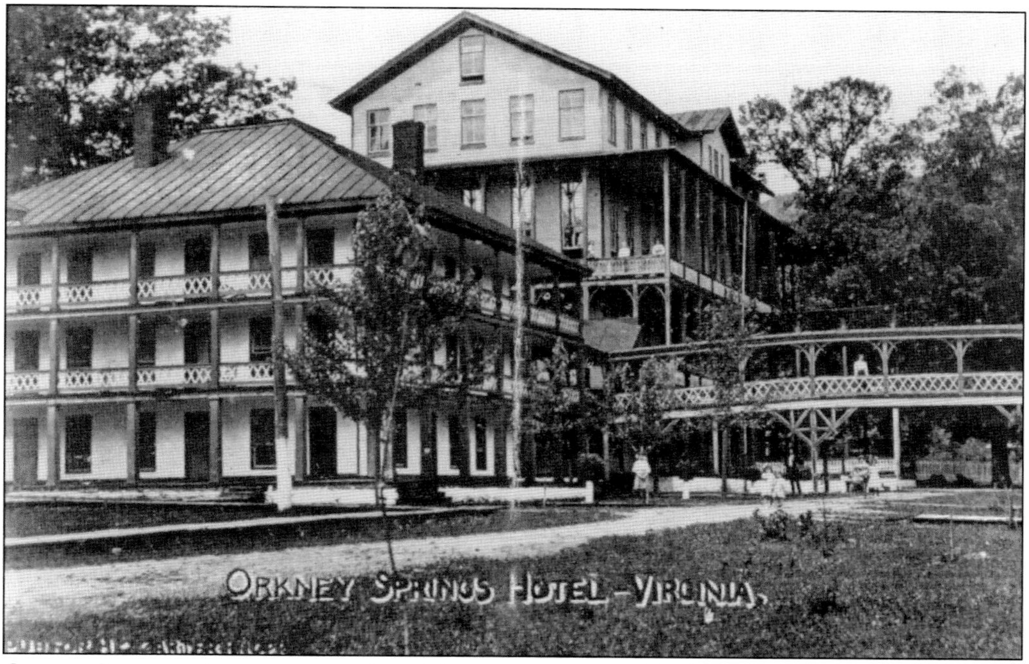

ORKNEY SPRINGS HOTEL AND THE BEAR WALLOW SPRING. In 1775, Dr. John McDonald, a physician and churchwarden of Frederick Parish, purchased 350 acres of land. Upon his death, Maj. Peter Higgins laid out a fort-like plan for the town of Orkney Springs in 1808. At the center of the plan is an oblong common labeled "public square." Four springs are in the square; they are named Methodist Springs, Lutheran Springs, Chalybeate (iron) Springs, and Tea Spring. Bear Wallow Spring and many others are nearby, and those who came to drink or bathe stayed over. Several log hotels were built prior to the Civil War. After the war, several three-story buildings and seven cottages were constructed. (SMOC.)

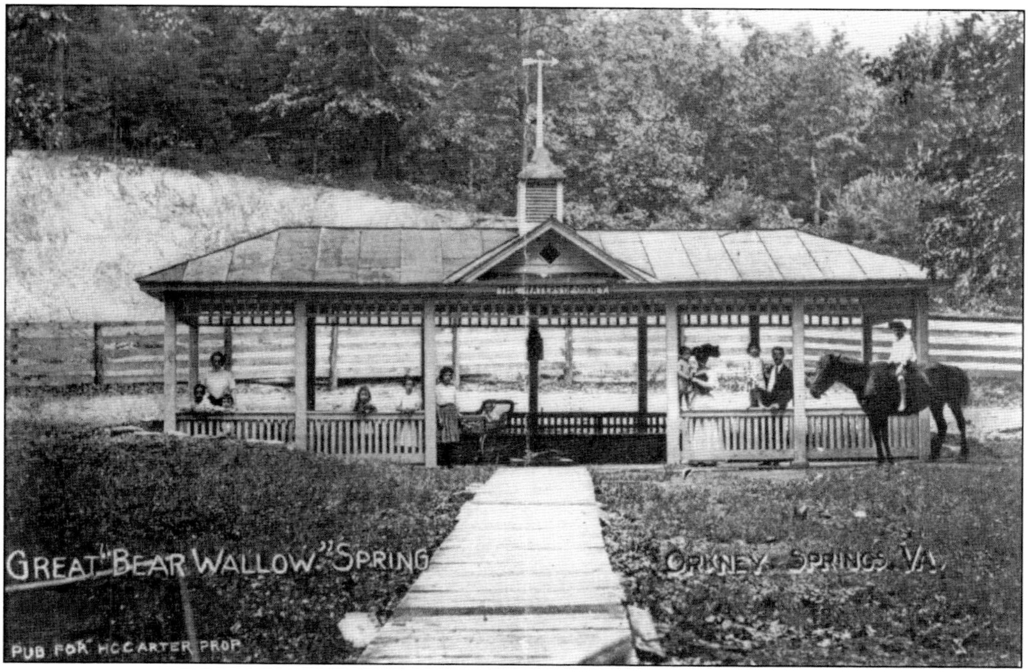

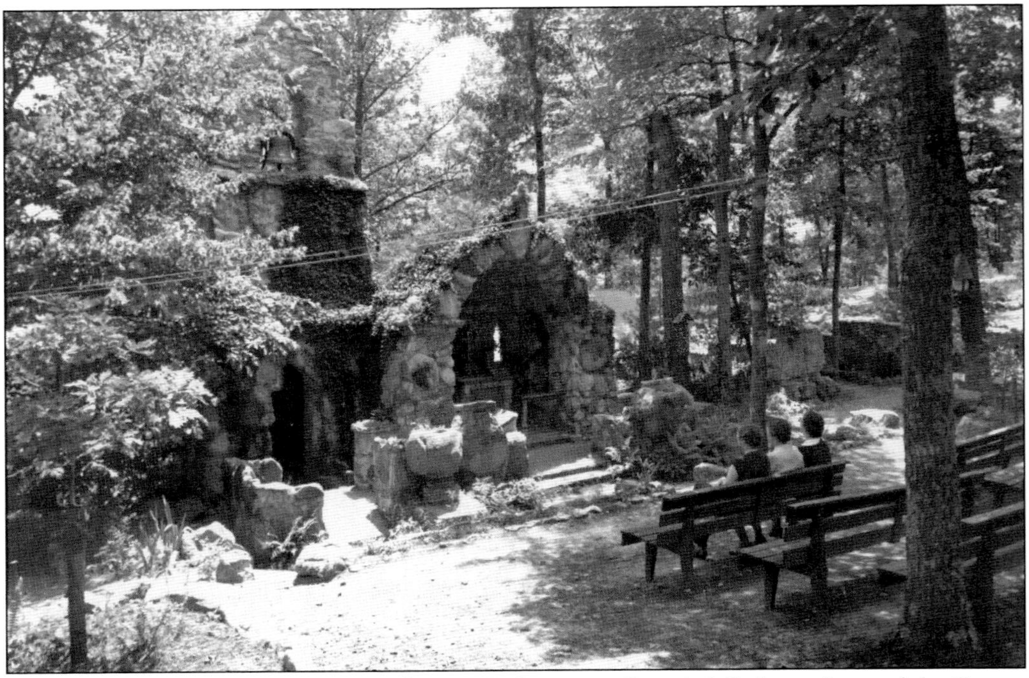

Shrine Mont. Seventeen miles west of Mount Jackson over Supinlick Ridge and toward the George Washington and Jefferson National Forest is Orkney Springs. At the tiny village past the hotels and up into the trees one can find Shrine Mont, the Cathedral Shrine of the Transfiguration. The Reverend Edmund Lee Woodward, M.D., built with love and his own hands a shrine where "we may be delivered from the inquietude of this world and behold the King in His beauty." The sanctuary was built to provide a place of worship and to commemorate a pious previous owner Bishop Gibson. The stone tower is 35 feet high. The altar is to the right of the bell tower, and a tree-sheltered amphitheater contains weathered benches for resting. (SMOC.)

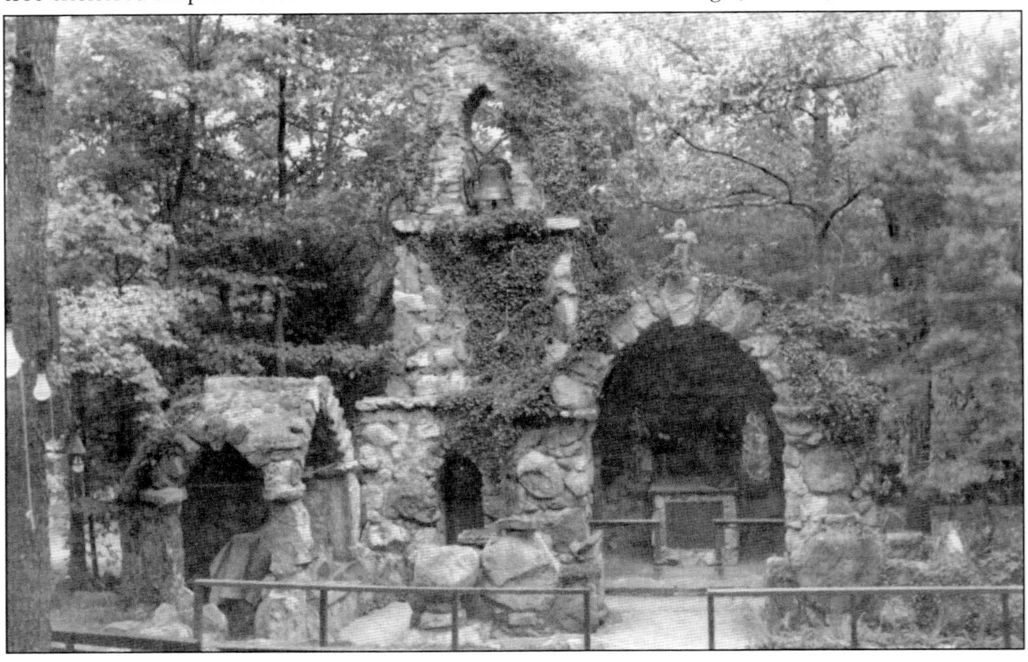

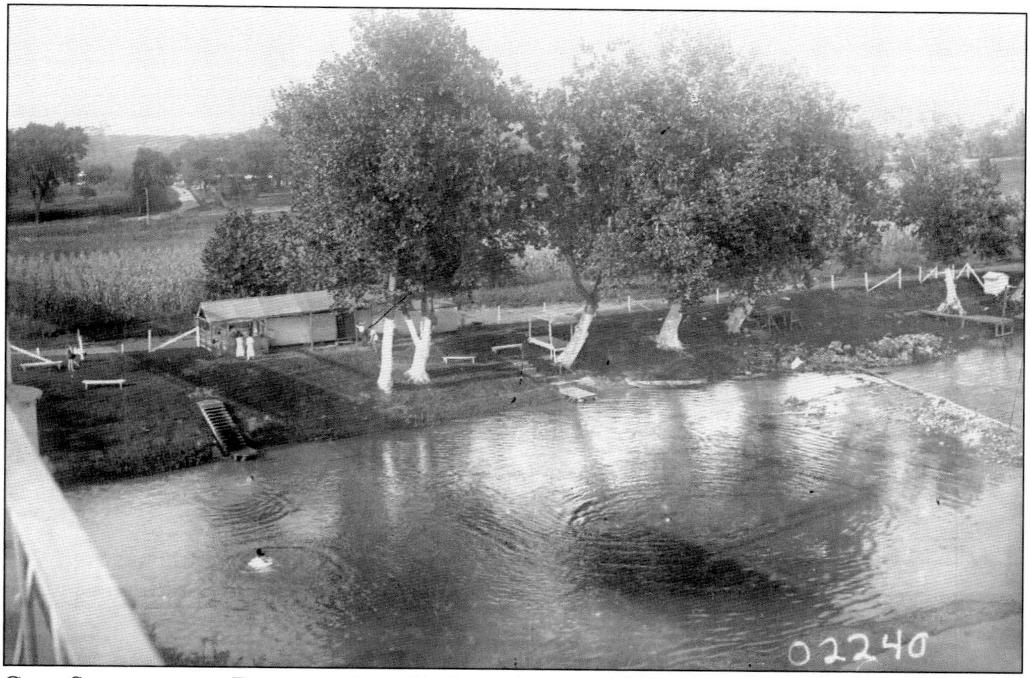

CAMP STRAWDERMAN POOL AND FLAG. Twelve miles west of Woodstock in the George Washington National Forest is a summer oasis for girls ages 6 to 19, established in 1929. To get to the camp, one must drive through the waters of Stony Creek. Rich in pioneer traditions, the farm has original log cabins, a bathhouse, a counselor's lodge, a trading post, and stables, and most are either old or built in a rustic style. The swimming pool is a section of Stony Creek dammed to provide required depth for the annual water ballets the girls perform. The camp provides horses, crafts, trails, and boating, and the food is grown in the large gardens. Counselors create a friendly family environment in the cabins with a unit of eight campers and two counselors. Some families have the tradition of offering this camp experience to all their daughters. (SCHS.)

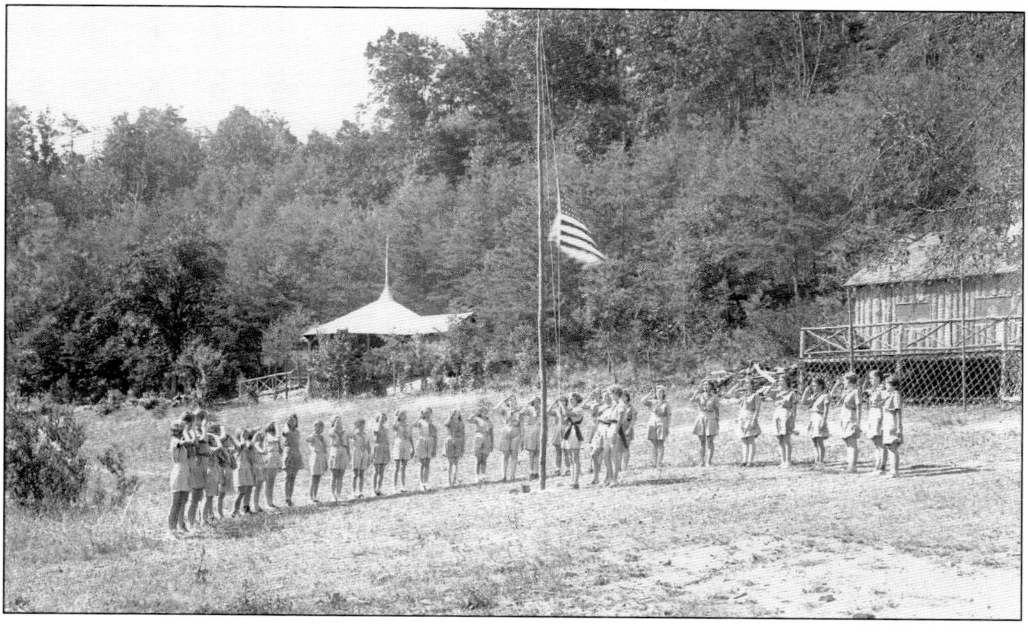

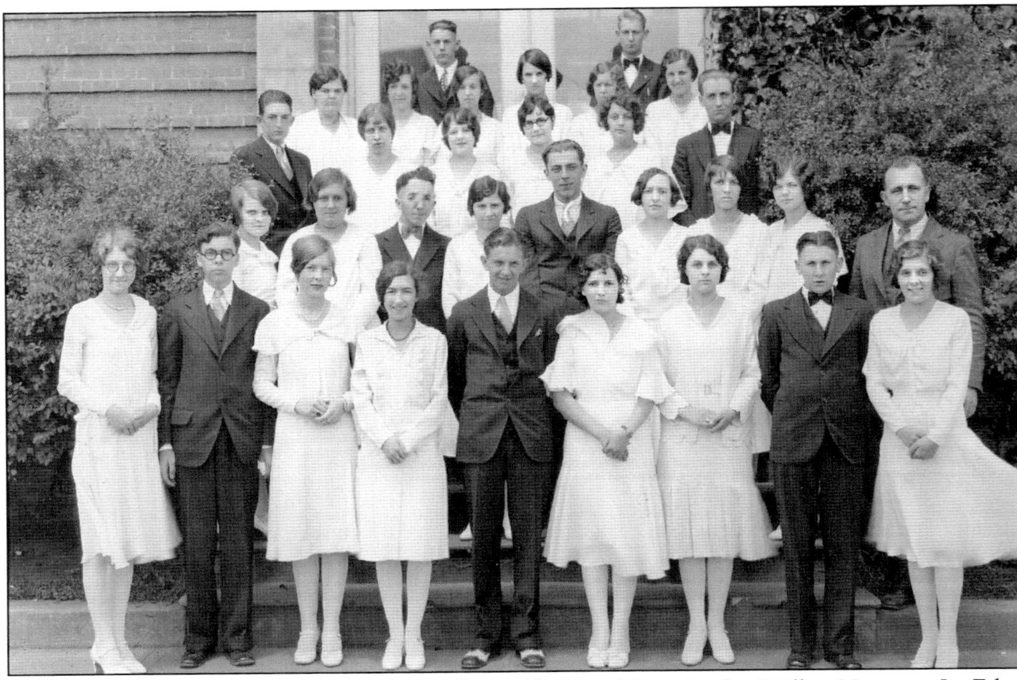

WOODSTOCK, 1930. Pictured from left to right are (first row) Ione Beyler, Wilbur Newman Jr., Edna Miller, Virginia Stickley, J. Pence, Joyce Williams, Eliza Fleming, Robert Ramey, and Romaine Foster; (second row) Grace Stoner, Emma Rush, Louis R. Marston, Martha Hooper, Homer Golliday, Winifred Burner, Eunice Miller, Martha James, and principal M. C. Hollingsworth; (third row) Edward Wickhaus, Hazel Spiggle, Fleta Hepner, Mary Harris Clem, Mary Funkhauser, and Samuel Stickley; (fourth row) Lucy Gaunt, Helen Rush, unidentified, Violet Sine, Lucy Plaugher, and Virginia Coverstone; (fifth row) Wilson Stickley and Charles Clem. (SCL.)

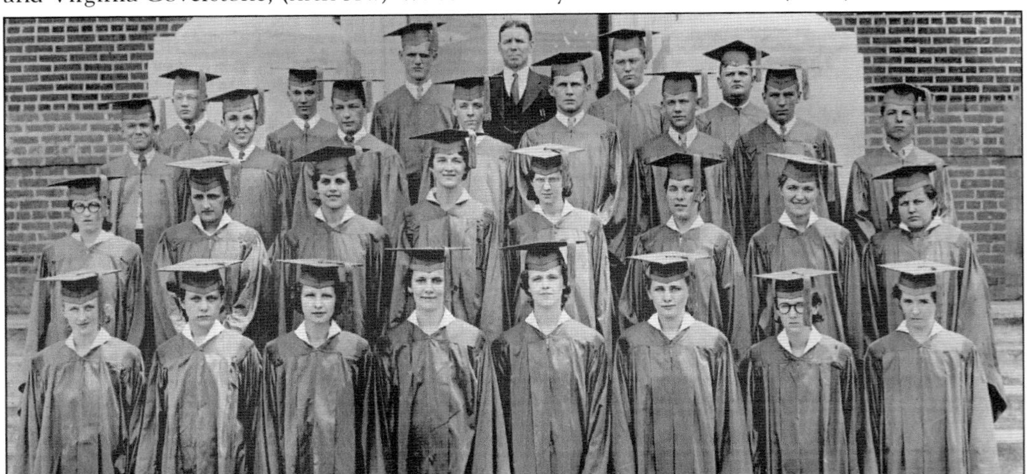

TRIPLETT, 1933. From left to right are (first row) Helen Shutters, Eleanor Holtzman, Frances Smoot, Elizabeth Younger, Helen Bowman, Maizie Barb, Wilda Hupp, and Lettie Swartz; (second row) Edith Harpine, Antionette Evans, Audrey Nell, Virginia Dellinger, Audrey Miller, Evelyn Miller, Eleanor Vehrencamp, and Thelma Sibert; (third row) Orey Rinker, Roger Mays, Ben Newland, Richard Burkett, Graham Stoneburner, Ned Tabler, Douglas Evans, and Paul Zirkle; (fourth row) Elwood Baker, Floyd Whitmer, George Lorentz, principal H. M. Painter, Jesse Sine, and Glen Estep. (JW.)

Five

Celebration and Recreation

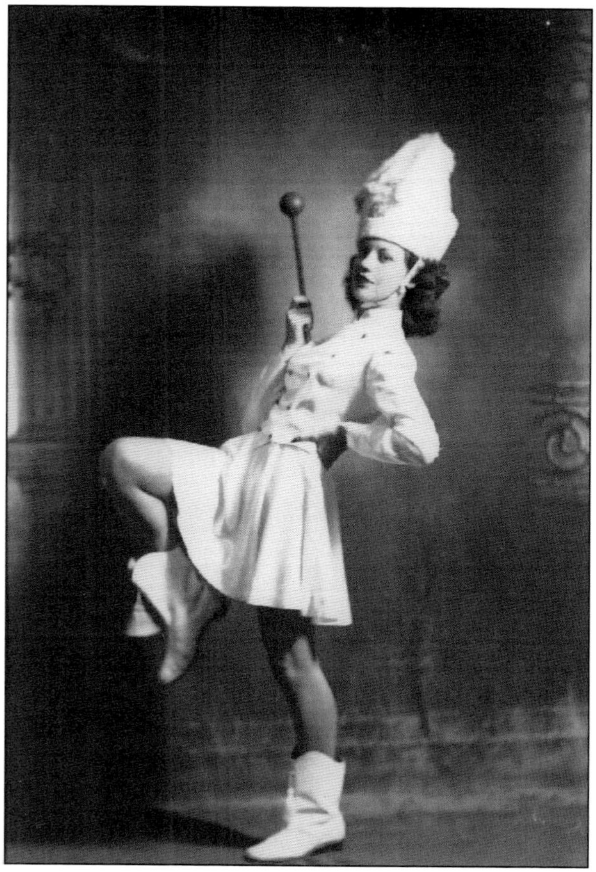

Juanita on Parade. Shenandoah County established traditions from the earliest times, and residents have created new ways to celebrate. Court days, patriotic parades, Memorial Day celebrations, church picnics, harvest festivals, fireman's parades, and the county fair are occasions to compete and collaborate. Memorial Day became an official holiday in 1868 to commemorate the lives of the soldiers who were killed in the Civil War. (Courtesy of Juanita Joan Stickley Anderson Hafer.)

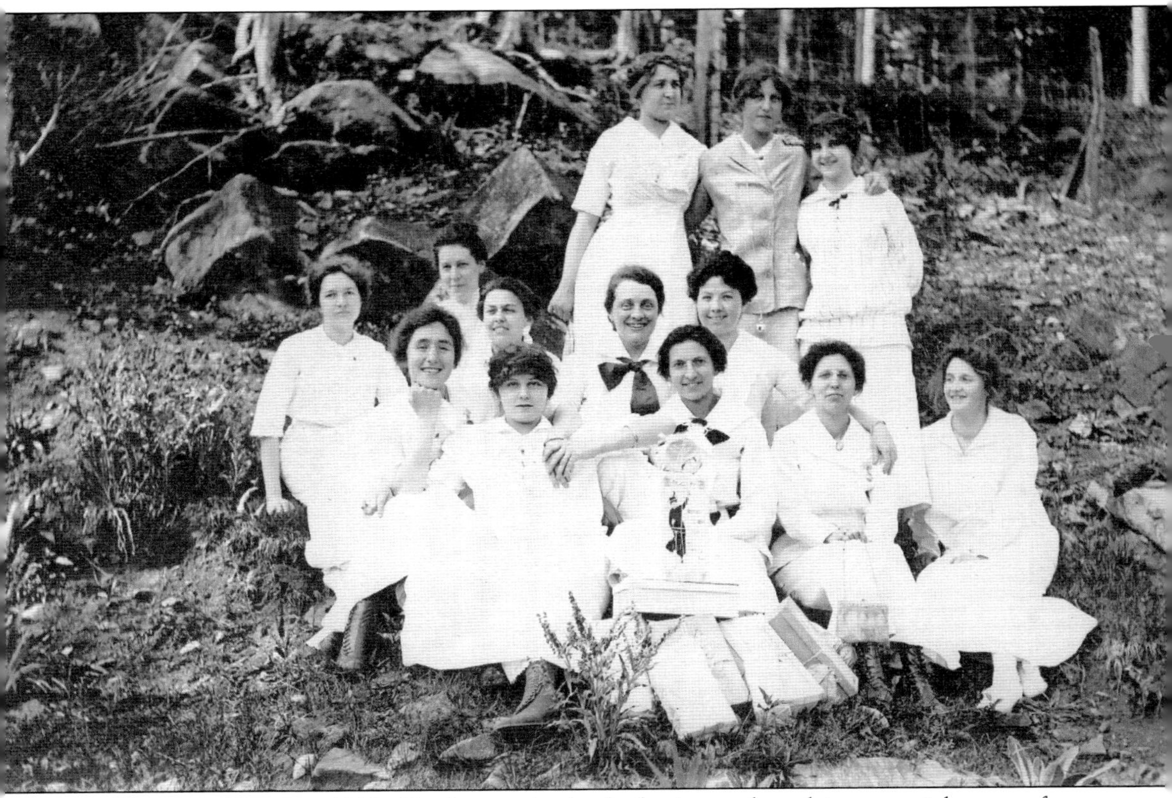

VOTE FOR WOMEN, 1913. Getting out in the fresh air together, this congenial group of women, dressed for town, has each brought food. After a hearty breakfast, they started out in Edinburg and walked 5 miles to Woodstock, where they opened their shoeboxes to have lunch. The women spent time in Woodstock and caught the night train back to Edinburg. Getting the right to vote was a topic of much discussion in the local newspapers and at social events. With a photographer on hand, they took the opportunity to make their wishes known, as can be seen in the small suffragette poster. Among those pictured are Marguerite Holtzman, Ameilia Whissen Coffman, Marguerite Hisey, Julia Whightman Wharton, Clara Evans, Katherine Snyder, Ella Belew, Elizabeth Murphy, Hattie Whissen, Trilby Hisey, Agnes Hopewell Tate, Lou Hopewell, and Bertha Hisey Walters. (SCL.)

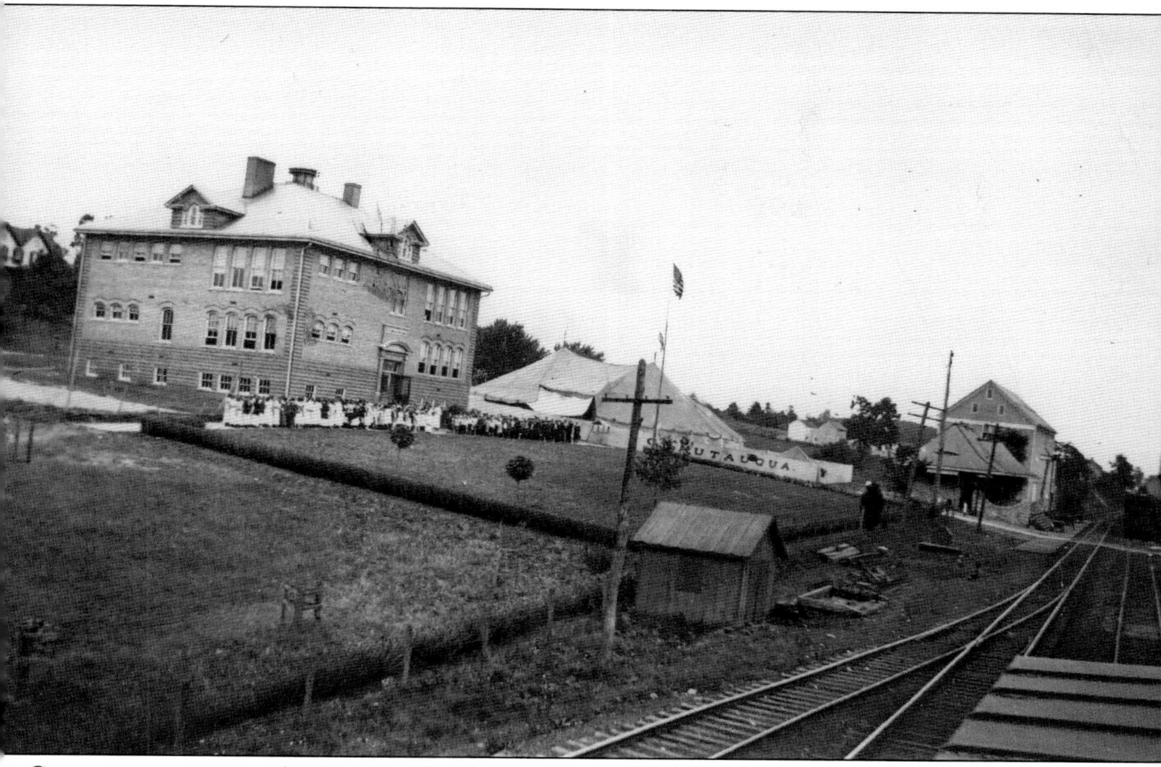

CHAUTAUQUA, 1920. The Woodstock School is seen with the Chautauqua tents, train station, and the Boyer Warehouse in the background. The large crowd gathered in front of the school includes participants in the local program. While the main organizers came from Chautauqua County in New York State, where the educational and entertaining cultural events organized in 1874, many of the players, singers, and performers were recruited locally. For an entire week, they worked together and rehearsed, and then they performed for the public. News articles and auditions created a large audience. From the July 24, 1925, *Shenandoah Herald* comes the following: "Chautauqua time is over. Monday night was the last session of our very successful entertainment, the Radcliffe Chautauqua. This is the first year our town has ever had a Chautauqua, everyone is enthusiastic for their return next year . . . there was a children's parade, which was very comic, and afforded much fun for both young and old." Little Dorothy Shrum and Derwood Johns won first prizes. (WMSC.)

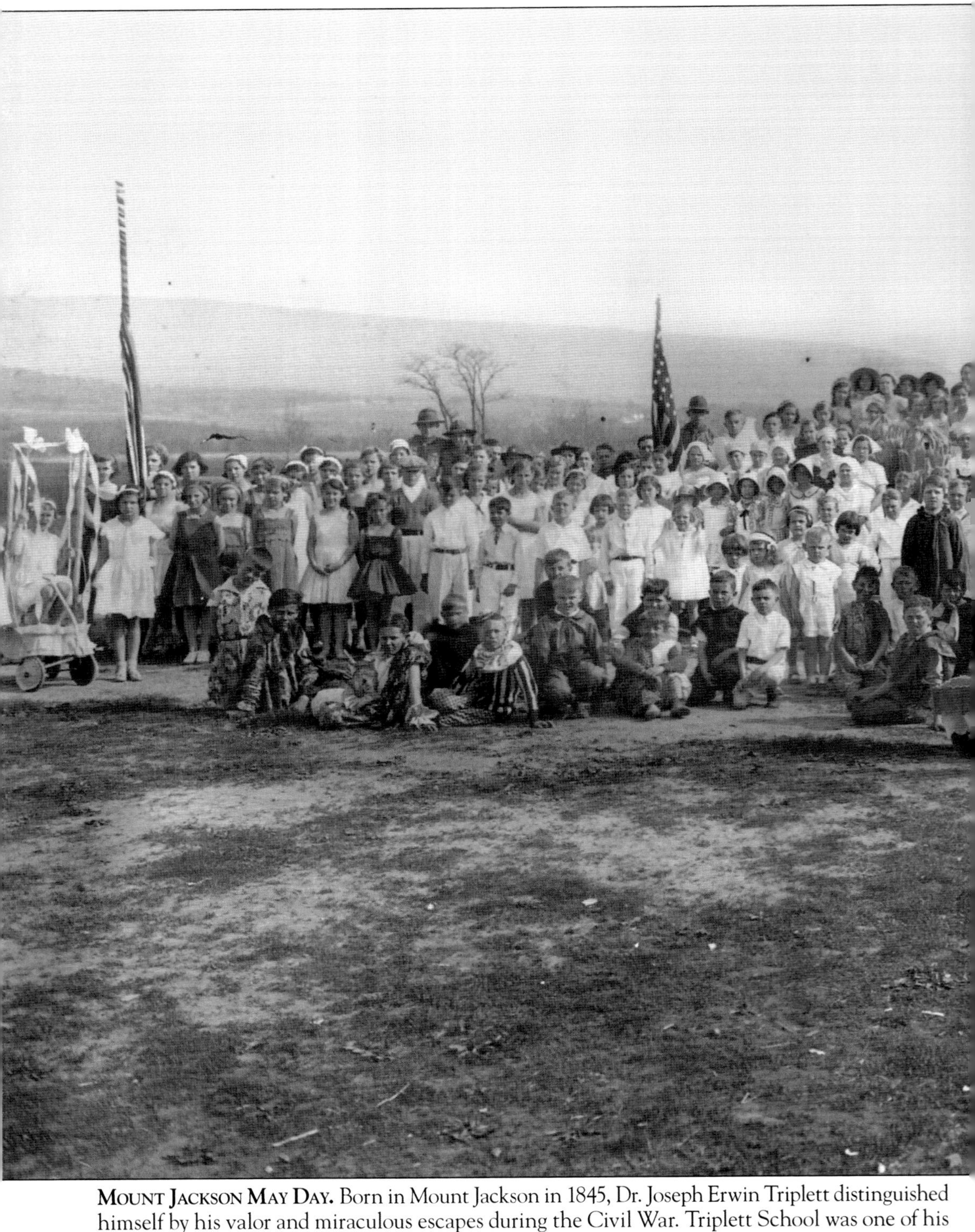

MOUNT JACKSON MAY DAY. Born in Mount Jackson in 1845, Dr. Joseph Erwin Triplett distinguished himself by his valor and miraculous escapes during the Civil War. Triplett School was one of his philanthropic causes. Although he never married, the educational advancement of the children of Shenandoah County was among his numerous accomplishments. After the May Day parade, around 1930, the students are assembled behind Triplett School. The theme was "How to fight

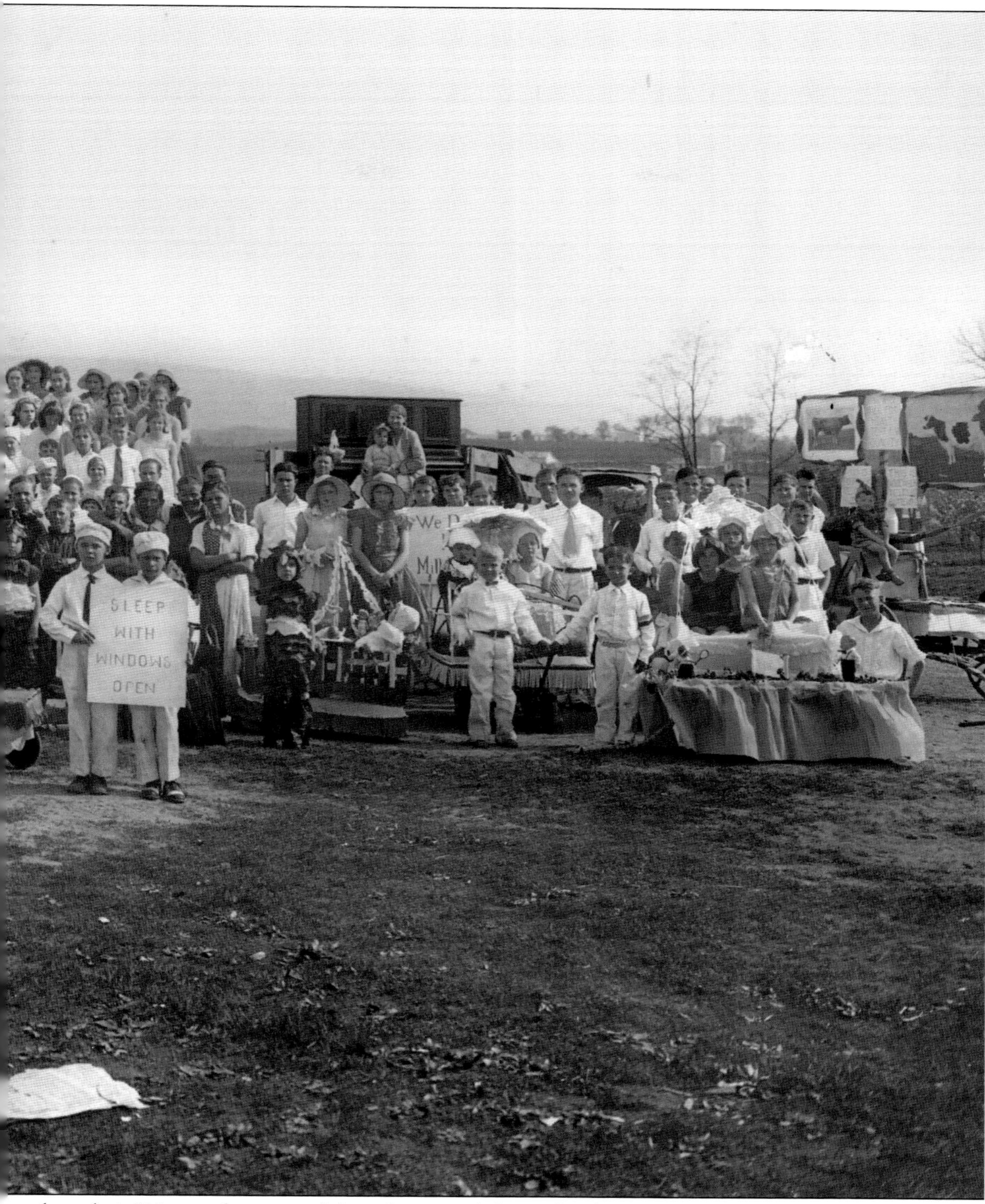

tuberculosis." Nurses, doctors, and the military are fighting the clown germs. "Sleep with windows open" is the title for the little house on wheels. The children are pulling wagons and floats, including the cows, to remind people to drink milk. Seen by the maypole, the girl in the dark dress wearing white shoes is Elesta Bowman Robinson (Miller). This photograph was purchased from her estate. (PPS.)

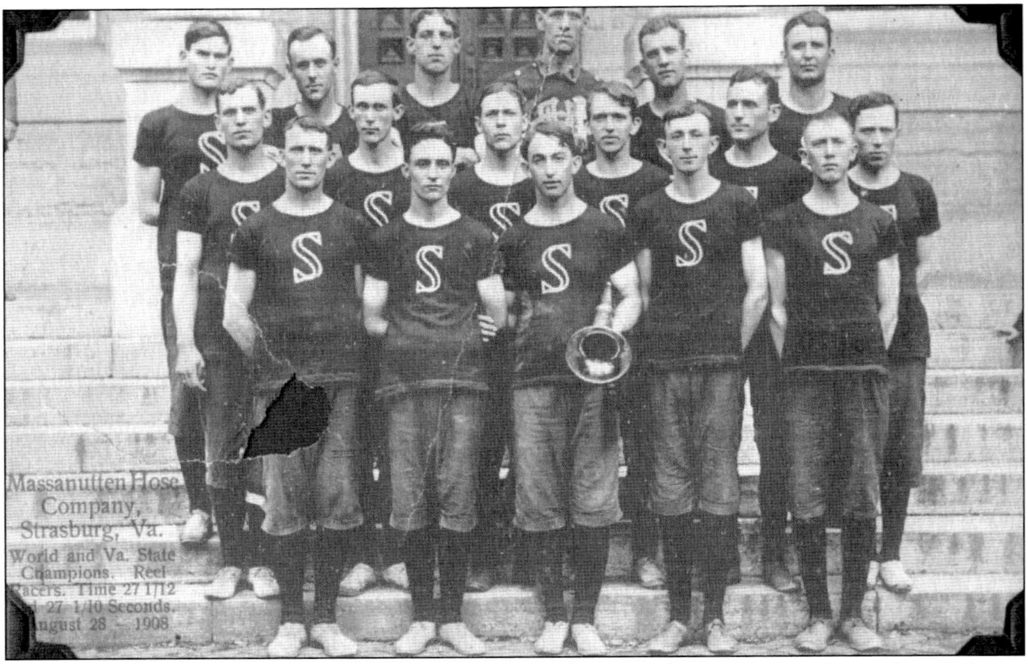

Strasburg Reel Racers. Competitions among neighboring fire companies have changed over time. Today the equipment commands attention. In the early 1900s, the men and their strength were more important. Massanutten Hose Company of Strasburg won the world and Virginia state Champions for Reel Racers award on August 28, 1908. The brass nozzle of the fire hose is under the arm of racer Louis Mackir. The others are unidentified. (JMC.)

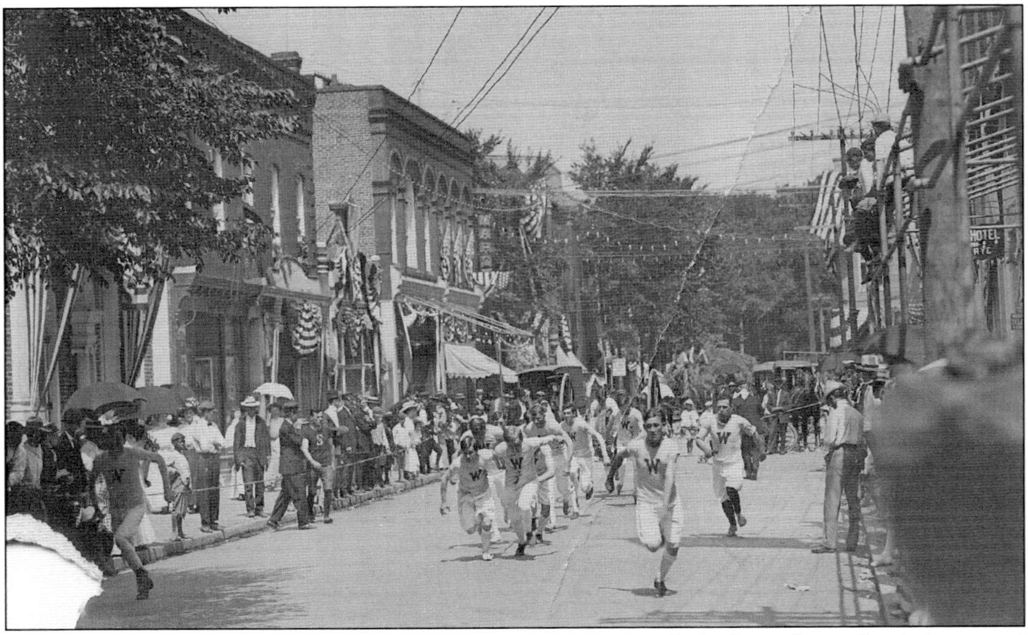

Pulling the Pumper. The Woodstock team is straining to pull the hose that is loaded on a rail above the axle with two huge wheels that may be seen above the heads of the runners. This event demanded strength and teamwork on the part of the competitors. The spectators are restrained for safety by ropes above the street curbs. (WMSC.)

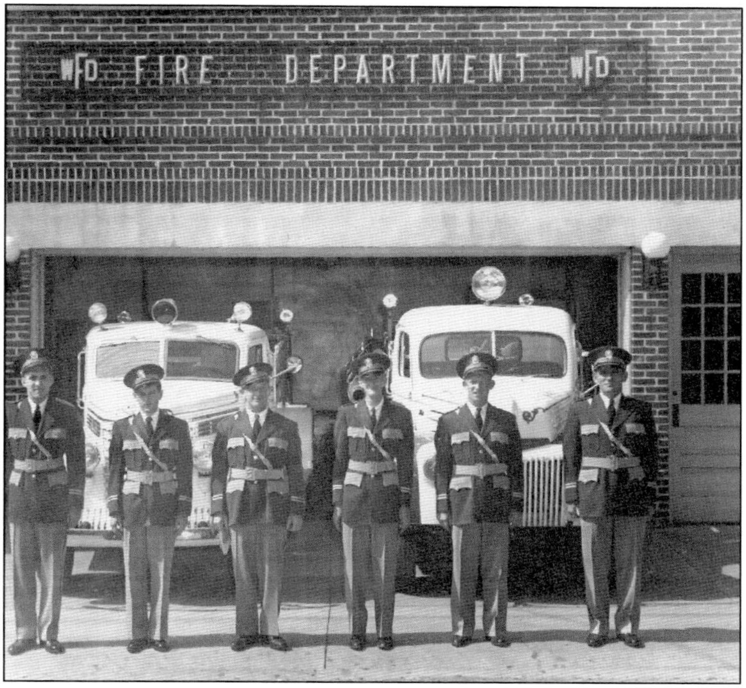

Woodstock Fire Department. This Woodstock Fire Department photograph was taken in May 1952. Shown from left to right are Daniel S. Hottle, Charles L. Wolverton, Henry "Dutch" Phillips, Raymond "Skilly" McInturff, Carl F. Miller, and Chester Rittenour. The fire station was built in 1930. This photograph has lost some of the image on the left side. The monogram for the sign above the door is "WFD Fire Department." (HRM.)

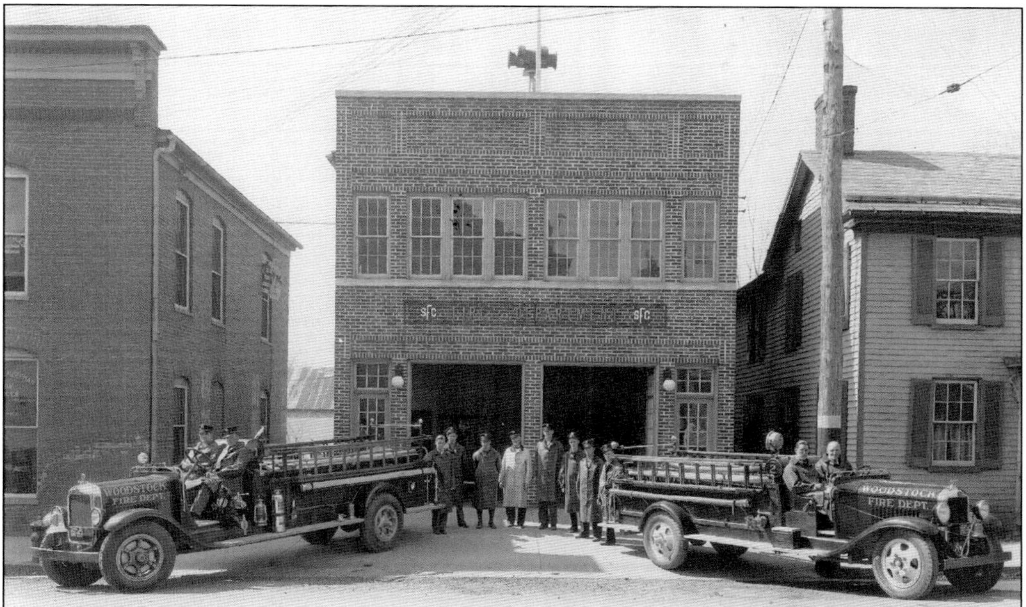

Shenandoah County Fire Department. In front of the older fire station are red fire engines with bells on the front, lanterns on the side, and marked "Woodstock Fire Department." The initials on the building are "SFC," for Shenandoah Fire Company, and remain on the fire department sign above the doors. The second floor of this building has always been a meeting space for community functions. (WMSC.)

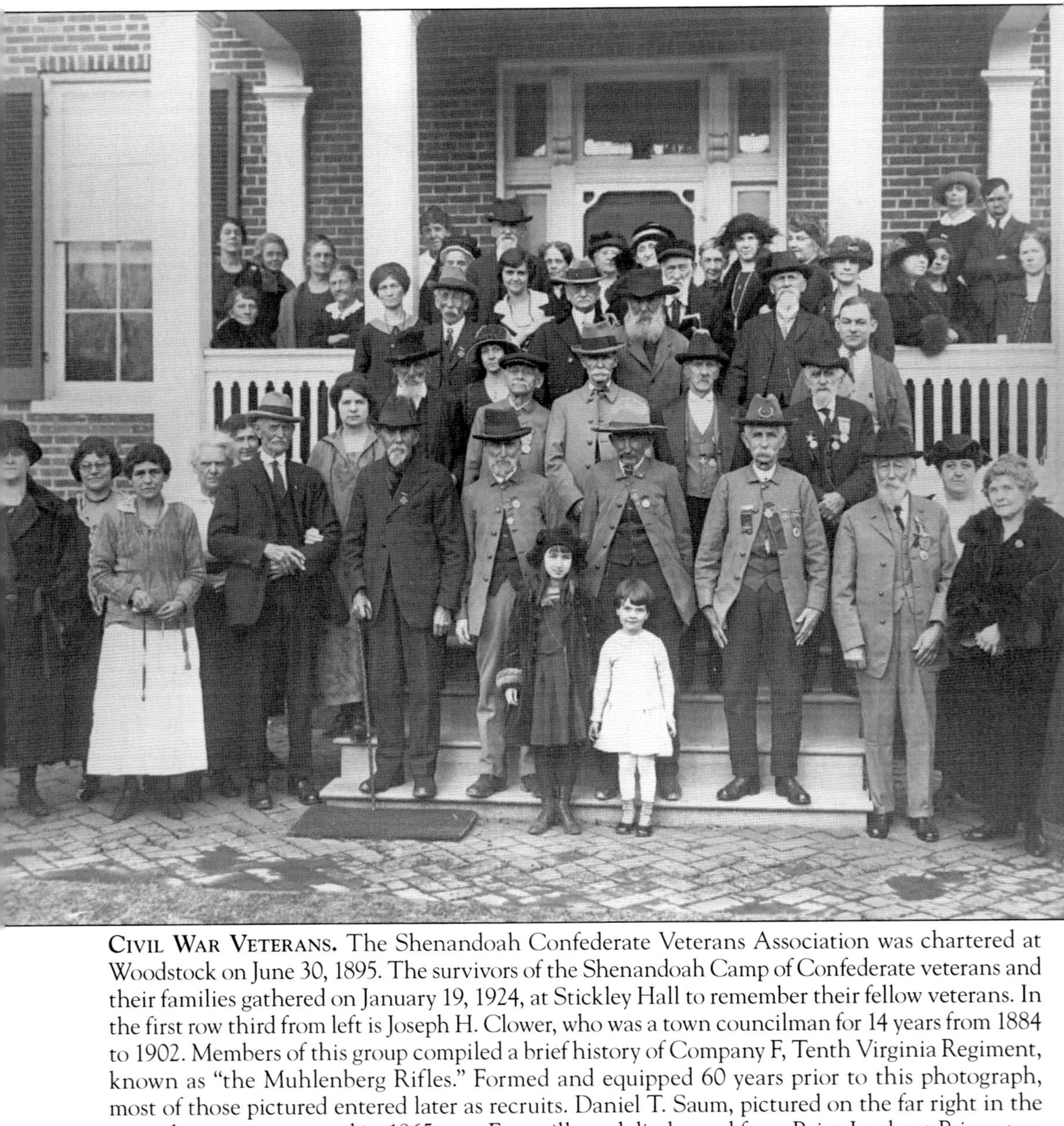

Civil War Veterans. The Shenandoah Confederate Veterans Association was chartered at Woodstock on June 30, 1895. The survivors of the Shenandoah Camp of Confederate veterans and their families gathered on January 19, 1924, at Stickley Hall to remember their fellow veterans. In the first row third from left is Joseph H. Clower, who was a town councilman for 14 years from 1884 to 1902. Members of this group compiled a brief history of Company F, Tenth Virginia Regiment, known as "the Muhlenberg Rifles." Formed and equipped 60 years prior to this photograph, most of those pictured entered later as recruits. Daniel T. Saum, pictured on the far right in the second row, was captured in 1865 near Farmville and discharged from Point Lookout Prison two months later. James H. Rodeffer, farthest left in the third row, was wounded at Chancellorsville. He served as mayor of Woodstock three times. James S. Kibler, second man in the second row, was wounded at Chancellorsville and imprisoned at Fort McHenry and Fort Delaware. (Courtesy of Jeremy McCleary.)

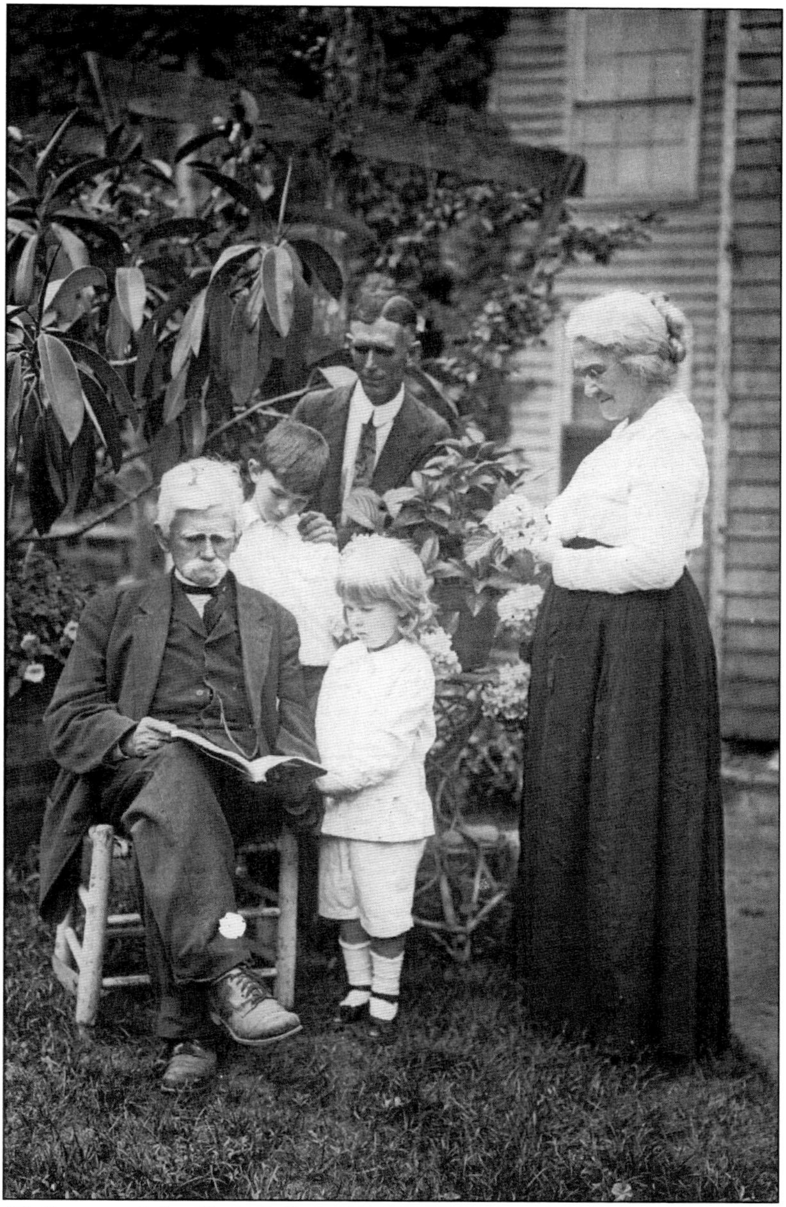

CAPT. JOHN H. GRABILL. John H. Grabill was born in 1839 in Mount Jackson, son of Ephraim Grabill and his wife, Carolyn Donaldson. He was educated in Woodstock schools and at Harrisonburg Boys School. He graduated from Dickinson College in Pennsylvania in 1860 and served with distinction in the Stonewall brigade as a Confederate soldier. He married in 1868, and in 1869, he became owner and editor of the *Shenandoah Herald*; his association with the newspaper continued for over 50 years. He was appointed superintendent of schools for the new Shenandoah County Public School system on September 23, 1870, and became responsible for the integration of schools to allow equal access for all students. He published his "Quote of a Diary of the Stonewall Brigade" in 1909, and he continued in the printing and publishing business in his retirement. In this photograph, he is shown with his wife, Mary Lytle Hollingsworth Grabill, David Walton, John Grabill, and Philip "Pete" Magruder Grabill. Survived by his eight children, he died at his home in Woodstock in 1922. (JH.)

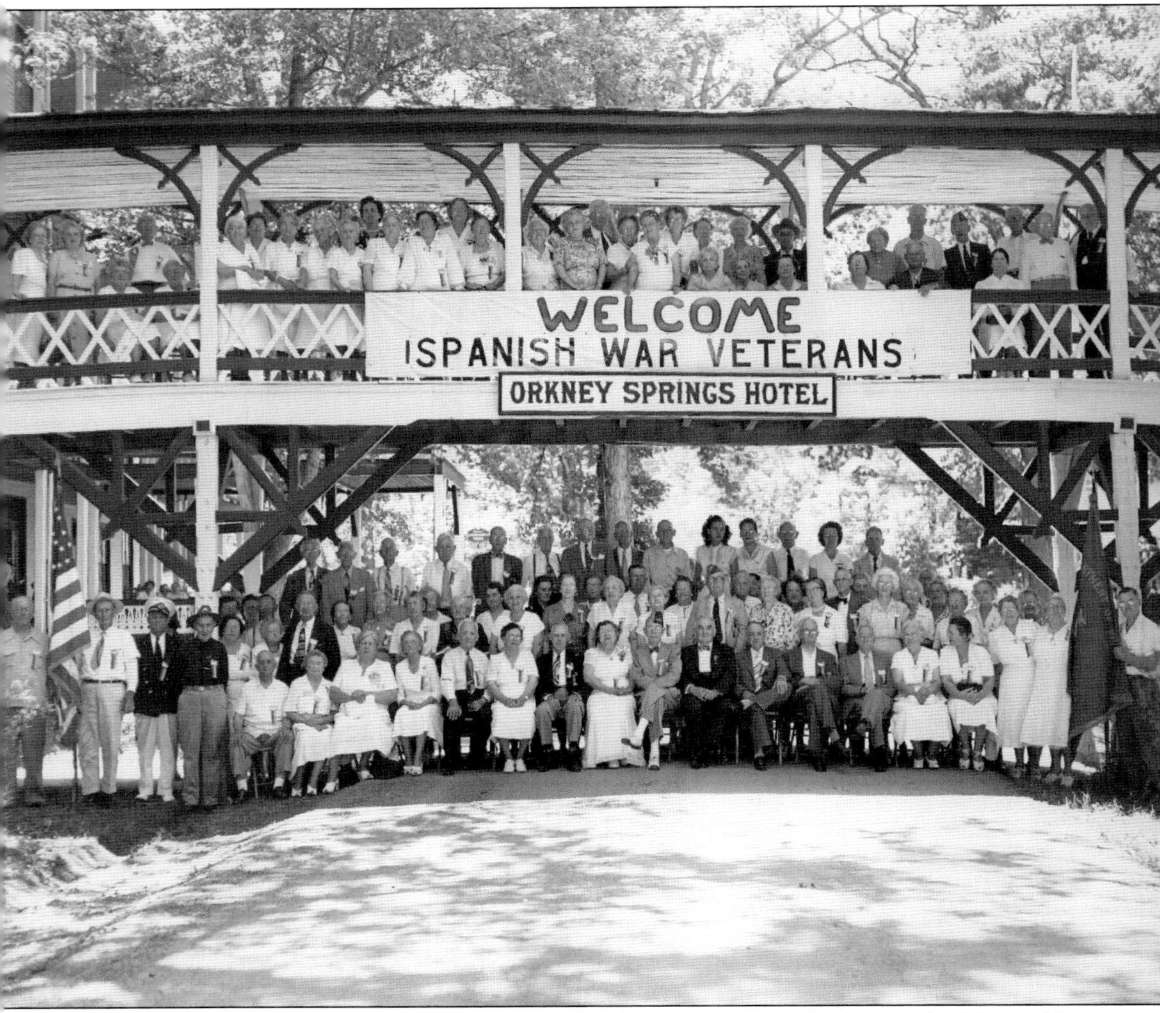

WELCOME SPANISH WAR VETERANS. A similar photograph was published in the *National Tribune* "Stars and Stripes" insert on August 30, 1951. A banner was hung on the bridge between the Virginia House and Maryland House in Orkney Springs for the celebration. In the previous war with Mexico (1846–1848), possibly 30 Shenandoah County men served. The following names were found in the March 9, 1848, *Woodstock Sentinel*: Isaac Bowman, James Henretty, Daniel S. Lee, Levi McInturff, Richard Pennell, Lemuel Spengler, Joshua Stover, W. G. Wharton, French Gray, Ephraim White, Isaac Lindamood, William Ripley, Philip Pitman, James D. Miller, and B. Franklin Bogan. The following Mount Jackson riflemen were also listed: William Y. Lovell, H. Holt, O. C. Billings, J. C. Dickinson, and H. Bowman. The September 5, 1848, *Woodstock Sentinel* reported on a celebratory event held in Strasburg that included an address by S. H. Dosh, music, singing, a procession through town, and food from tables spread under the trees. (SCL.)

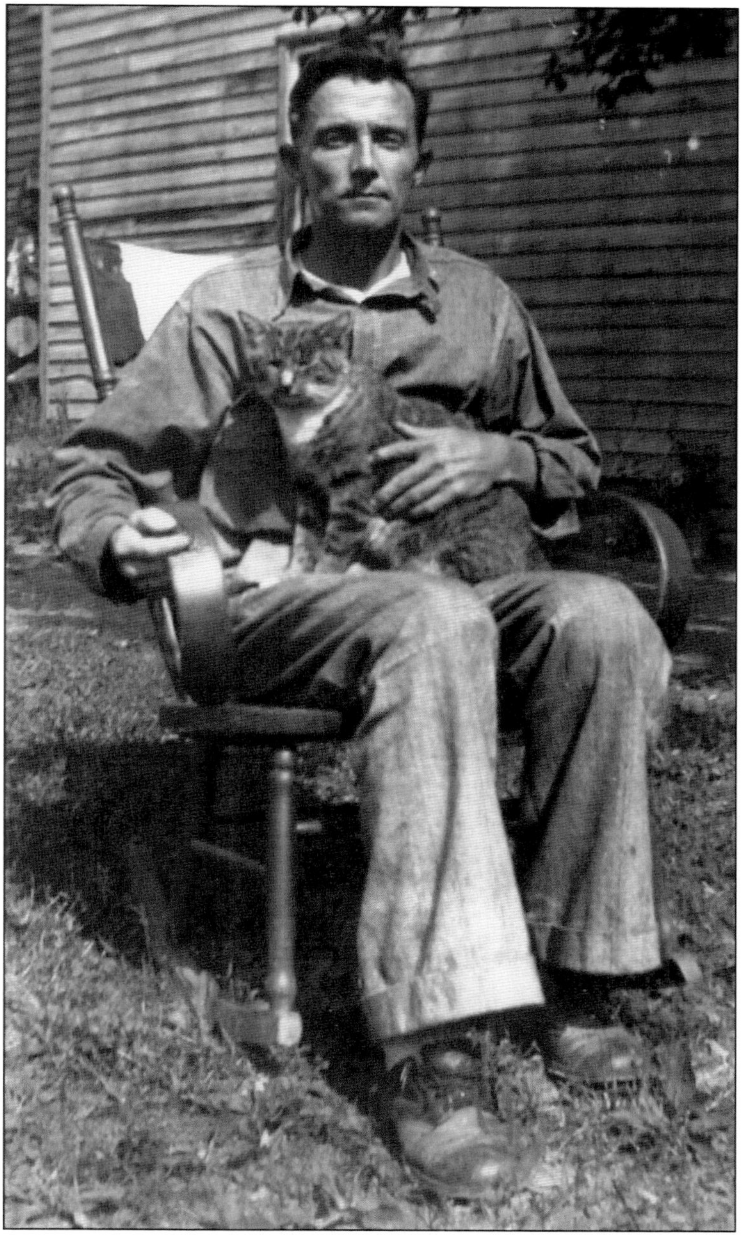

CPL. CHARLES ARCHIE JOHNSON. Charles Archie Johnson was born in Grottoes, Rockingham County, in January 1896, and he enlisted on June 5, 1917. He was a miner with brown eyes and light brown hair and was single at age 21. Serving in France, he was gassed and his lungs were damaged, but he finished out the war and returned home. He got a job at the manganese mine in Fort Valley, where he spotted Clara Cave, the cook's daughter. They married and had six children, even though he was gradually becoming more disabled. Johnson received a small pension, and Clara supplemented that with the family garden. This last picture of him with his cat Tiger was taken in June 1937. Although his wife and children lovingly cared for him by bringing him ice cream and fanning him to keep him cool, he died in September 1937. Beatrice, the oldest daughter of Johnson, always thought she was her father's favorite child. Now at age 91, she has come to realize that each of her five siblings believed the same thing. (Courtesy of Beatrice Johnson Ritenour.)

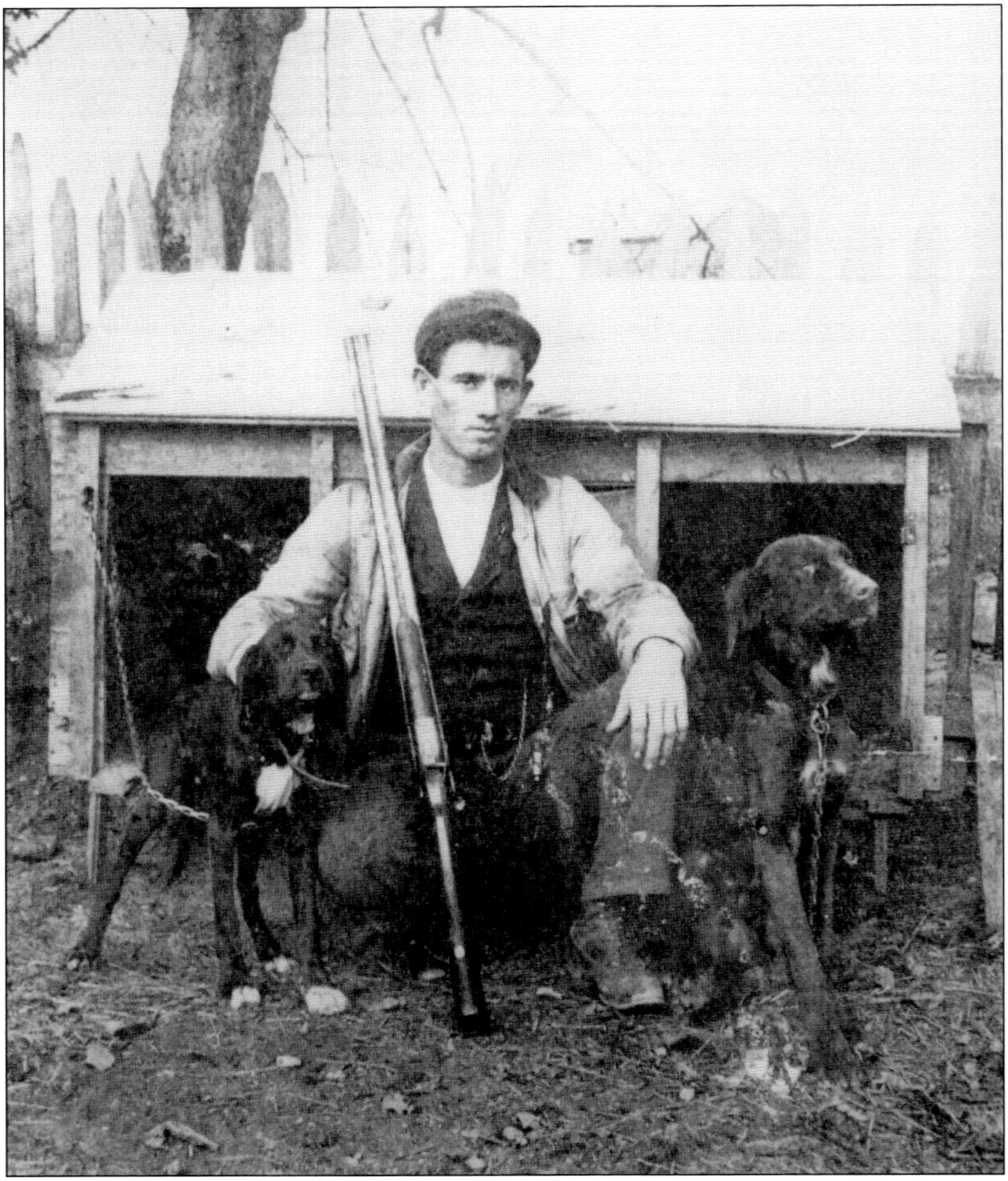

Linden Arthur Sheetz. Linden Arthur Sheetz is seen with his gun and two of his hunting dogs in 1890. He was born in Edinburg, and the story is told of two little boys in diapers, Bud Whiteman and Jack Hutchinson, who were missing from home. Everyone searched frantically for them until Sheetz remembered the children loved his hunting dogs and that they were probably headed towards Massanutten Mountain. He found them searching for his dogs. Sheetz served in World War I. The Shenandoah County Exemption Board published in the *Strasburg News*, "The 1917 military draft numbers totaled 1,475. Of that number, 324 will be called upon to report for examination." The *Edinburg Sentinel* published excerpts of letters from local boys serving overseas, including this one: "Tell father hello . . . we are at the front and see lots of air battles every day, and I have seen many big shells come over. The boys have names for the big shells, such as Kid Shrapnel, the Berlin Express, the Cook Shack Special, and so on. Your son, Don Leslie Sheetz." (SCL.)

Six

BONE AND MUSCLE OF THE NATION

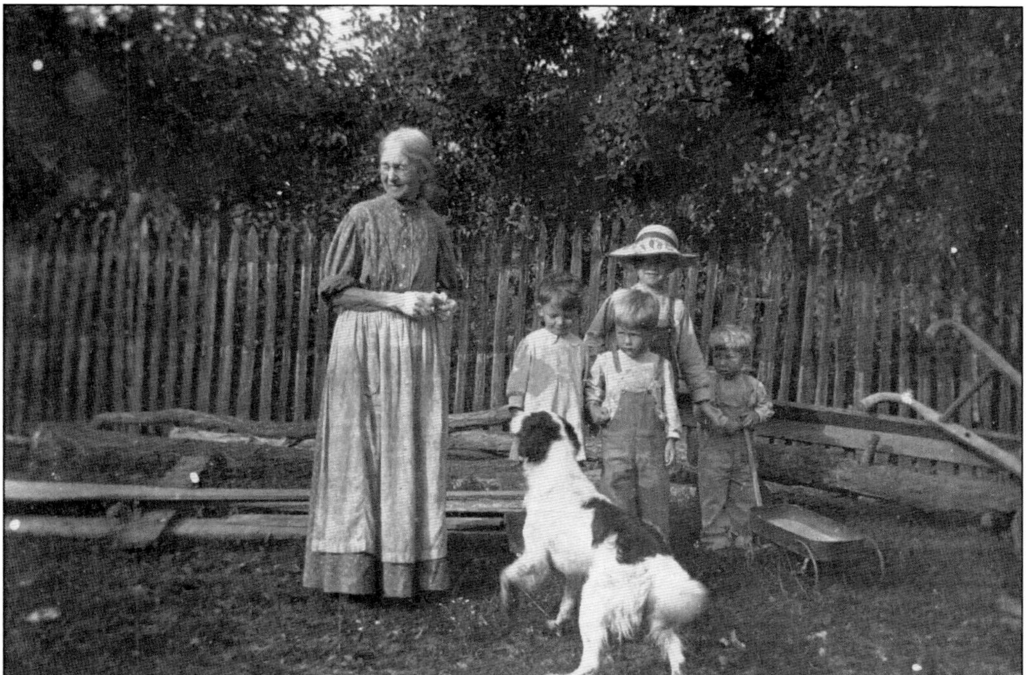

MAMA STICKLEY WITH ASA'S CHILDREN. At the Virginia House of Delegates on January 28, 1835, Philip D. C. Jones of Shenandoah County said, "You know I am from old Shenandoah, the tenth legion of Democracy; my people have always held their political principles undefiled. They think, and so do I, that the doctrine of Mr. Jefferson is correct, that the laboring people are the bone and muscle of the nation." (GRS.)

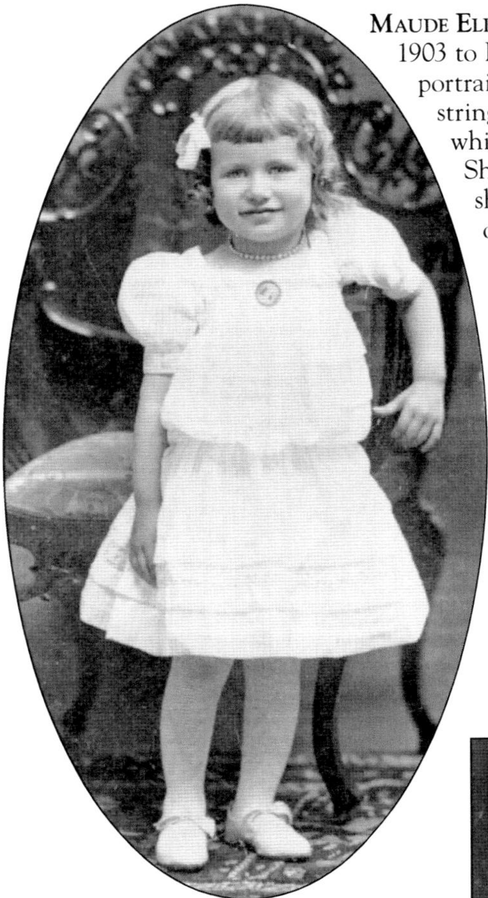

MAUDE ELIZABETH CLEM. Maude Elizabeth Clem was born in 1903 to Philip B. and Sadie Coffman Clem. They had her portrait made when she was three years old. She wore a string of pearls and brooch on her white organdy dress, white stockings, white shoes, and a bow in her hair. She married Galen Franklin Wakeman in 1923, and she is the mother in the Wakeman family portrait on page 81. (WF.)

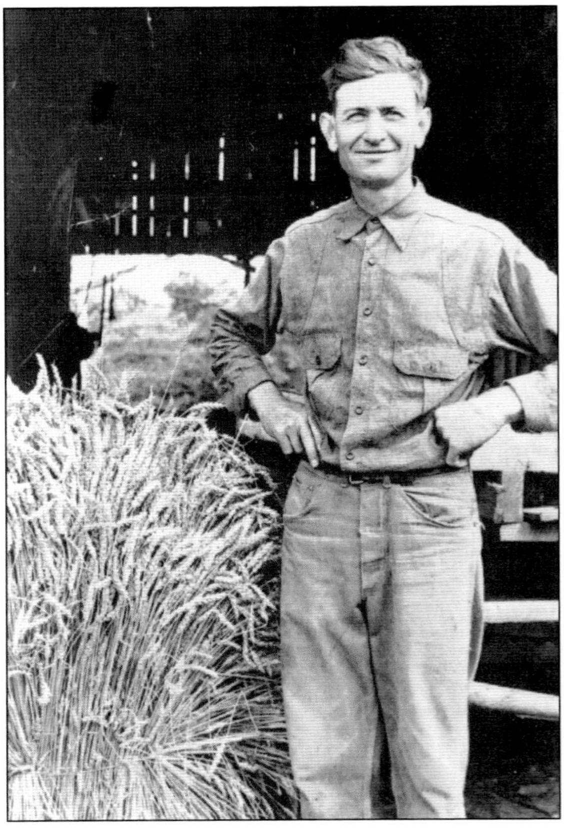

GALEN WAKEMAN AT THE BARN. Galen and Maude lived at Wakeman's Grove with their eight children and foster son. Wakeman is shown in 1950 next to an abundant shock of grain. J. Ozias Wakeman, his father, donated the land and helped to raise the funds to build Wakeman's Grove Church of the Brethen, which opened in 1901. In 1904, Lemuel Wakeman became the church's first ordained minister. (WF.)

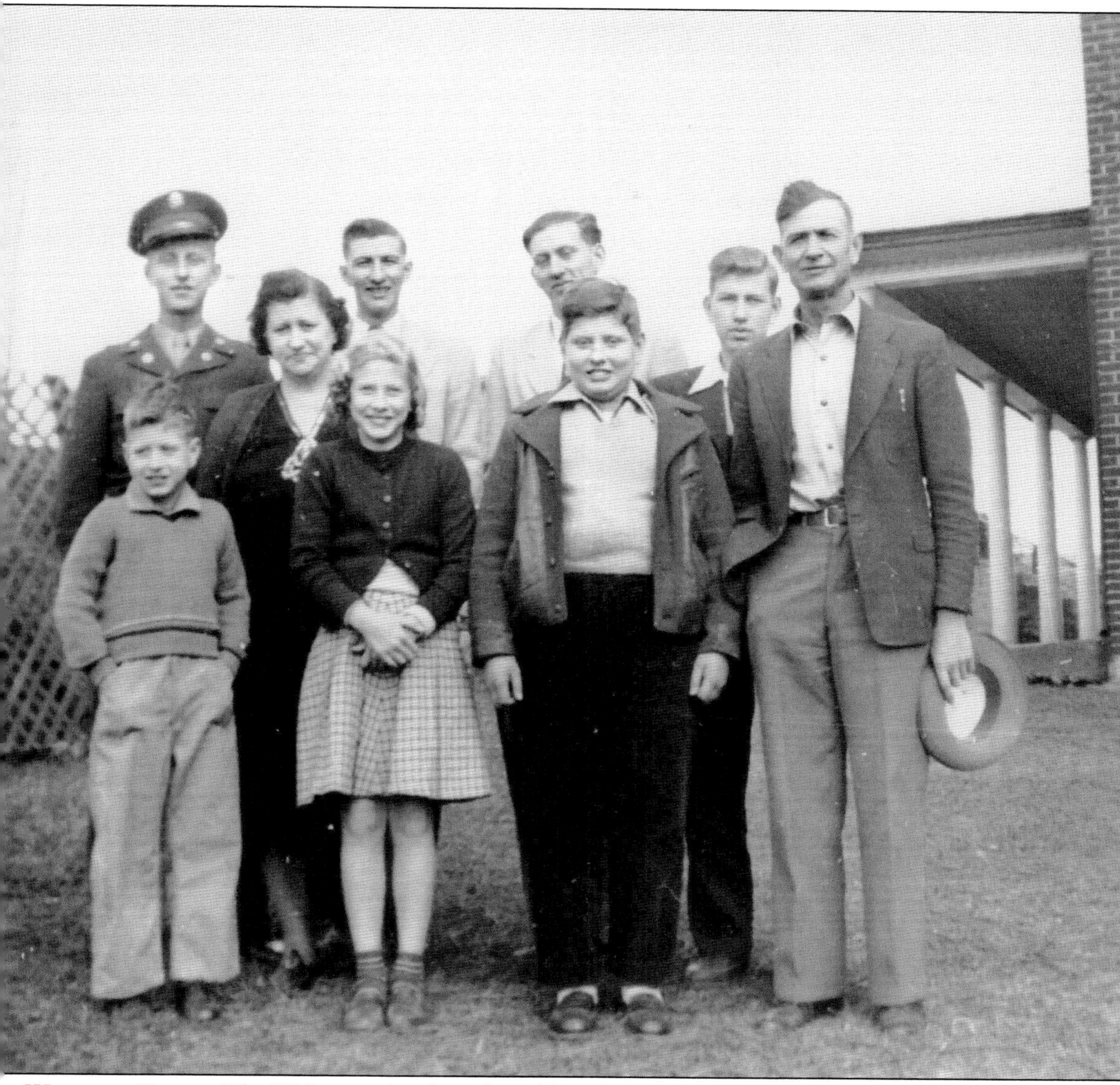

WAKEMAN FAMILY. The Wakeman family gathered for Christmas in 1948 at the Wakeman home place on Swover Creek Road west of Edinburg. They celebrated the holiday and the return of Stanley from boot camp. He is seen on the far left in the back row next to Ray, Galen Earl, and Paul. In front are Nelson, mother Maude, Fay, Robert, and father Galen Franklin. This pre–Civil War home has caverns nearby where Civil War soldiers hid their horses. Galen's great-great-grandfather Jonas Washington Wakeman bought the house at auction in front of the courthouse, sight unseen. By the time they arrived at the auction, the farm they wanted was already sold, so they bought this one near Wakeman's Grove instead. Galen, his father, grandfather, and great-grandfather were all born in this house. Galen and his family supported the Wakeman's Grove Church of the Brethren and worshipped there on Sundays. (WF.)

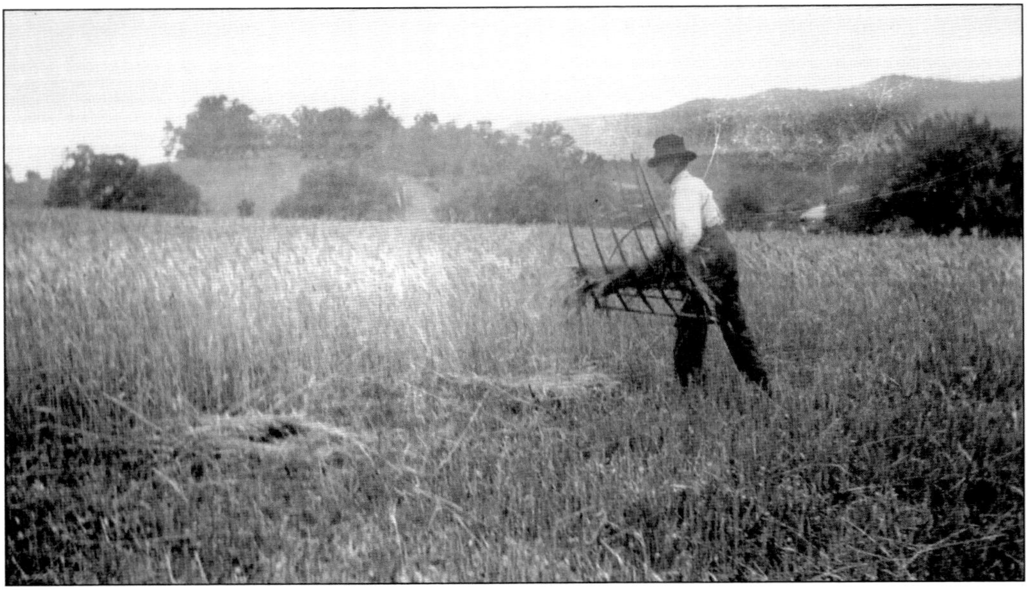

Cutting Grain with Cradle and Three Horses and Three Farmers. The John Connor family used three, but often four or six horses were used to pull heavy combines on their farm at Buck Hill. Above, the cradle is being used by one of the Connors to collect cut grain and drop it in a pile. Below, son Fred Connor is driving the horse team as they pull the combine. John and his son Carl are bringing the sheaves to the combine. The grain heads are thrown into the combine where the grain is shaken into a container and straw falls out of the end. The straw is either gathered for bedding the animals or is spread on the field. Grains harvested by combines include wheat, oats, rye, and barley. Dry crops are easier to cut than green ones. (JCH.)

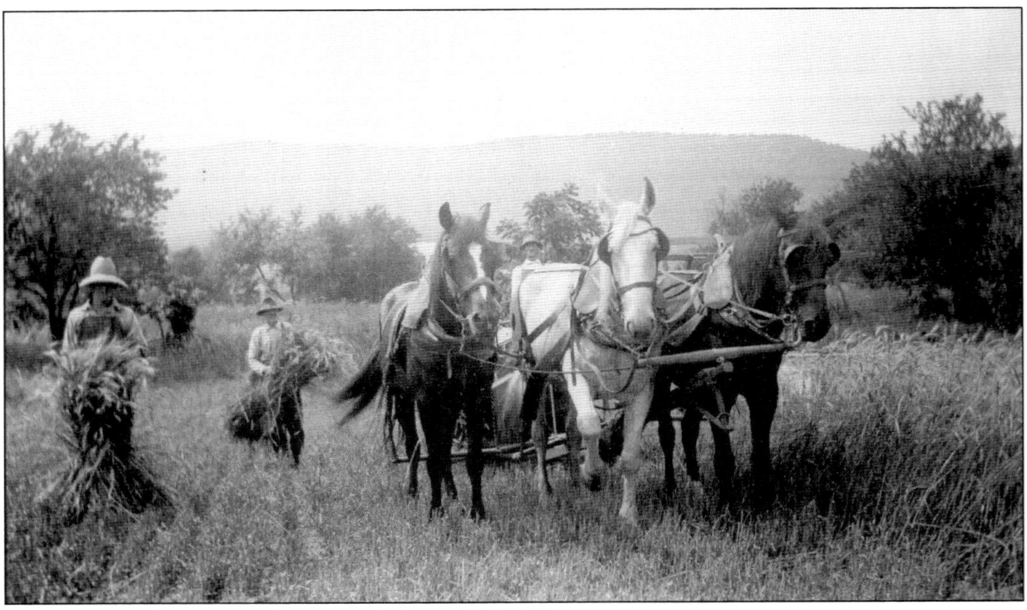

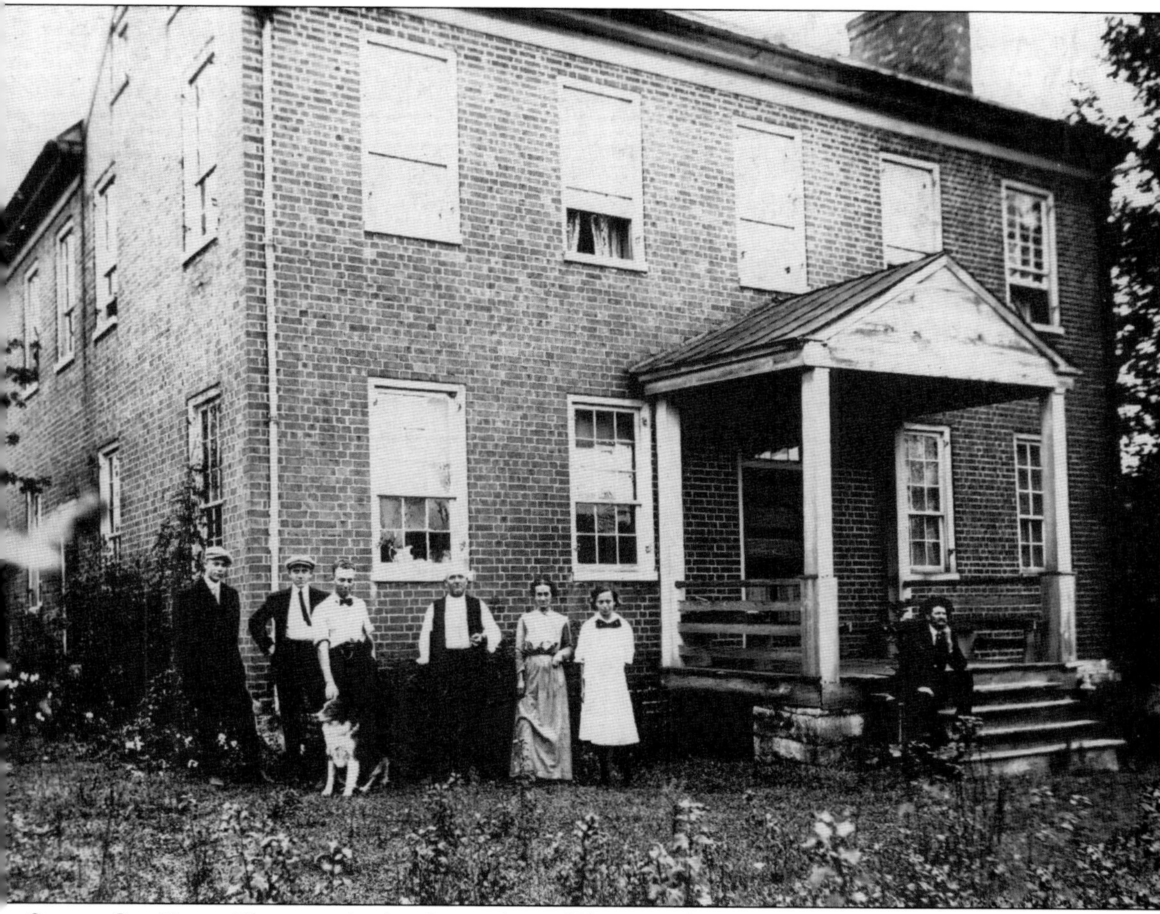

Spring Oak Farm. These are the family members of Eleazer and Lillie Ship Haun. They are shown on their farm on Coffmantown Road near St. Luke, just west of Woodstock, which is now known as Spring Oak Farm. In front of their large brick house are Garrett H. Haun, Alger Haun, Jacob Haun with dog Tyler, Eleazer Haun, Lillie Ship Haun, and Hazel Jane Haun, who later married C. H. Zigler. The man on the steps is unidentified. Eleazer, son of Jacob and Frances Elizabeth Zimmer Haun, got married at age 27 in 1890 to the 22-year-old Lillie. Eleazer was a successful cattle dealer and farmer. During the summer, his family lived on the farm, but in the winter months they lived in Woodstock so the children could go to school. The Haun-Carrier Cemetery is located on this property. Eleazer's father, Jacob, was one of the seven wounded passengers in the 1876 train wreck when Narrow Passage Bridge collapsed. He was severely injured about the head but recovered. (JH.)

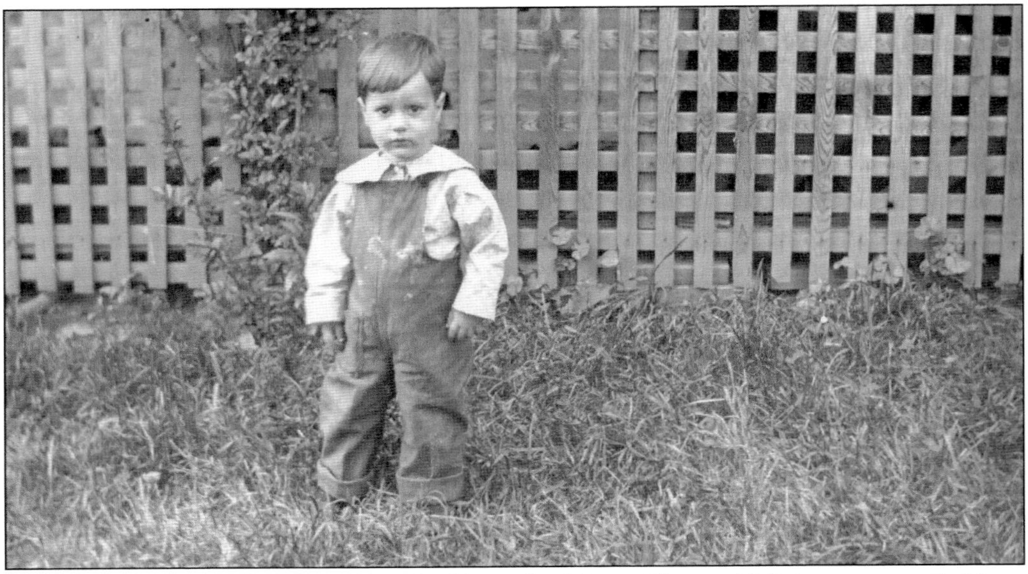

THE LITTLE FARMER BOY. This postcard, addressed to Mamie Sheetz of Edinburg, was mailed from Maurertown. The message is "Aunt Annie, come down soon, May." This photograph is one of many taken by Perry Crabill, who was fascinated by the camera. A large collection of his images has been donated to the Shenandoah County Historical Society. Some of them are printed for the first time in this book. (SCL.)

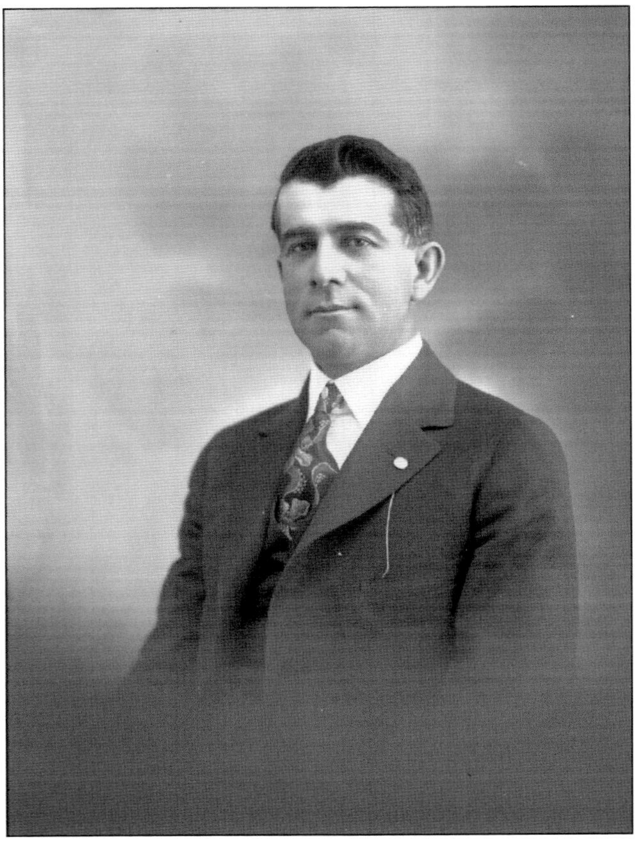

GARNETT PAINTER. Born in 1880 at Indian Fort Stock Farm in Hamburg, Painter owned the farm near Bowman's Crossing, where he raised purebred Hampshire sheep and short-horned cattle. In 1927, he married Ida Henkle Bowman and built a home where they lived until his death in 1960. His nephew Herbert Garnett Painter owned the farm until he passed away in 1998. His heirs still raise sheep here at Paintertown. (SCHS.)

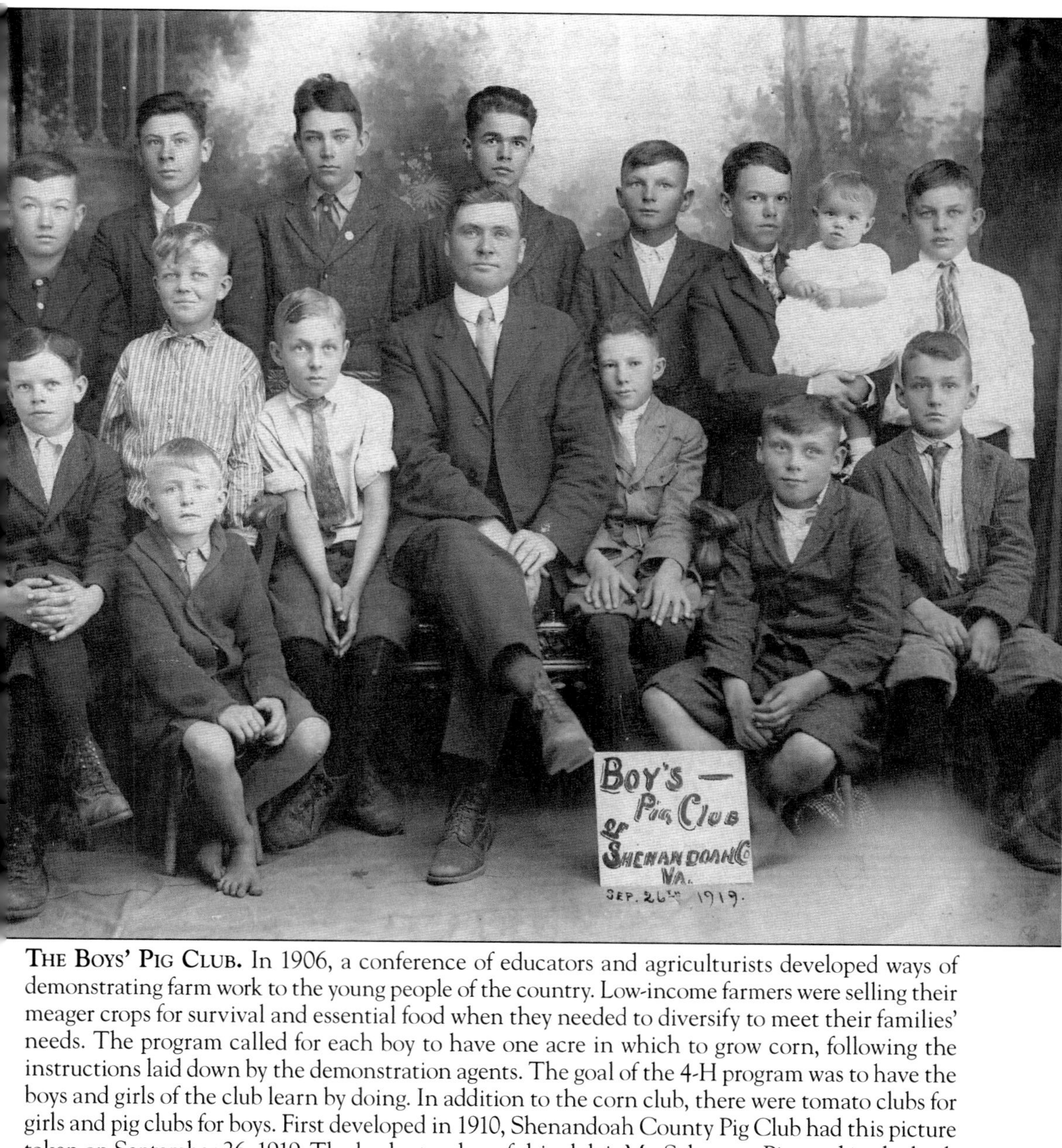

The Boys' Pig Club. In 1906, a conference of educators and agriculturists developed ways of demonstrating farm work to the young people of the country. Low-income farmers were selling their meager crops for survival and essential food when they needed to diversify to meet their families' needs. The program called for each boy to have one acre in which to grow corn, following the instructions laid down by the demonstration agents. The goal of the 4-H program was to have the boys and girls of the club learn by doing. In addition to the corn club, there were tomato clubs for girls and pig clubs for boys. First developed in 1910, Shenandoah County Pig Club had this picture taken on September 26, 1919. The leader-teacher of this club is Mr. Schwartz. Pictured in the back row from left to right are two unidentified boys, Elmer Lee Colley, two more unidentified boys, Gordon Bowman (holding his little sister Helen), and unidentified. Others in the photograph are William Wetzel, William Logan Sr., Emmert Hoover, and Courtland Bowman. (WF.)

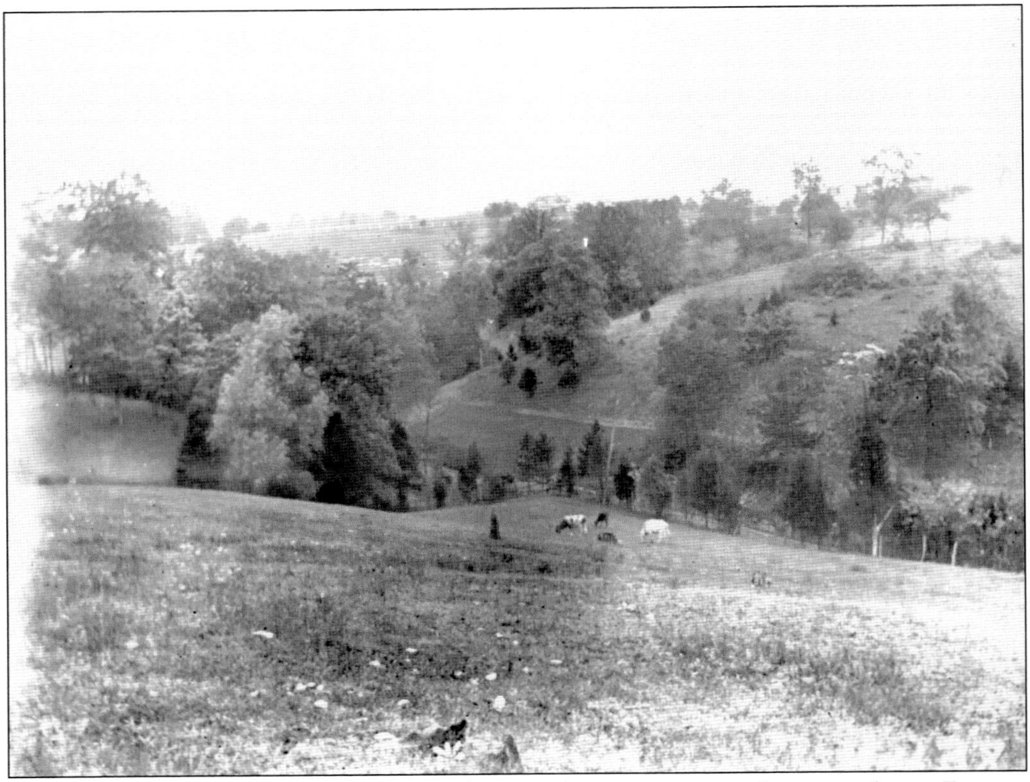

Pasture with Cows. Stonewall Magisterial District has mountains to the east and west. Farmers built their homes near the river in the flatlands, allowing the animals to graze on the hillsides. Here are cattle grazing in the pasture. The farmers were careful about maximizing the advantages of each part of their acreage, so they pastured their cattle on the hillier parts that could not be used for planting crops. (PCC.)

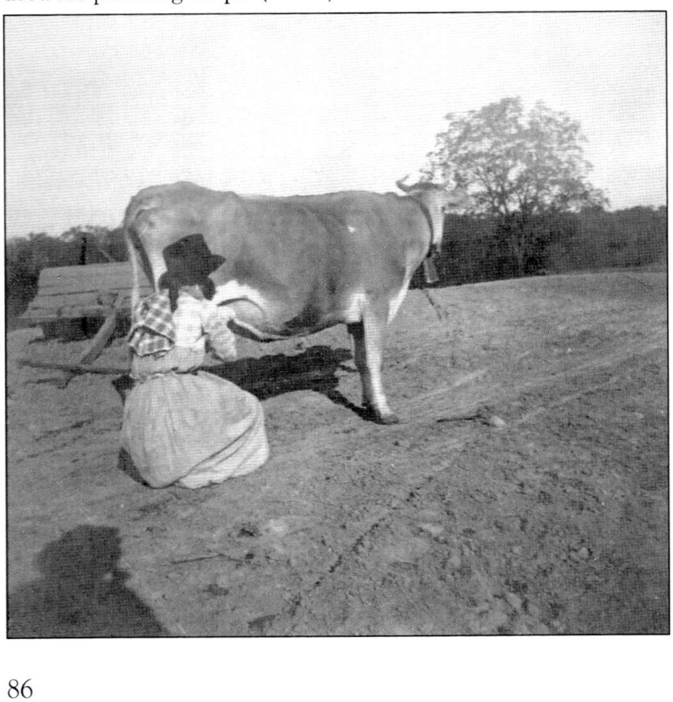

Mary Painter Milking Her Favorite Cow. After 40 years as a teacher and principal in schools in Clarke and Shenandoah Counties, Erasmus Painter bought Burner's farm in 1885. He and his wife, Martha, resided there until his death in 1917. Their son Otis and his wife, Bessie, remained on the farm in Clary, where they cared for Martha until she died in 1942. Otis's sister Mary lived with them. (JPM.)

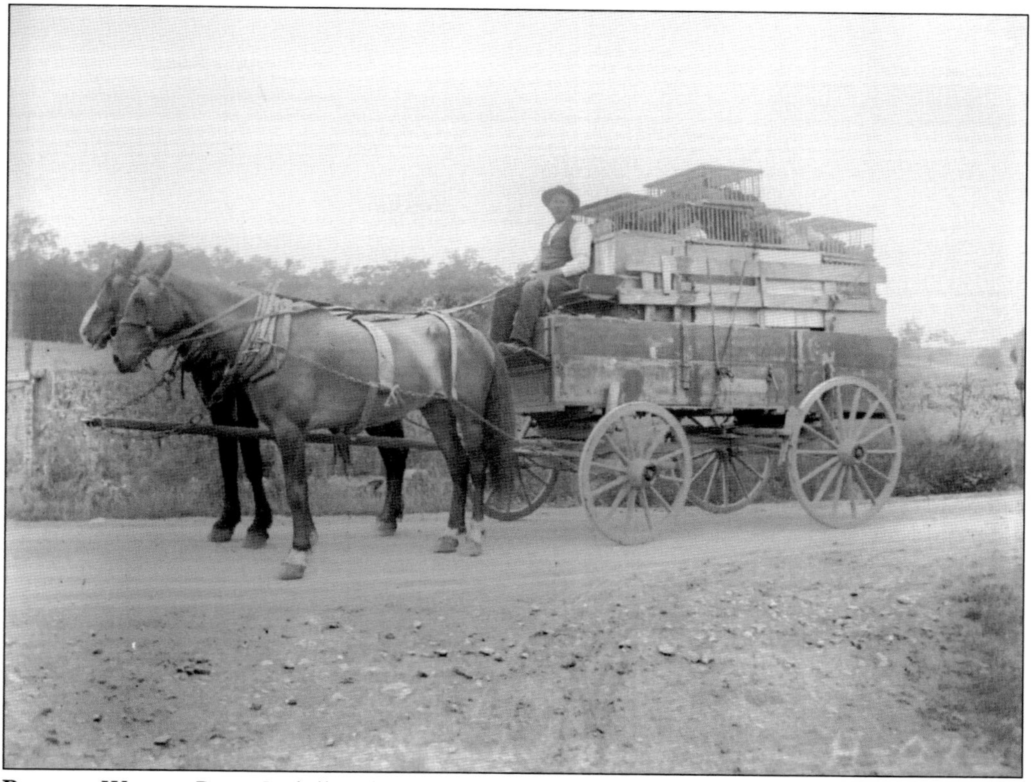

POULTRY WAGON. Perry Crabill, a photographer who grew up in the Stonewall Magisterial District of Shenandoah County, took up the art of making pictures when it was new, and he had a passion for capturing the ordinary. When someone new came by, he captured them on film. The driver of this wagon is not known, but raising poultry continues to be an important part of Shenandoah's agricultural success. (PCC.)

FARRIER AND HORSE. The farrier, or blacksmith, is at work in the doorway of the barn, probably at Crabill farm. From his box of tools, he has selected the proper one to clean the horse's hooves; perhaps he is replacing the shoes. His dusty, sweaty clothing is in contrast to the sleek, shiny horse and makes a nice textural contrast with the raw barn wood. (PCC.)

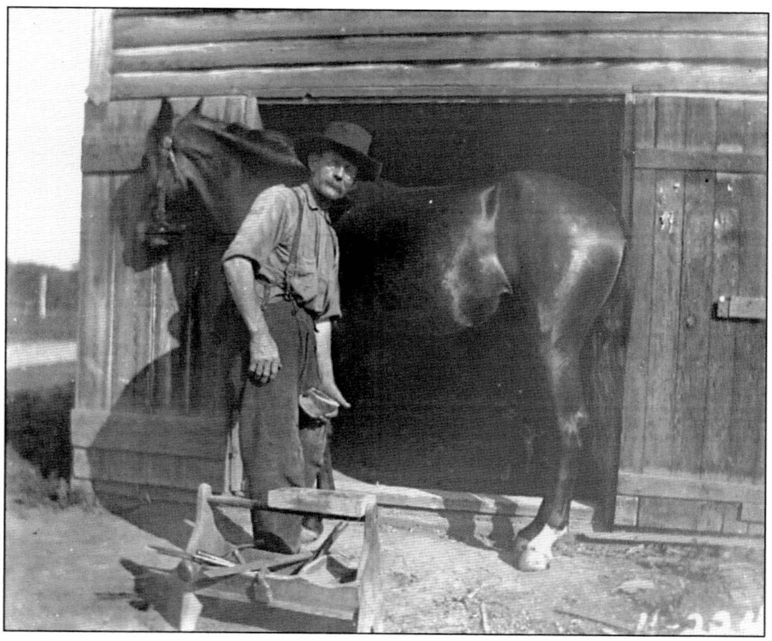

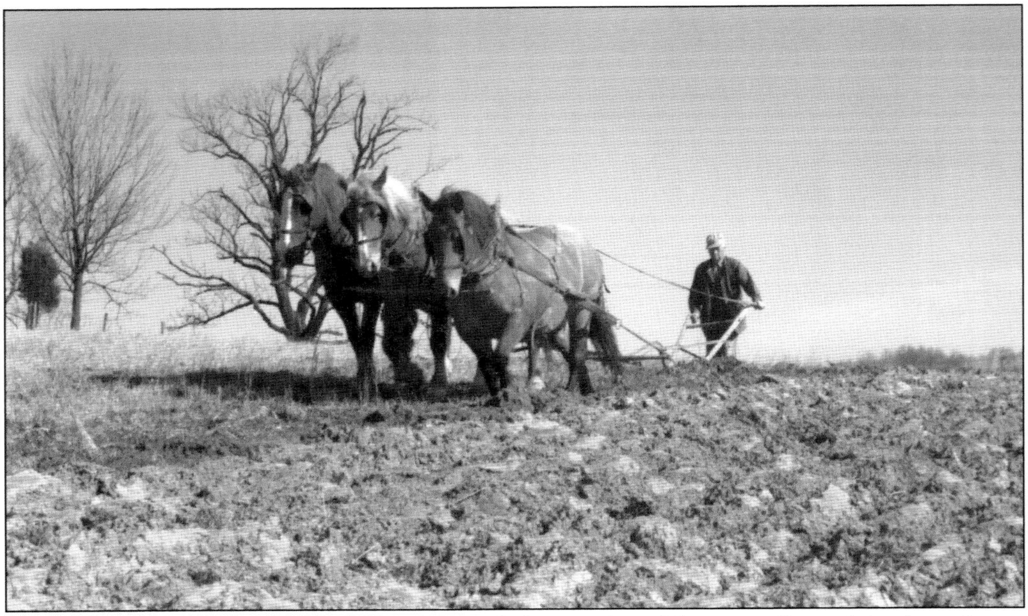

Three-Horse Team. Like his father, Kenneth Painter loved farming. One of the best things about the farm he purchased from his grandfather was the horses. Painter refused to give up his horses even after other farmers had switched to tractors. He is shown here plowing the field behind a team of three sturdy horses. He entered his horse and wagon in Toms Brook parades for many years. (JPM.)

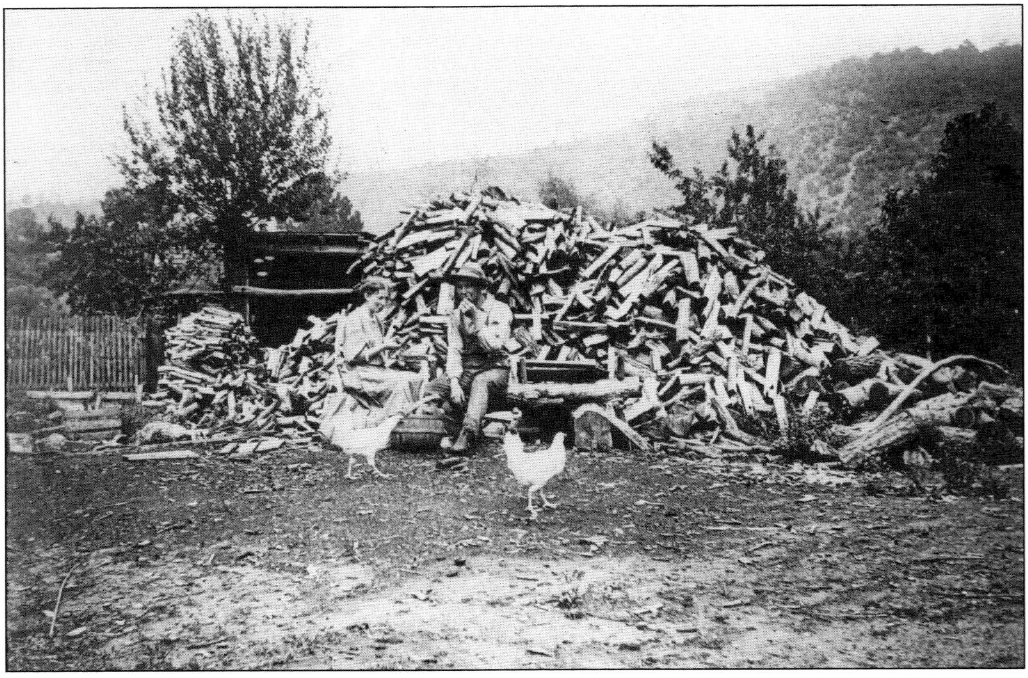

Eating Peaches at the Woodpile. On Bellview Farm, this young couple is taking a break. A disorganized pile of wood has been dumped here; larger pieces still need to be sawed. The couple appears to be snacking on peaches, and the two chickens are searching for food. Behind them on the left is a neatly stacked pile of wood, the woodshed, and the fenced garden. (GRS.)

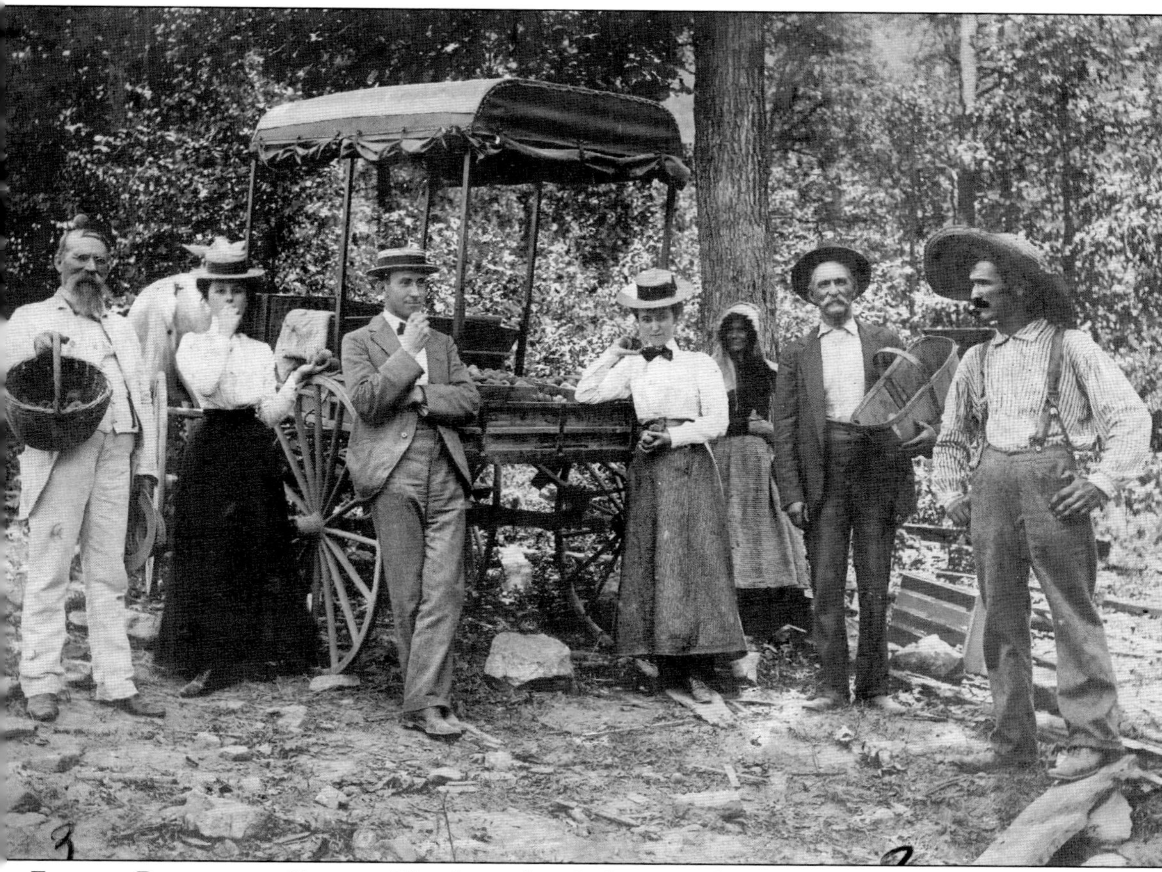

Erasmus Painter and Friends. The three identified men in this picture are George F. Shaw, Henry Burgess, and Erasmus Painter (with the market basket). One of the young women is Erasmus's daughter Agnes MacAtee Painter. The story passed down in the family is that Erasmus enlisted in the Confederate army in June 1861. He was wounded in Manassas on August 28, 1862, and taken prisoner in Woodstock on November 10, 1863. He was moved to the Wheeling prison and then to Camp Chase in Ohio, and his final incarceration was at Fort Delaware. The death rate there was 20 percent, and Erasmus was forced to eats rats to survive. While there, he was befriended and fed by Agnes, the young daughter of the prison's overseer. In return, he gave her his Roanoke College label pin and promised her if he had a daughter he would name her Agnes. In 1866, the first child born to Erasmus and his wife, Martha, was named Agnes MacAtee Painter. (JPM.)

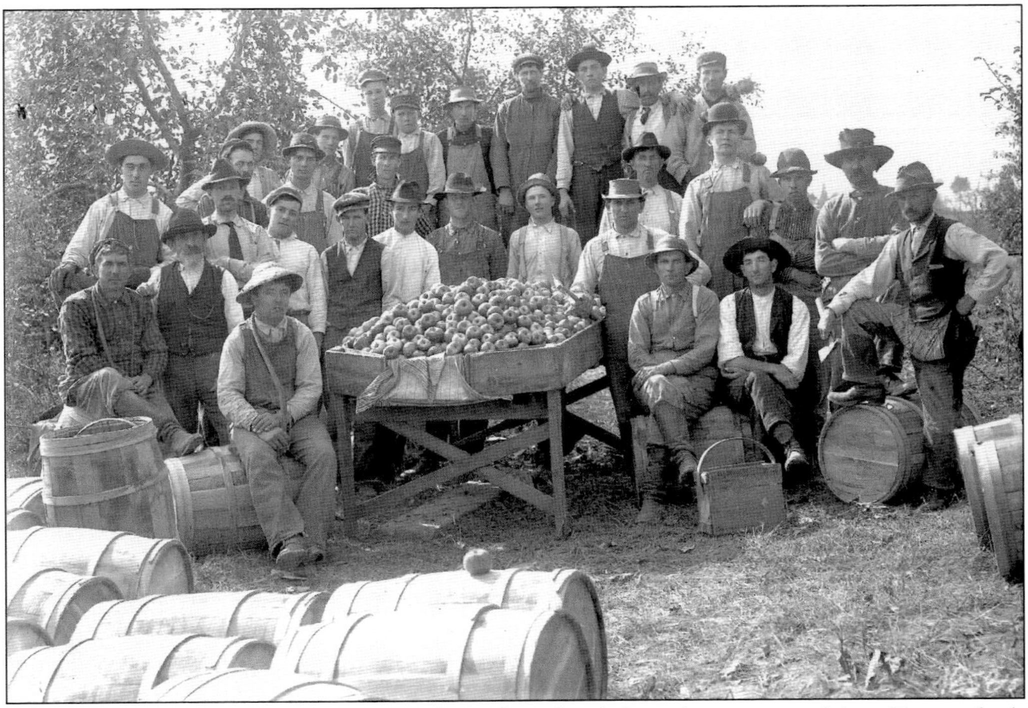

APPLE WORKERS. Since 1890, apple and peach orchards have been successful in Shenandoah County. The first fair was held in October 1886, and the competition for the best fruit continues. The workers in the above image are displaying apples in humorous ways. They are probably at the Asa A. Sheetz orchard west of Woodstock on Narrow Passage Creek. Pictured are Edgar and Darus Kibler; Asa, Jacob, John and Noah Sheetz; Russell and Hugh Peters; and John Swartz. The others are unidentified.

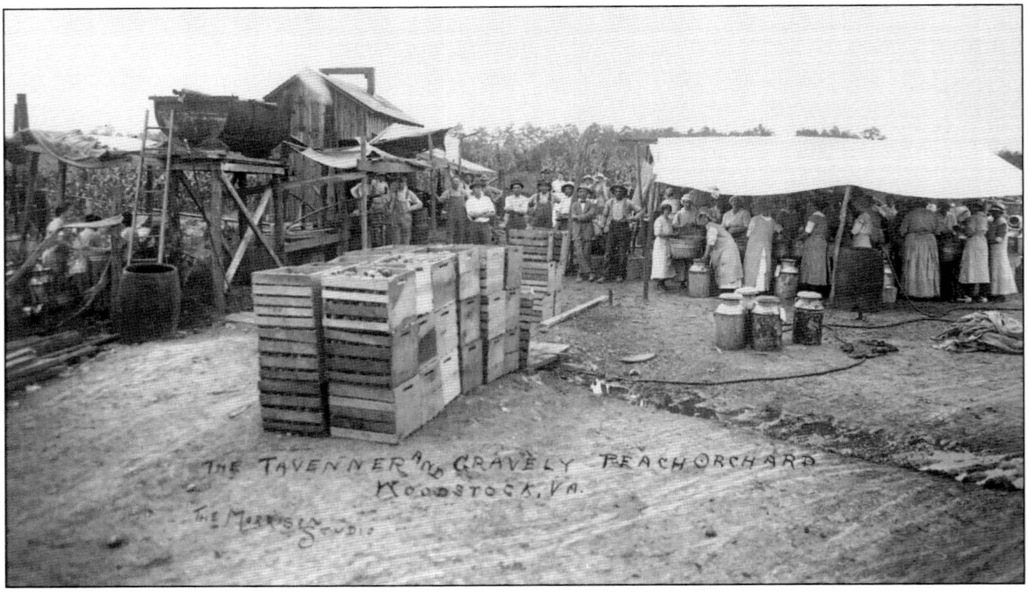

TAVENNER AND GRAVELY PEACH ORCHARDS. In 1910, Judge Frank S. Tavenner and James G. Gravely formed an association for growing and packing fruit. Their high standards and innovative methods have made Tavenner and Gravely Pack famous. (Both SCHS.)

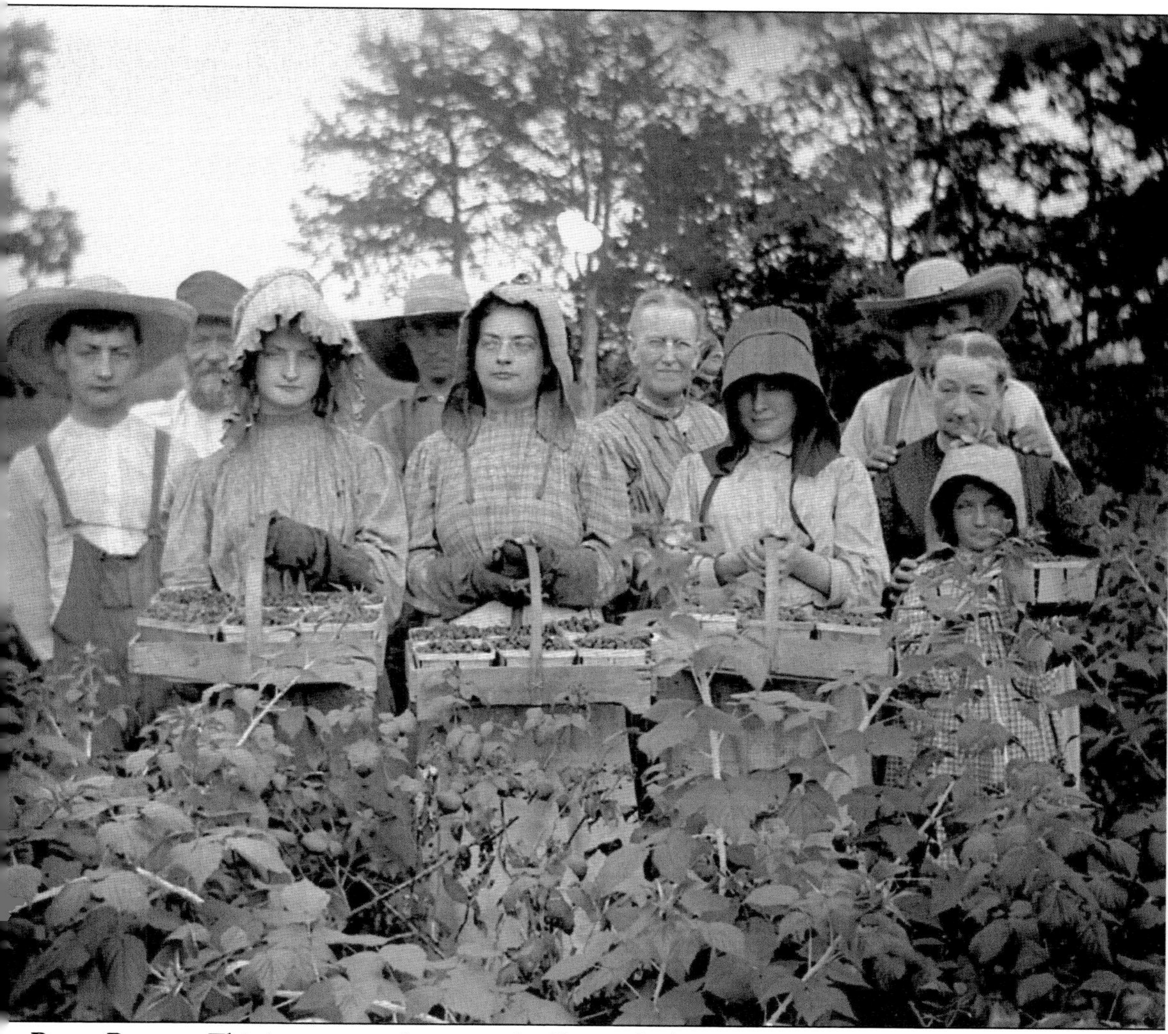

BERRY PICKERS. This image was taken near the Shenandoah River. The women workers in the first row are holding carriers containing six quarts of raspberries. The little girl is holding up one quart. All four of them are wearing protective bonnets on their heads to keep the raspberry bushes from scratching their faces. Two of them are wearing heavy gloves to protect their arms and hands. Behind them are the other berry pickers and probably the owners of the farm. In the foreground are the raspberry canes, developed from native species, with the slender, upright shoots spread rapidly by sucker plants. Raspberries grow best in cool temperate areas in fertile, moist, well-drained soil. The bushes are pruned in spring to promote production. There is a limited production in the second harvest season and full production in the third and fourth seasons. Well-taken-care-of red raspberry bushes that are mulched with straw can yield from 3,000 to 3,500 quarts of fruit per acre. (PCC.)

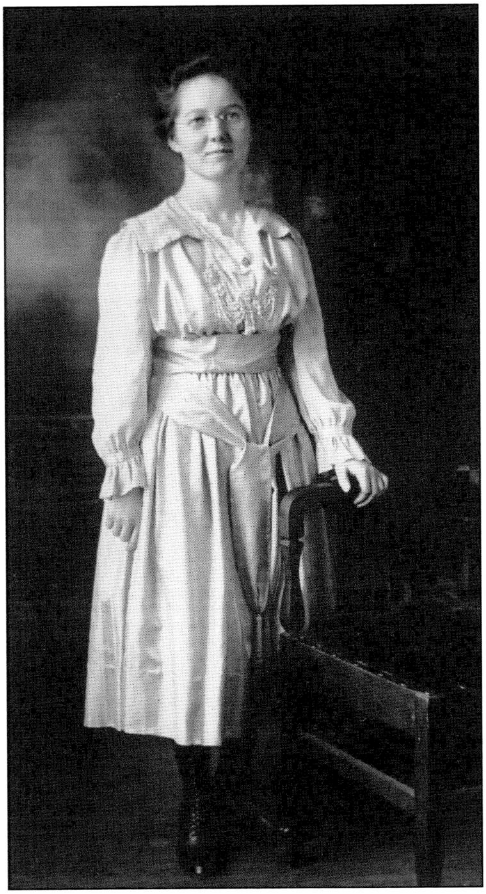

Lucille Lorraine Stickley and Bellview Farm. Located south of Cedar Creek, this farm began in 1745 when Squire David Stickley acquired 440 acres. The farm was inherited by five succeeding generations up to Walter E. Stickley. He and his wife, Mary Susan Hinkins Stickley, seen in the meadow between the house and barn, lived here and raised their four children, Lucille, Boyd, Fred, and Douglas. Lucille continued to live on the farm with her parents, and she bought out the shares of her siblings. She recorded events on her camera. Her nephew Ralph and his wife, Gloria, are now the keepers of the memorabilia of the Stickley farm and family. The name of Bellview has been part of the farm since before 1923, when the Rand McNally Standard Map of Virginia shows it as a stop on the Southern Railway. (GRS.)

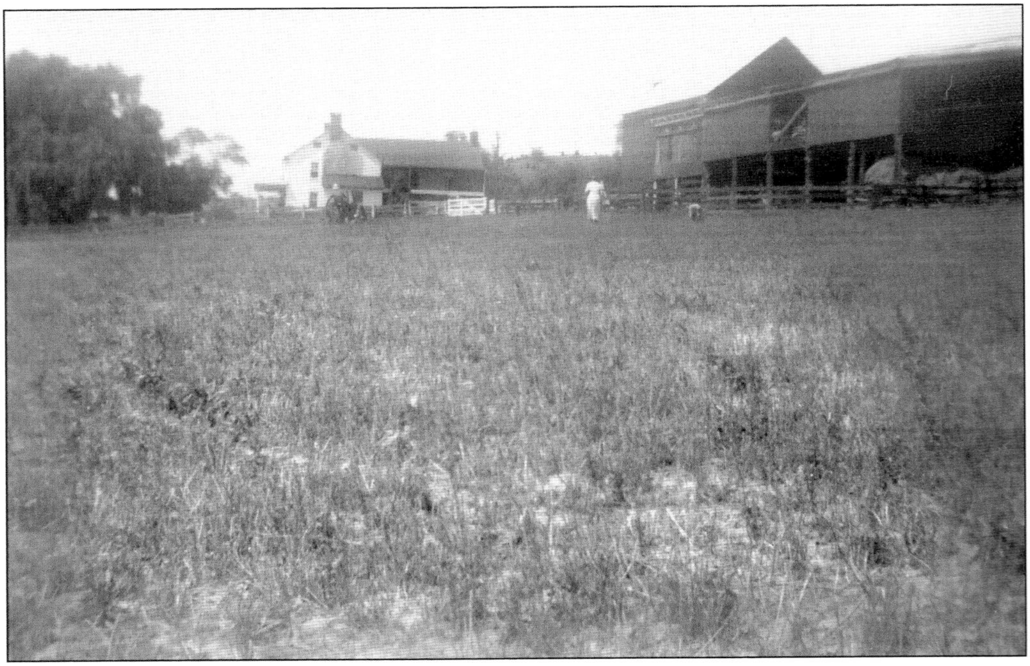

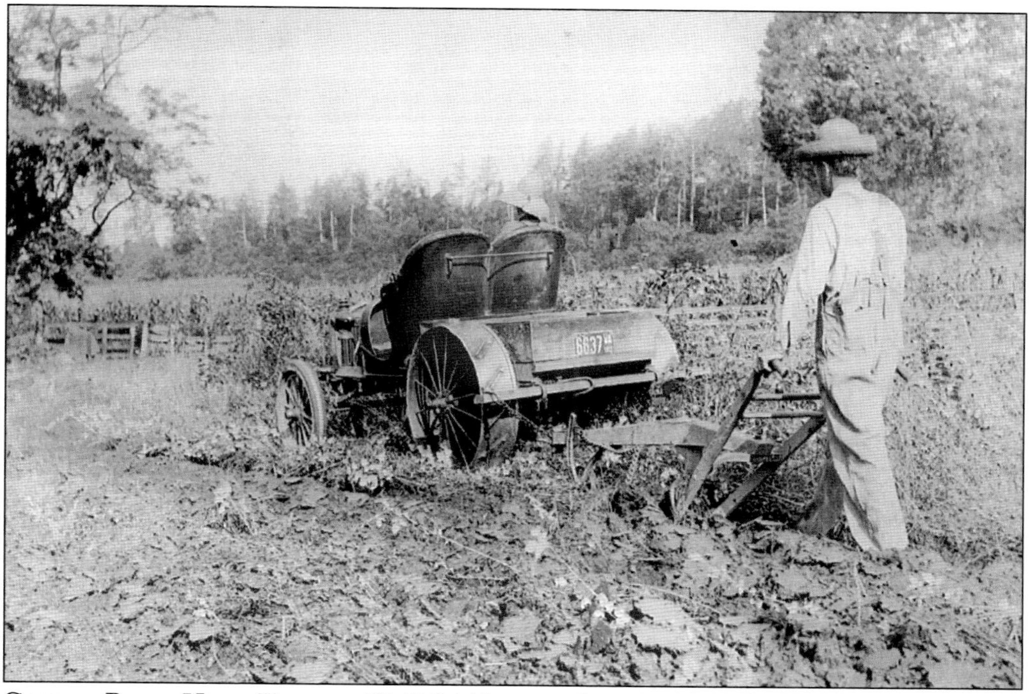

Goodbye Buick, Hello Tractor. W. C. Stickley was a farmer interested in inventing ways to make work easier. He made a new tractor by re-creating his old Buick. He is seen holding the plow while his wife, wearing a straw hat, does the driving. W. C. changed the back wheels to provide better traction. The wide metal wheels allowed him to get onto the ground earlier in the spring. (GRS.)

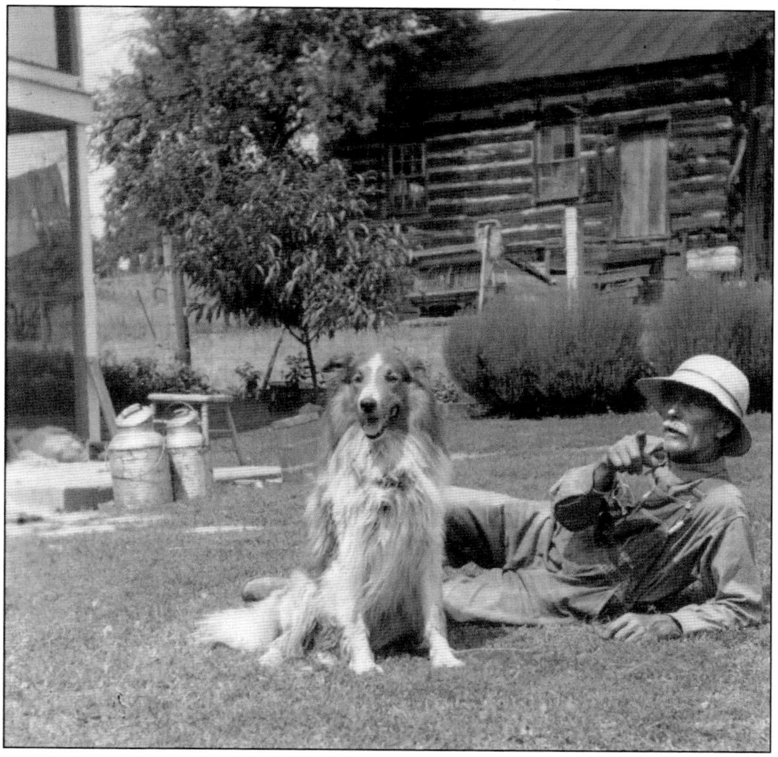

W. C. Stickley at Bellview. This photograph of W. C. provides a closer look at the man behind the farm. He and the dog are seen in the yard at Bellview farm. The early log cabin is still on the farm; it has been used for many purposes over its 200 years. The two shiny objects in the left background are milk cans with their lids ajar. (GRS.)

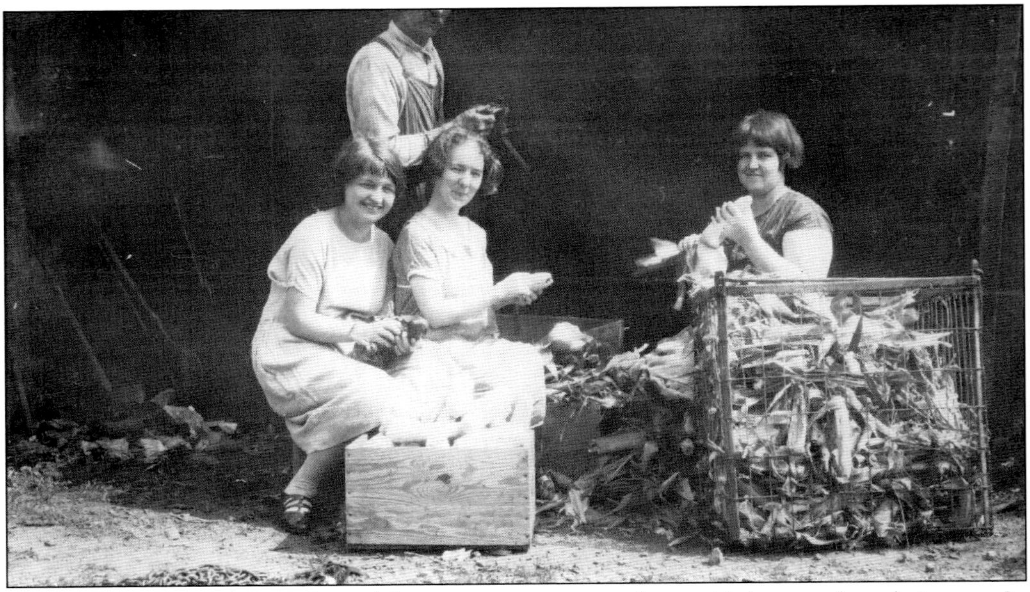

Helpers Shucking Corn. One of the major crops on any farm with hogs and cattle is corn. In recent years, there is a great difference between the corn one feeds to the hogs and that which one serves to guests. Perhaps this was not always the case. The girls, although unidentified, are Lucille Stickley's friends. W. C. Stickley is instructing this happy trio in the proper technique for shucking corn. (GRS.)

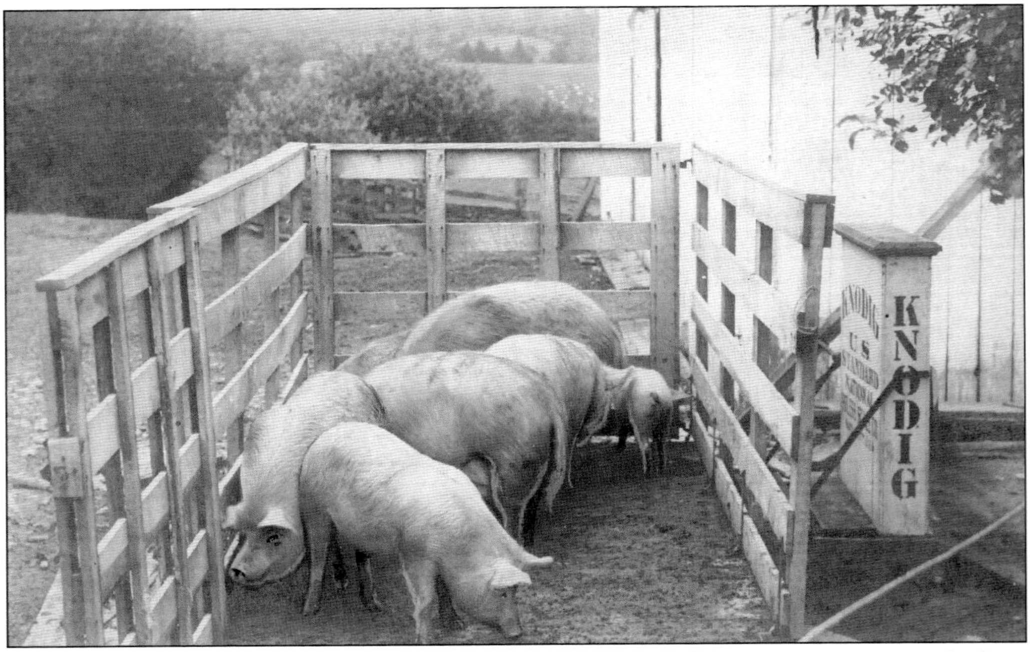

Hogs and the Knodig. The hogs in the pen have been fattened up on corn grown on the farm and are being weighed. The National Scale Company's Knodig was in the August 1907 *Agricultural Advertising* magazine. The box on the side of the pen is where the scale dial is located. The two iron levers support the platform that is the floor of the scale. (GRS.)

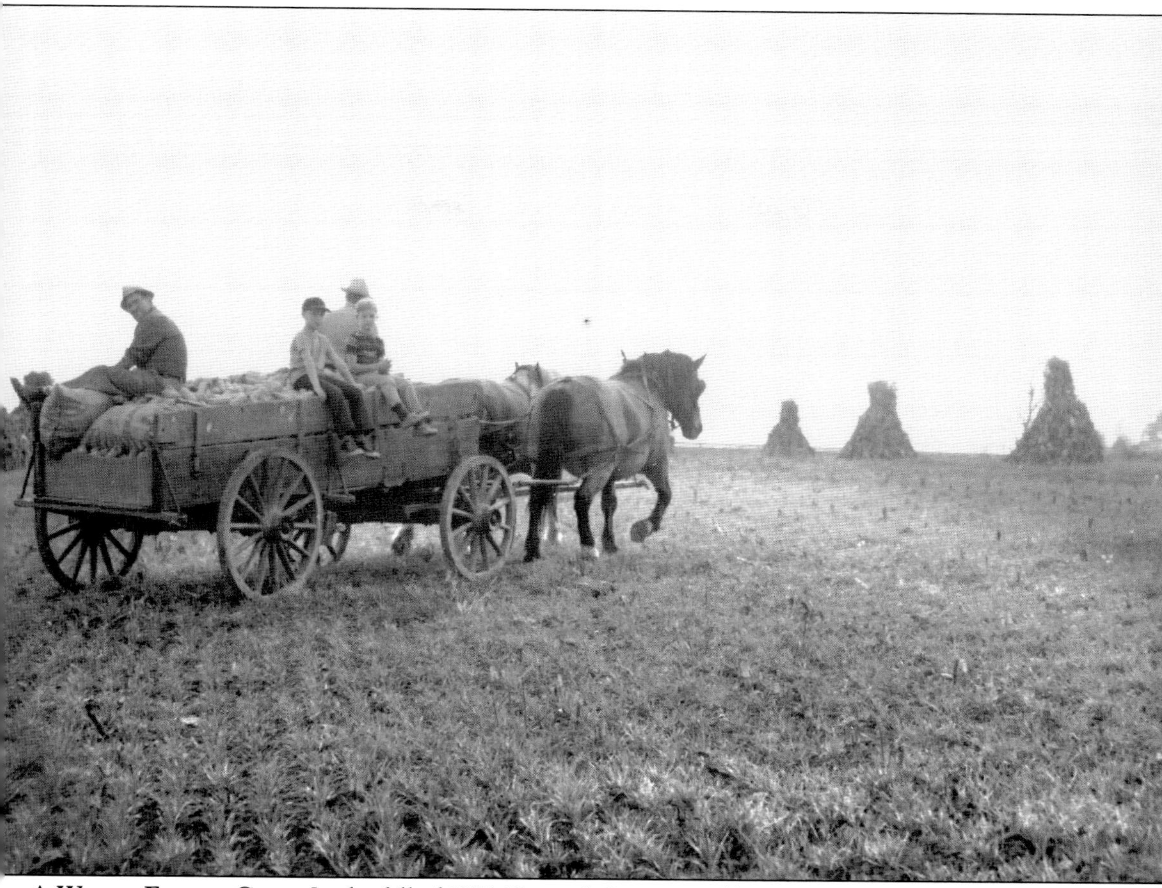

A Wagon Full of Corn. In the fall of 1975, Kenneth Painter and his team of sturdy draft horses hauled this load of corn fresh from the fields to the barn. His two grandsons Richard and Randy Stickles, ages nine and eight, respectively, and Alton Orndorff have been helping to gather the corn. Corn shocks stacked up to dry are in the background. Painter was known for his calm demeanor. When the 1976 bicentennial wagon train stopped in Strasburg to rest overnight, Painter visited the campsite. It did not take long for them to recognize his expertise with the horses. They were concerned about a team of obstreperous mules and how they would react during the trek over Paris Mountain to Leesburg. They asked Painter if he would be willing to drive that team. He agreed, and the trip was uneventful. (JPM.)

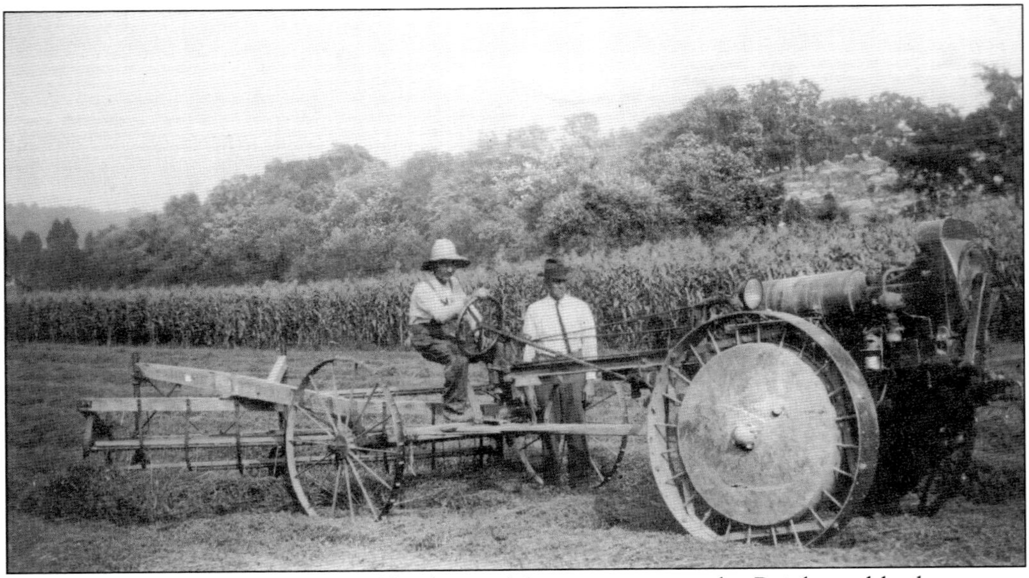

Homemade Tractor. W. C. Stickley learned from converting the Buick, and he has a new invention. The wheels are all larger, and the platform where the seat is mounted is much higher than his previous attempt. He seems to be showing it to a friend. The corn in the background is yet to be harvested, but he probably enjoyed every minute of his time on this high seat. (GRS.)

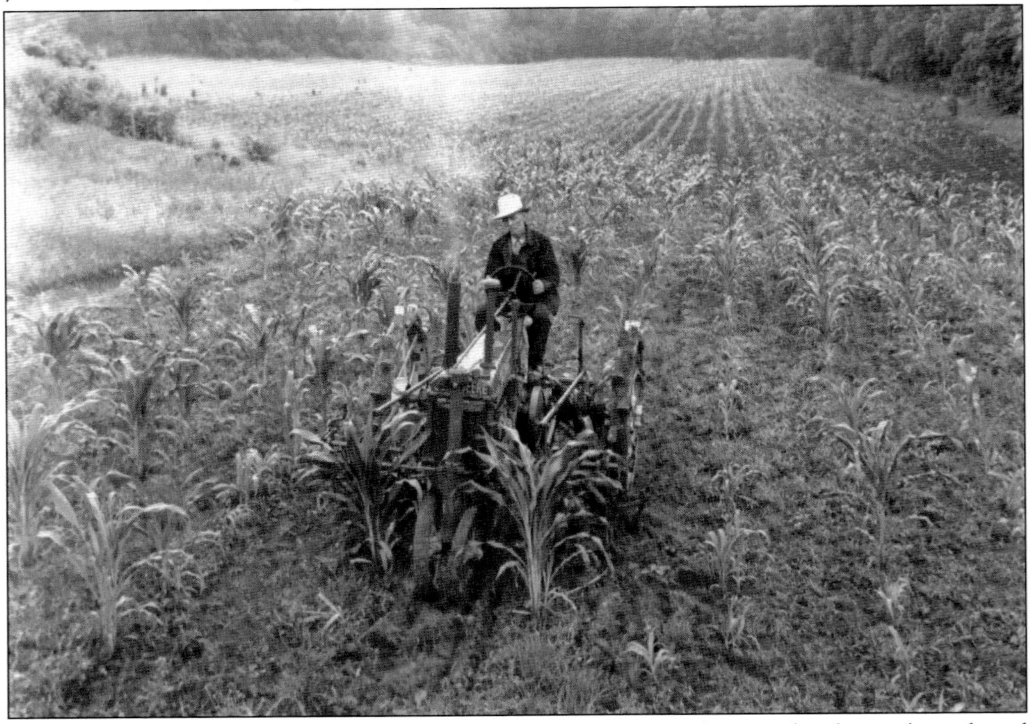

John Deere. This is the last in the series of Stickley's tractors. The corn has been planted, and it appears that now he is weeding between the rows. The narrow front wheels allow the driver to go precisely between the rows, something that neither of his homemade vehicles would have been able to do. This inventor yielded to the green giant of tractors, and it made him happy, according to family members who are preserving these photographs. (GRS.)

Seven

Forges, Furnaces, and the Fort

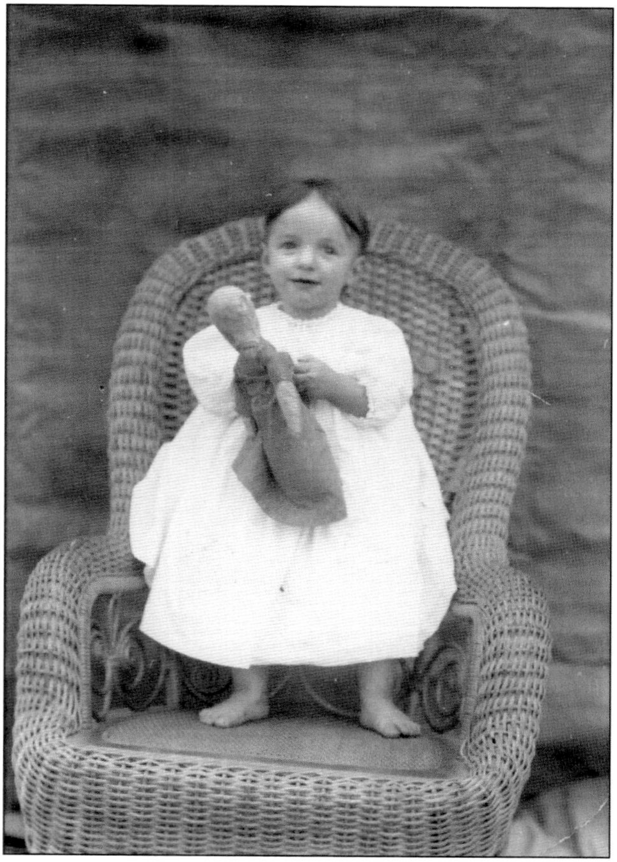

Ellen Rebecca Myers. By 1860, there were seven furnaces operating in Shenandoah County. Each of them burned dozens of cords of wood daily when they were "in fire." The rest of the year was spent cutting wood and hauling it to the furnace. Account books kept by the ironmasters list drivers and colliers who made the charcoal. This chapter focuses on family members who worked together. (SCL.)

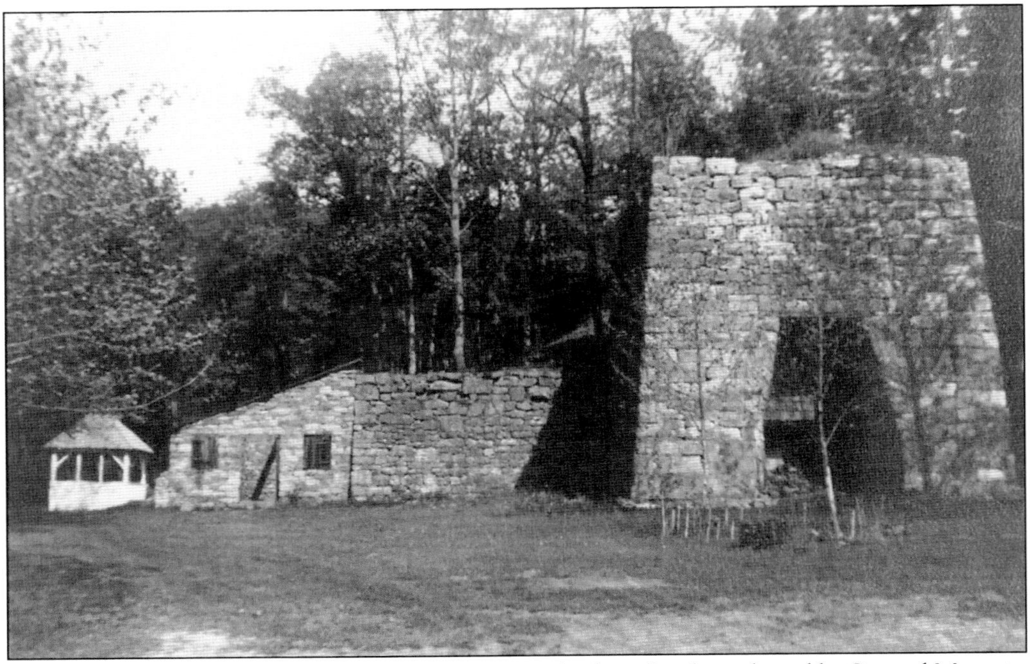

Henrietta Iron Furnace. Henrietta Furnace was built on land purchased by Samuel Myers in 1853. He named his furnace for his wife, Henrietta, but it was also known as Myers Furnace and Alum Springs Furnace. During the Civil War, Myers joined the southern forces. Much of the local iron was sold to Tredagar Iron Works in Richmond. (DBG.)

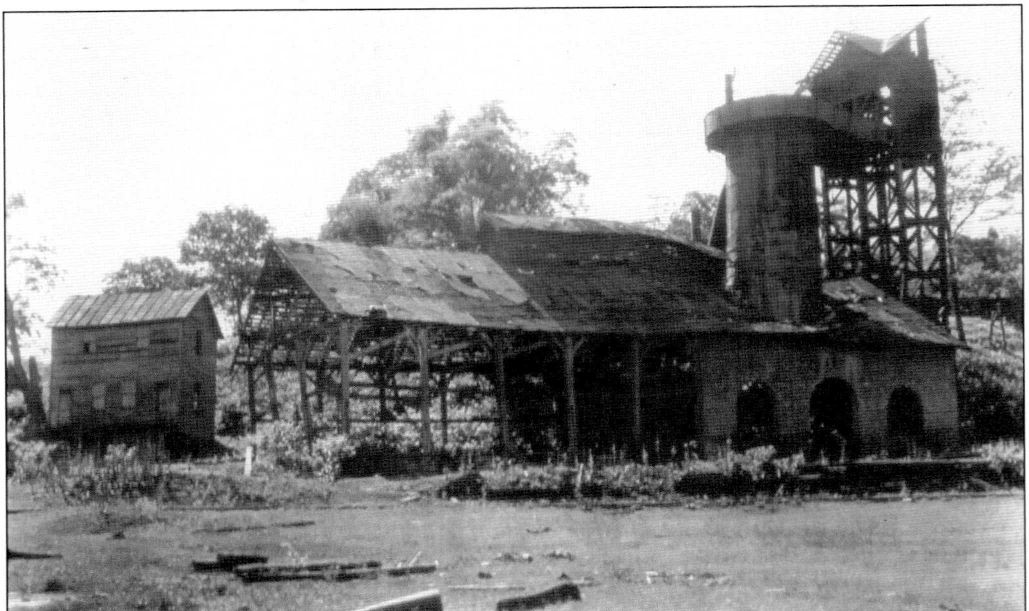

Liberty Furnace. Located on Stony Creek beyond Columbia Furnace, Liberty Furnace began operations about 1822 under Walter Newman's guidance. He already had Pine Forge on Smith Creek. Liberty Furnace was a large complex of buildings, with a charcoal house, a furnace stack, an office, a laboratory, and a casting shed, until it ceased operations in 1917, the last one in the county to do so. (SCHS.)

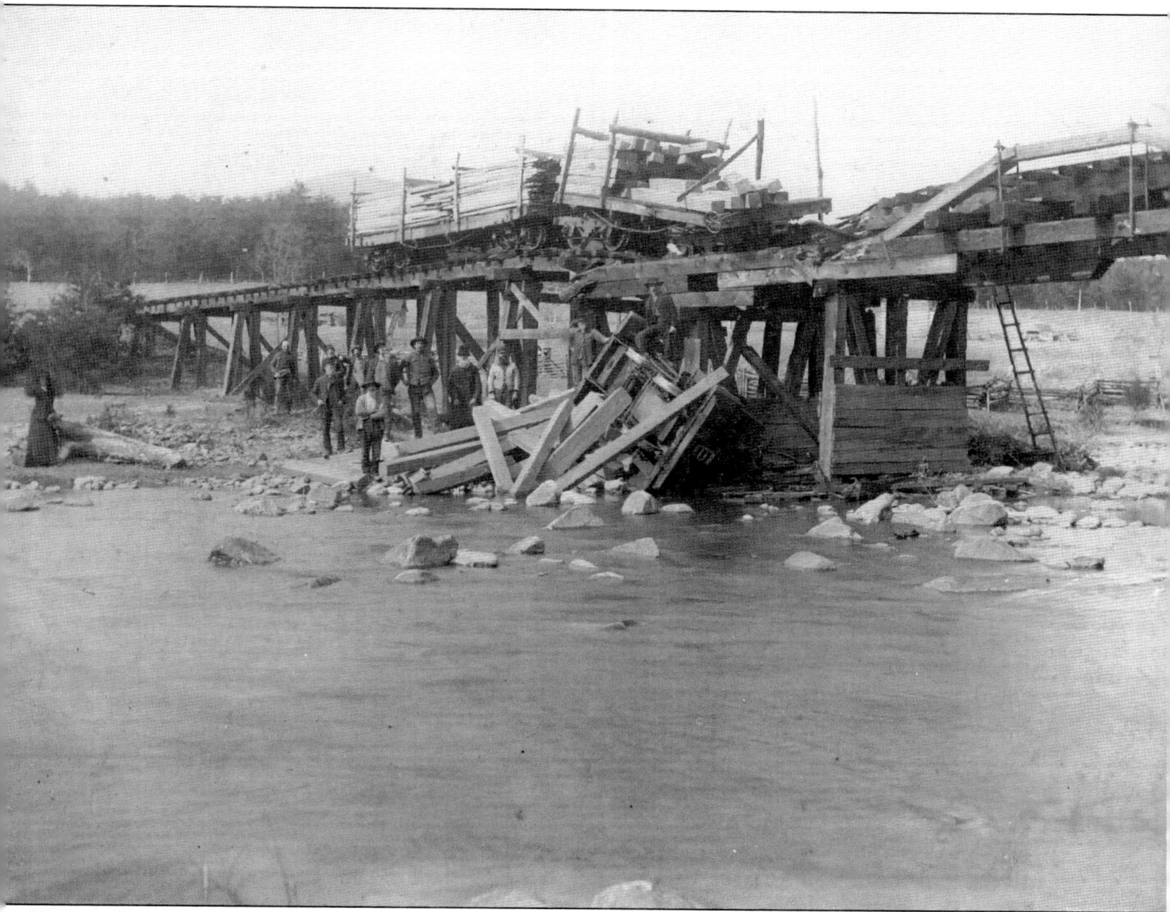

DINKY RAILROAD ACCIDENT AT STONY CREEK. This narrow-gauge railroad was built by the Liberty Iron Company in 1891 and operated from Liberty Furnace and Columbia Furnace, following Stony Creek to Edinburg. On special occasions, the dinky railroad provided excursion opportunities for the community. The dinky left Liberty Furnace each morning, carrying lumber, pig iron, charcoal, and bark to the Southern Railway yard at Edinburg, with stops at Columbia Furnace and Lantz Mill to pick up the mail. At 10:00 a.m. on March 2, 1911, while loaded with lumber, the bridge timbers gave way behind Fred Helsley's Store, and the dinky engine plunged into the creek. Engineer James Sine lost his life, and Thomas Foltz, a fireman, was injured. The engine and trestle were quickly repaired. Soon after the accident, Foltz was promoted to engineer, and Seward Sine was hired as fireman. Liberty Furnace and the dinky operated until the fall of 1917. (SCL.)

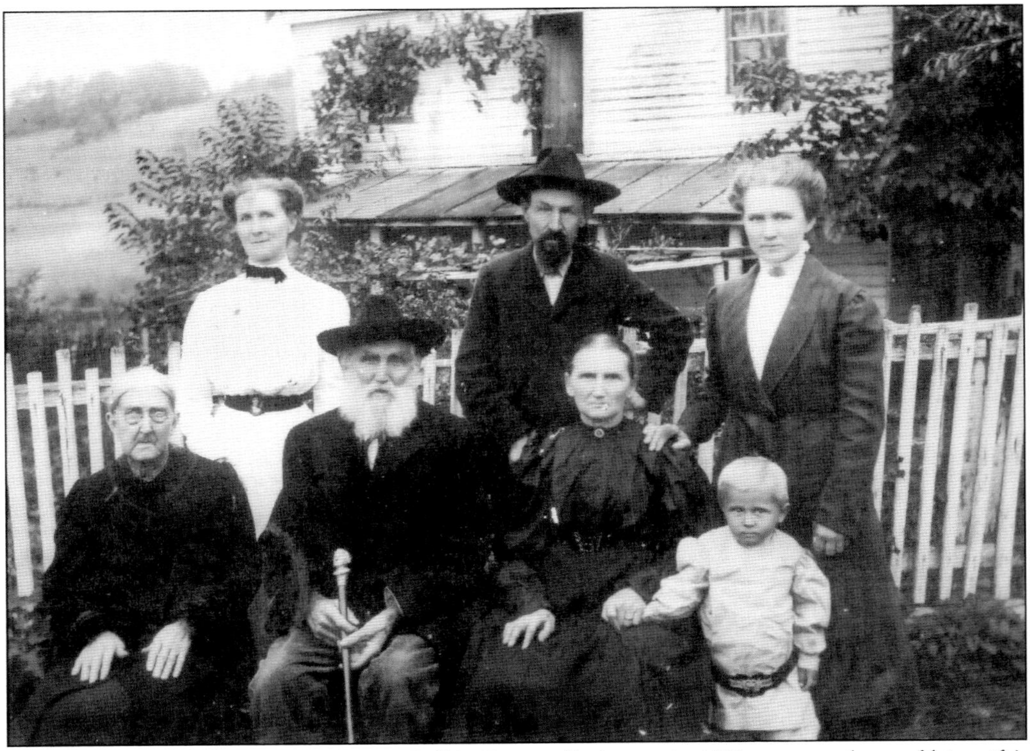

Ananias Polk Family. At Ananias Polk's Conicville home in 1911 are members of his wife's family. Polly Ann Hepner West Polk, wearing a family heirloom brooch with Martha Washington's image, is seated in front. Gideon Hepner, her father, holds another heirloom, his Jefferson Davis cane. On his left is Sarah Hepner, and behind them are Sarah Polk Smootz, Ananias, and Annie Smootz Pence Youngblood. The child is Annie's son Eugene Smootz. (MP.)

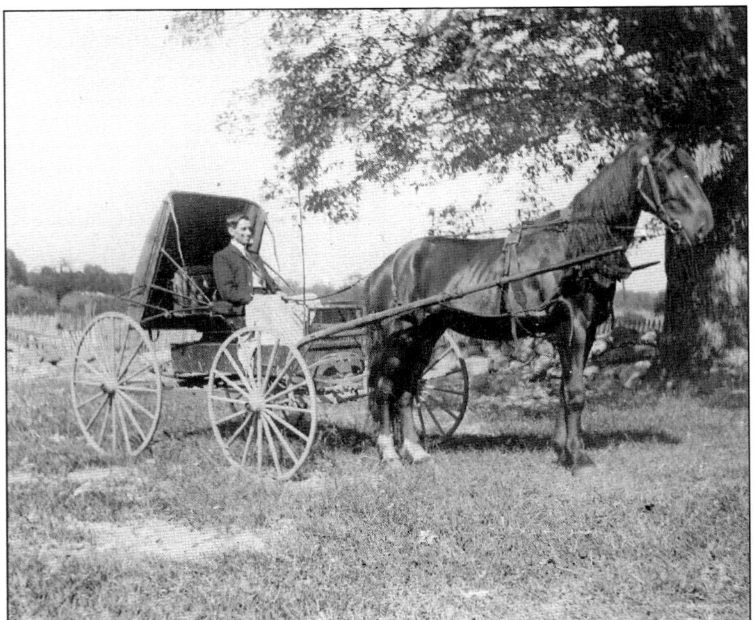

Patrick Henry Racey in Carriage. Patrick Henry Racey, born in 1887 at Columbia Furnace, was the youngest of St. Luke Racey and Lydia Ann Shireman's eight children. His father was a miner at Columbia Furnace and later a farmer in St. Luke. Patrick, a handsome lad, courted in an open carriage. He married Ada F. Orndorff; they had six children and lived in St. Luke where he was a farmer. (SCL.)

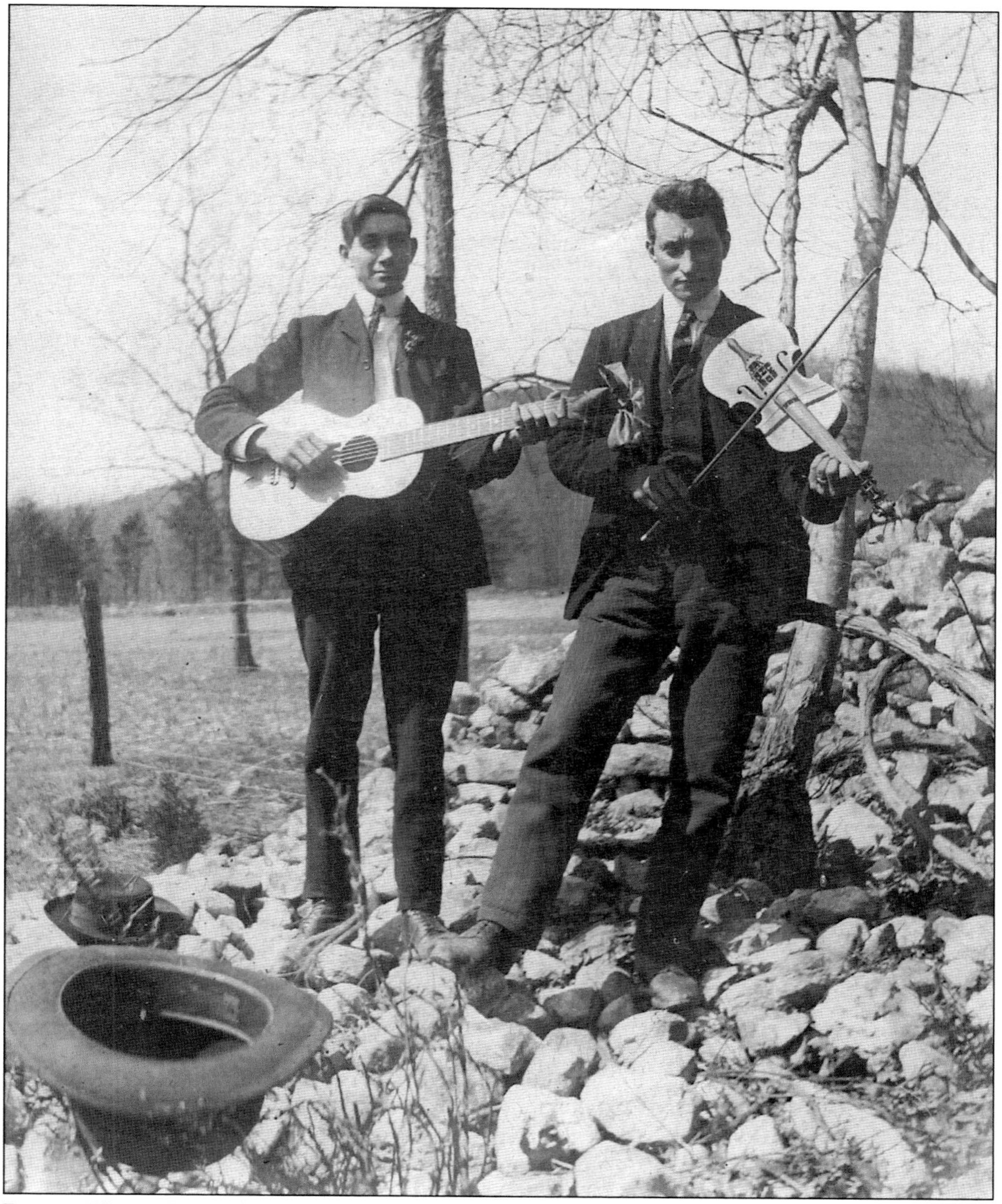

Patrick Henry Racey (Left) and Charlie Plauger (Right). These two men lived in Shenandoah County and made happy music together. They are seen in this rock pile with their hats in front of them as though they are looking for a handout. Patrick had music in his blood; he learned to play from his father's family in West Virginia. Patrick's uncle Joseph Racey worked hard as a coal miner in West Virginia. In the late 1920s, money was scarce and the coal mines were shut down part-time. Joseph had an idea to put enthusiasm back in their community: he formed a band with all of his sons. They cleaned and polished their barn and then held Saturday night barn dances at the Racey farm. Joseph and his six sons, who played banjo, guitar, violin, and mandolin as the Racey Ramblers, created the music. Patrick often joined in the music at these barn dances. Charles Franklin Plauger was 10 years older than Patrick. He married Grace May Munch in 1905; they lived in Fort Valley with their seven children. (HC.)

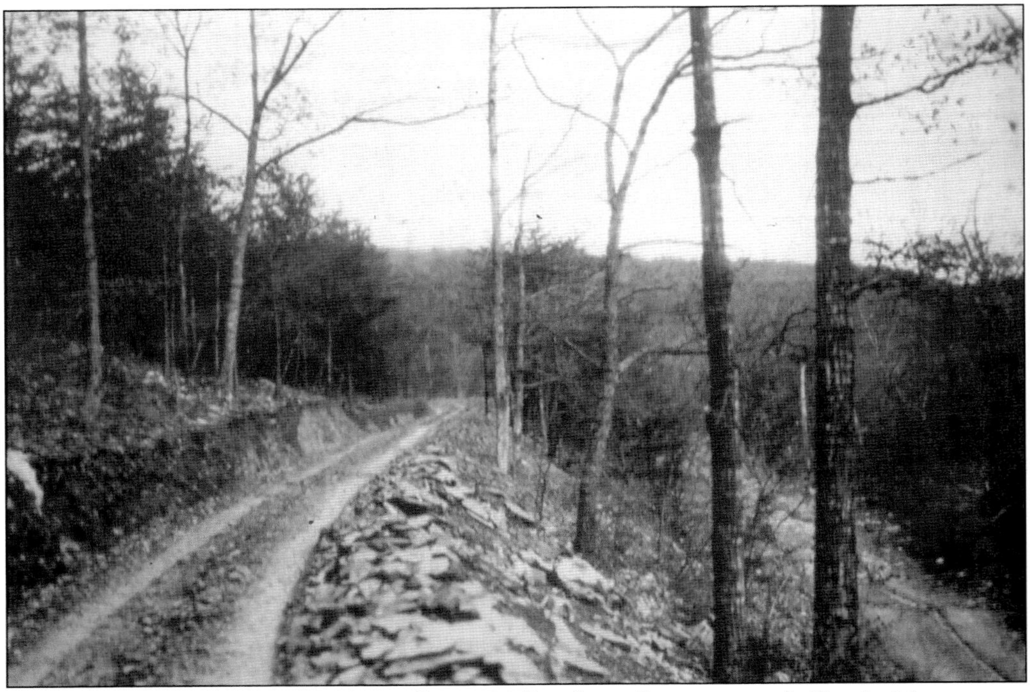

Edinburg Gap Road. First called Powell's Fort Valley, this valley is surrounded by the Massanutten Mountains and was surveyed by George Washington, who returned here after his defeat of General Cornwallis at Yorktown. The fort is accessed by Waterlick Road, Woodstock Tower Road, or the Edinburg Gap on Fort Road. It is this steep, curving, dusty road that brings the truck into the valley in this early-1900s image. (SCHS.)

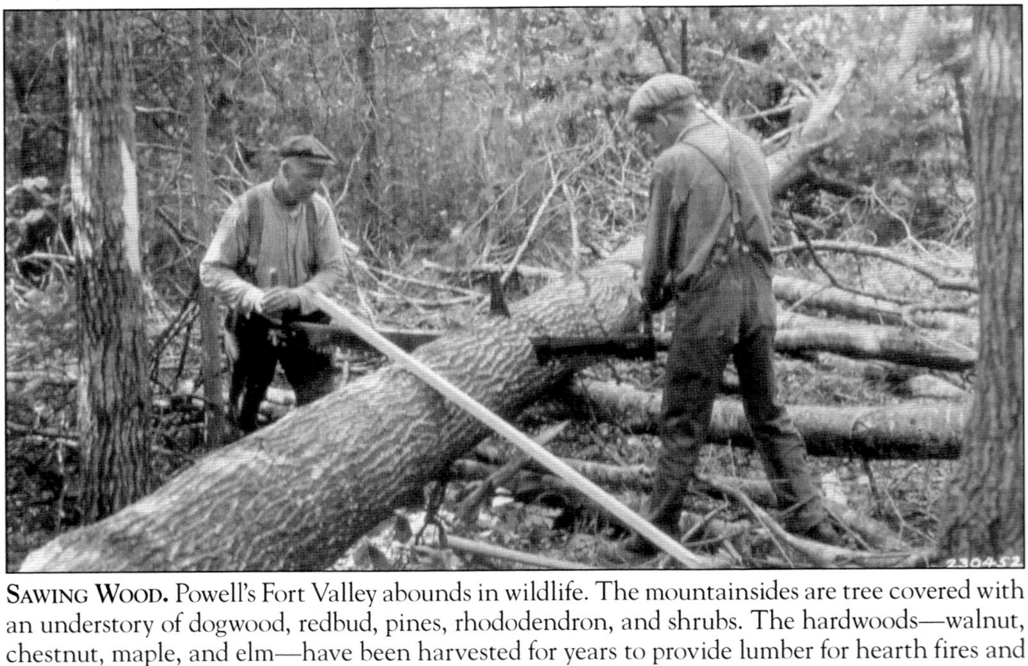

Sawing Wood. Powell's Fort Valley abounds in wildlife. The mountainsides are tree covered with an understory of dogwood, redbud, pines, rhododendron, and shrubs. The hardwoods—walnut, chestnut, maple, and elm—have been harvested for years to provide lumber for hearth fires and outbuildings. The technology for clearing and cutting has changed. This image shows men working with a two-man saw to make manageable lengths. (SCHS.)

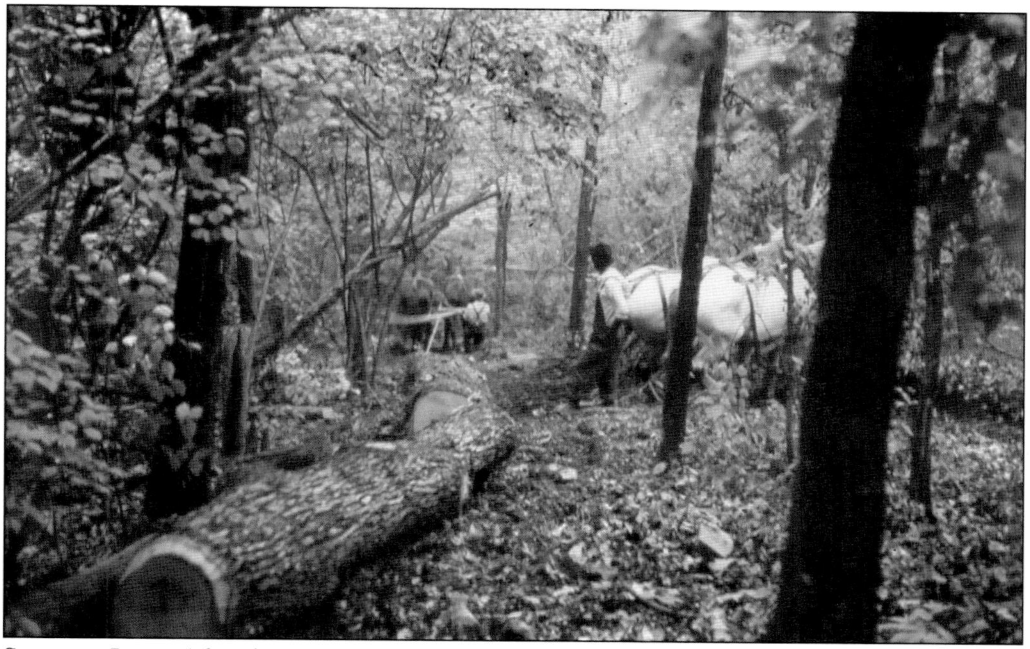

SKIDDING LOGS. After the trees are cut down and side limbs removed, they are secured to either a slide or by a harness and dragged preferably on level ground or a downhill slope to a conveyance with wheels, or to a body of water. The logs are then transported to the nearest lumber mill, where they are sawn into boards for construction of building and flooring. (SCL.)

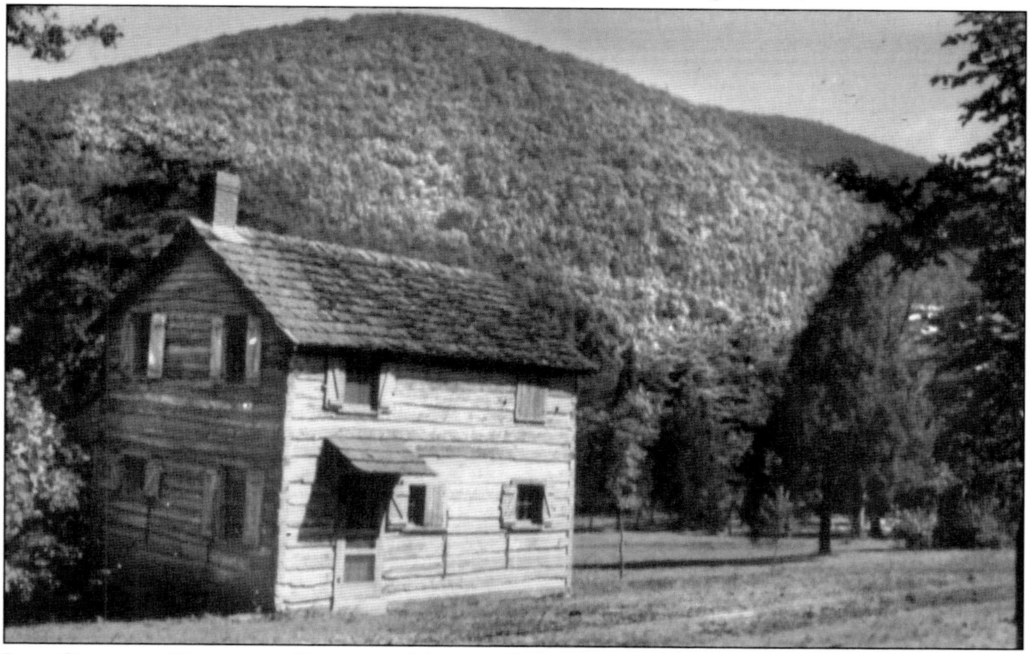

LOG CABIN AT ELIZABETH FURNACE. Many early homes in Shenandoah County were made of logs. This house at Elizabeth Furnace remains intact. Others have burned or been dismantled and the lumber used elsewhere. The house is located at the northern end of Fort Valley in the George Washington National Forest and was rehabilitated in 1995, part of the new interpretive exhibit on iron furnaces in the national forest. (SCHS.)

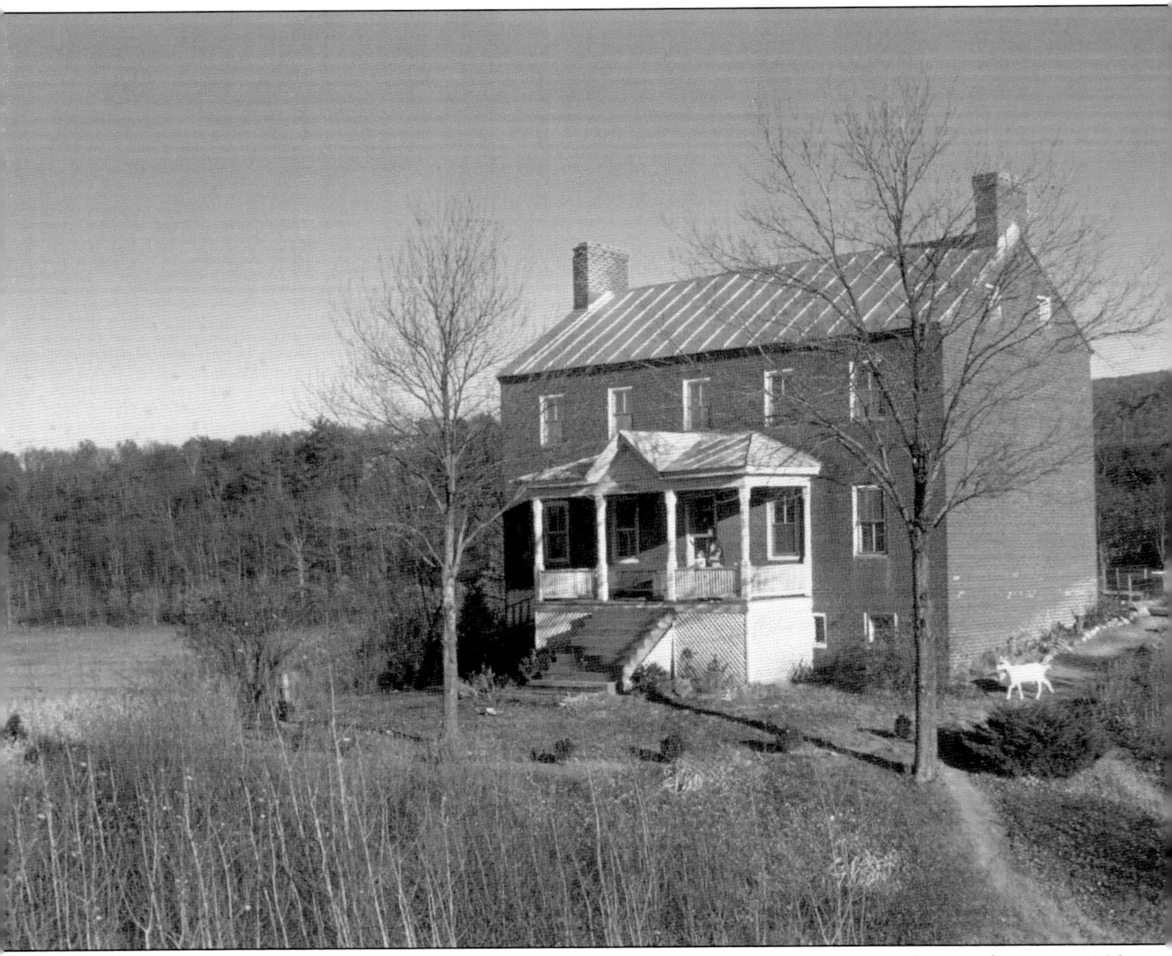

MUNCH HOME. The brick house on Seven Fountains Road, built by Daniel Munch Sr. in 1823, was the only brick house in Fort Valley. The brick was made on the property. Twelve-year-old Addison Munch and his friend Manoah Harmon carried the brick and mortar for this house. The Munch house has been lived in by members of the Cullers, Ritenour, and Munch families. According to Orie Munch, 39 children were born in this house to these families. Orie lived here with his mother, Estelle, and father, Eugene Munch, a schoolteacher and farmer. The current owners purchased the property in 1970. They raised their two daughters and assorted pets here, including the goat seen coming around the corner. (Courtesy of James and Meg Trott.)

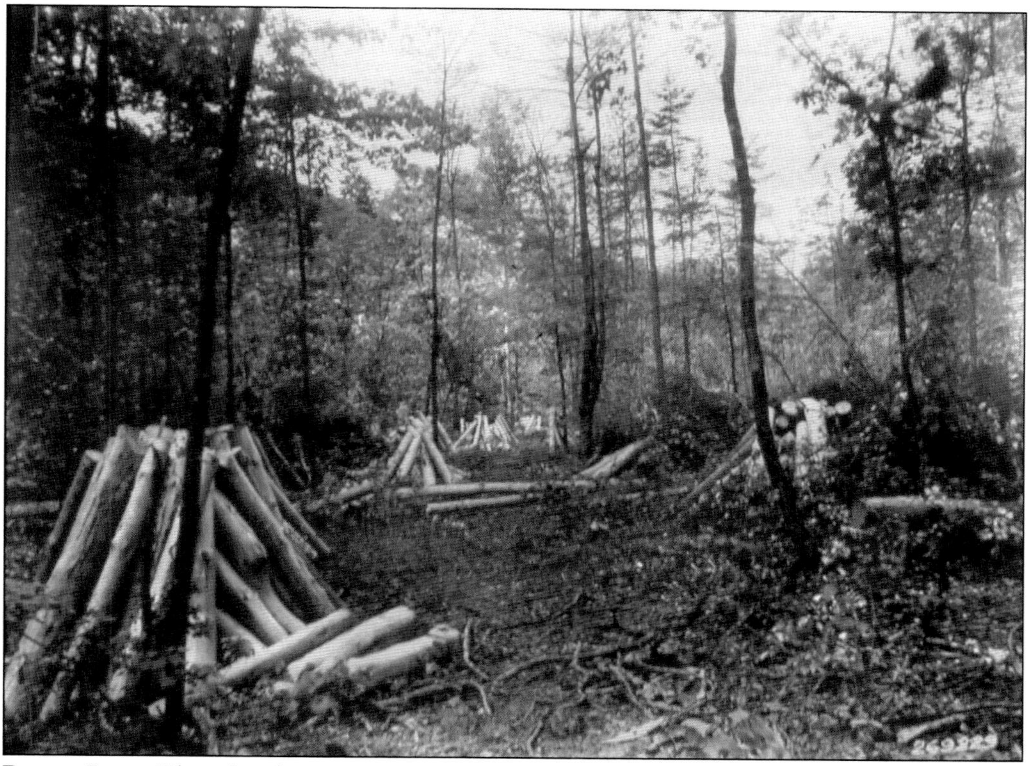

Peeled Logs. These logs have been peeled and are being prepared for use in charcoal making. The iron furnaces needed a hot fuel to melt the iron, and charcoal burns hotter than logs. Therefore the logs were treated by firing and turned into charcoal by the colliers who made their living stacking and charring the logs. Tanners used other peeled logs. (SCHS.)

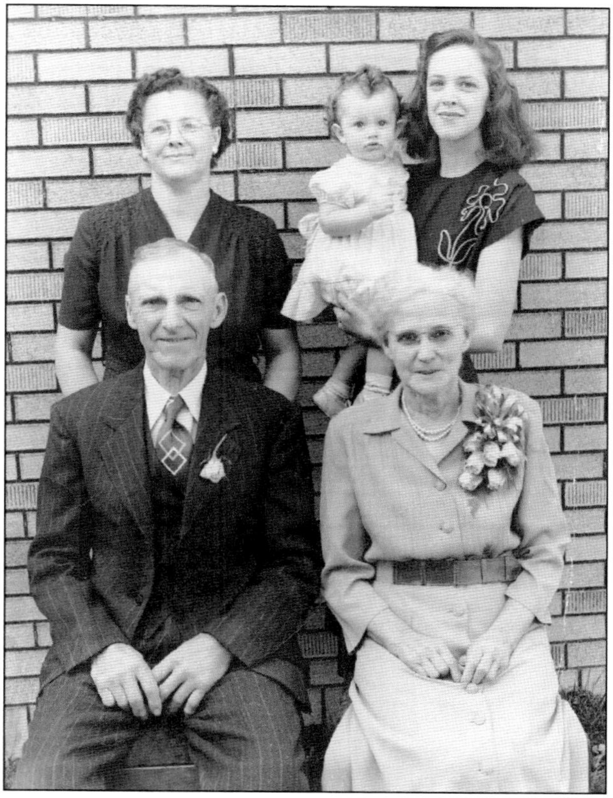

Fogle Wedding Anniversary. Addison Lee and Minnie Beatrice Cook Fogle celebrated their 50th wedding anniversary in 1948. They met when Addison came to Fort Valley from Hardy County to work for Minnie's father, William Newton Cook, stripping bark for tanning hides. The Fogles lived in West Virginia and Delaware before returning to Fort Valley to farm. They had seven children, Florence, Lester, Edna, Zirkle, Clara, Pauline, and Emogene. (WF.)

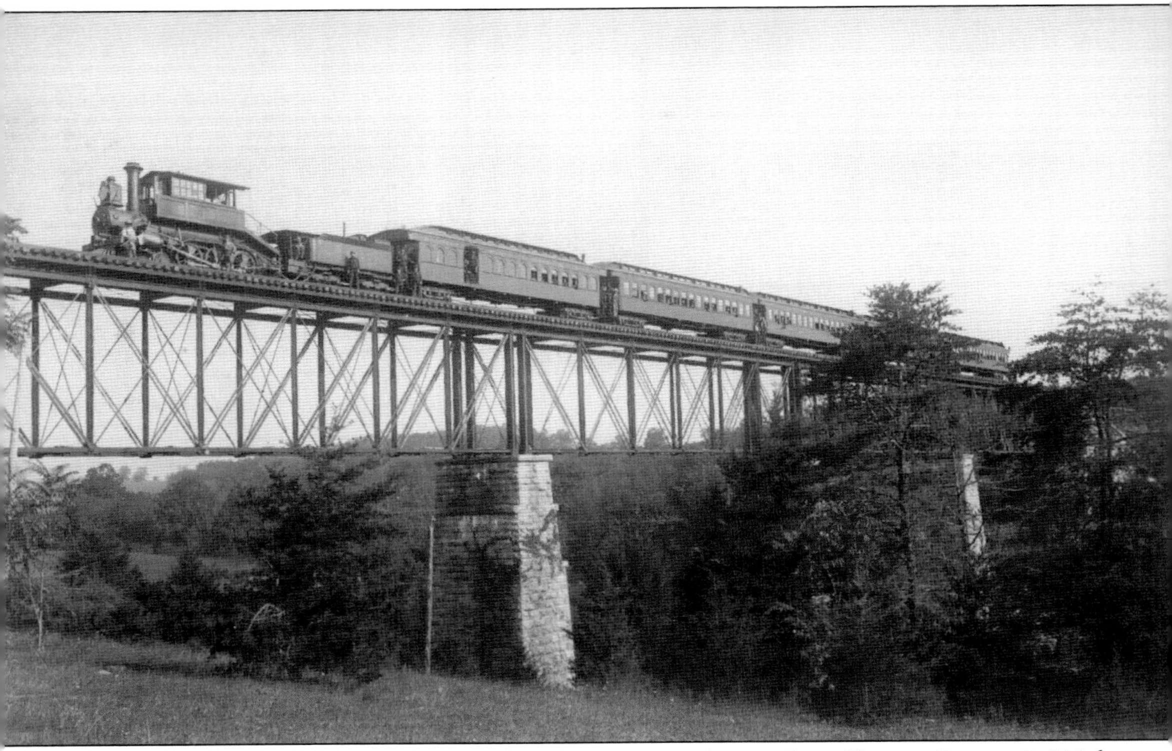

Trestle at Narrow Passage. A passenger train on the trestle at Narrow Passage is 114 feet above the water. The train is stopped so that photographer Warren Waltham can take a picture. The windows are open and passengers are looking out; other passengers are on the steps. The engineer and crew are standing beside the coal car. According to an account in the *Shenandoah Herald* on March 9, 1876, the old, wooden railway bridge crashed into the ravine under a heavy load of cattle, sheep, hogs, 500 barrels of flour from local mills, and many tons of pig iron. It also had one passenger coach. The entire train fell, and 11 of 18 men aboard and all the cattle were killed. W. A. Wightman of Woodstock, the Edinburg justice of peace, was among those killed. Lumber in the trestle was old, rotten, and considered unsafe. (SCL.)

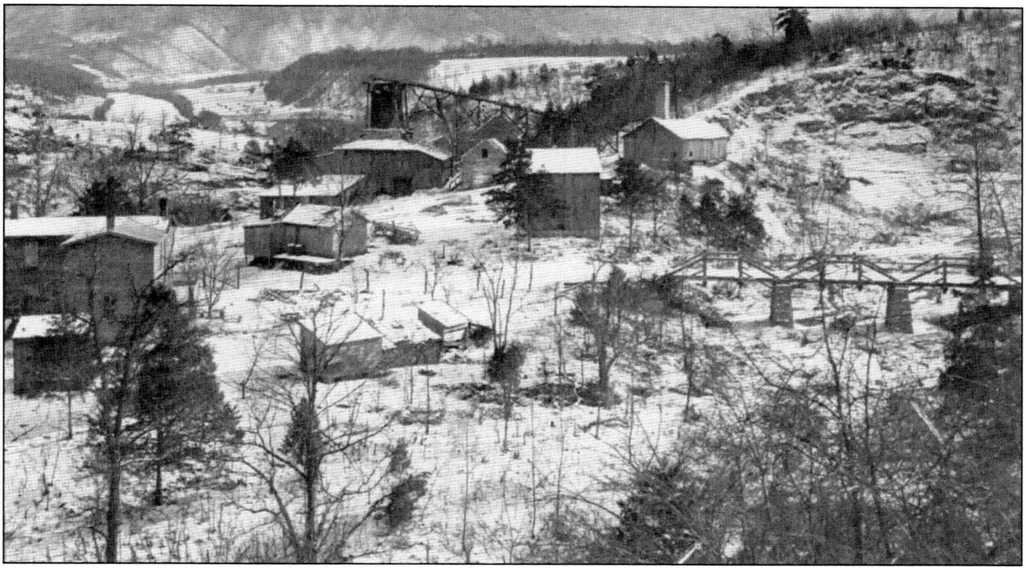

PUGH'S RUN IN THE SNOW. Pugh's Run, north of Woodstock, is usually a peaceful place. On the night of November 9, 1908, two Southern Railway freight trains met head on here. Two men were killed and four injured as the engines, traveling at 30 miles per hour, collided but stayed on the tracks. The cars loaded with coal and lime went over the east side of the tracks. (SCL.)

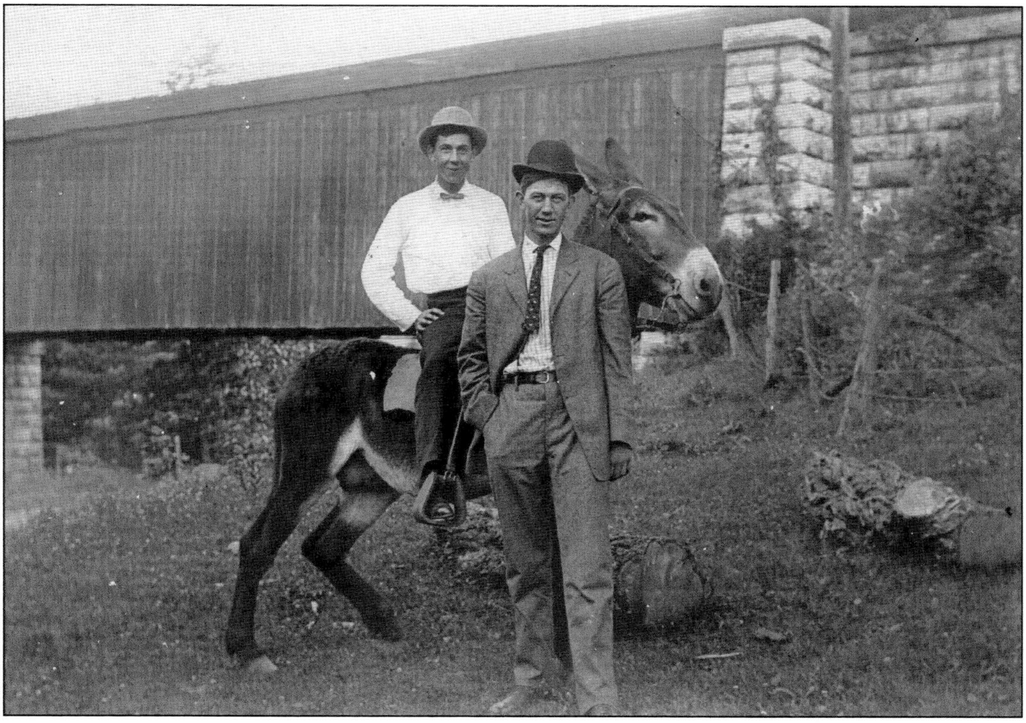

DONKEY AT RAILROAD BRIDGE. This amusing photograph by Perry Crabill shows the photographer and his friend Joe Cooper in front of the wooden railroad bridge across Pugh's Run. At 200 feet long and 70 feet from the creek bed at the highest point, it was completely destroyed on Sunday morning, August 2, 1915, when sparks from an extra freight train about 3:00 a.m. ignited the bridge. (PCC.)

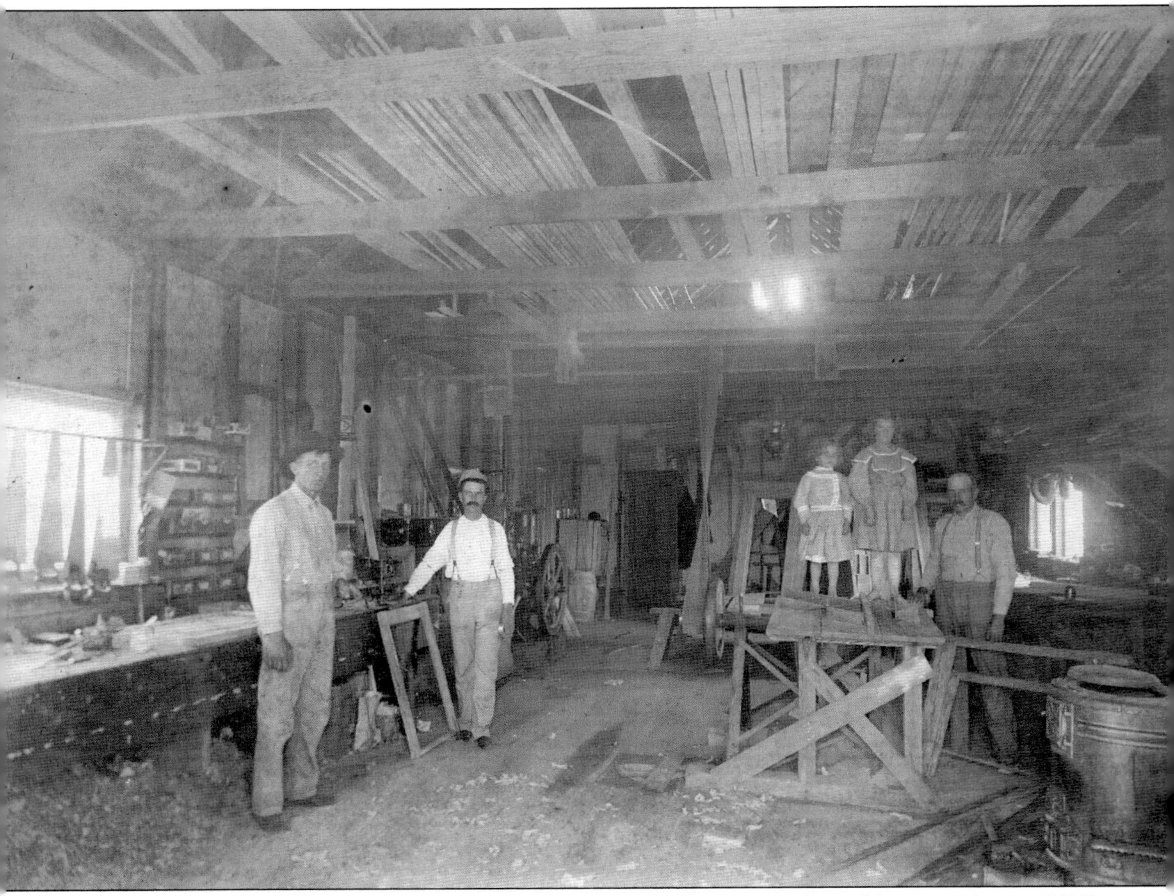

GEORGE WILLIAM STICKLEY'S WORKSHOP. James and Matilda Schull Stickley were George William Stickley's parents. They lived near Deer Rapids in the Davis Magisterial District. In 1869, George married Virginia Catherine Baker, and by the 1880 census, they had six sons. The workshop on their farm is where they made furniture and repaired doors, window frames, and so on around the farm. This workshop has become known for the chairs they made. The two men on the left may be George and W. D. Stickley. They placed business advertisements in the 1885 *Lake's Atlas*. If one looks closely at the image, saws are seen hanging in front of the windows, and cigar boxes are lined up on the wall against the workbench. This is a testament to the care and organization of the successful businessmen. No one else is identified. (GRS.)

Eight

A LIVING LEGACY

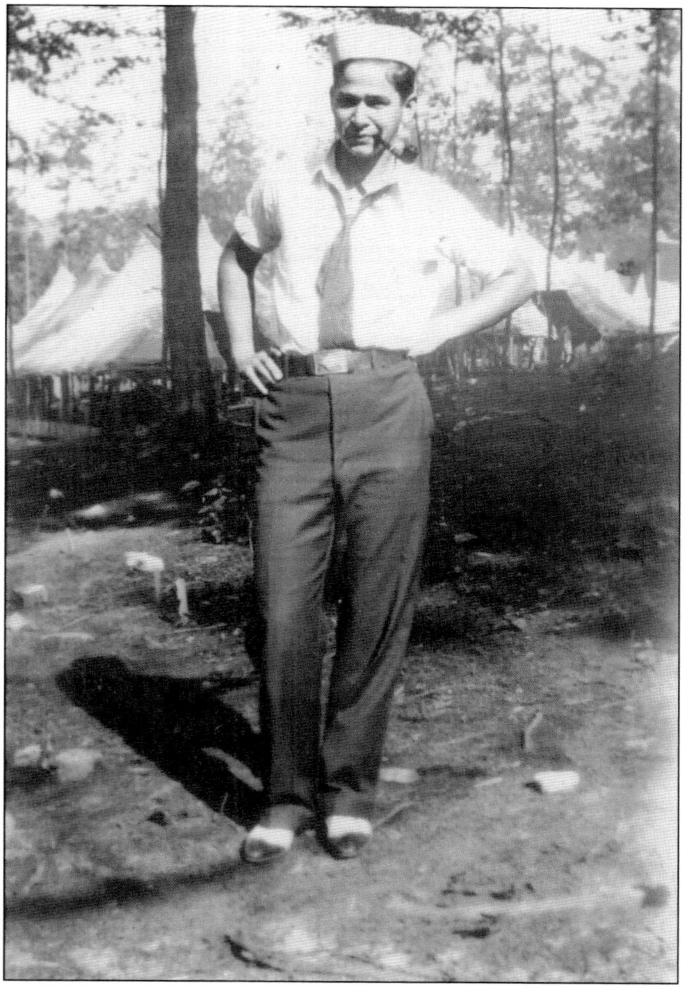

GARLAND HUDGINS. The George Washington National Forest at Fort Valley was selected in 1933 as the first camp of the Civilian Conservation Corps (CCC). To conserve natural resources and employ young men in a demoralized nation, Pres. Franklin D. Roosevelt conceived the idea of the CCC. Some of this chapter's photographs are from Garland Hudgin's scrapbook. (USDAFS.)

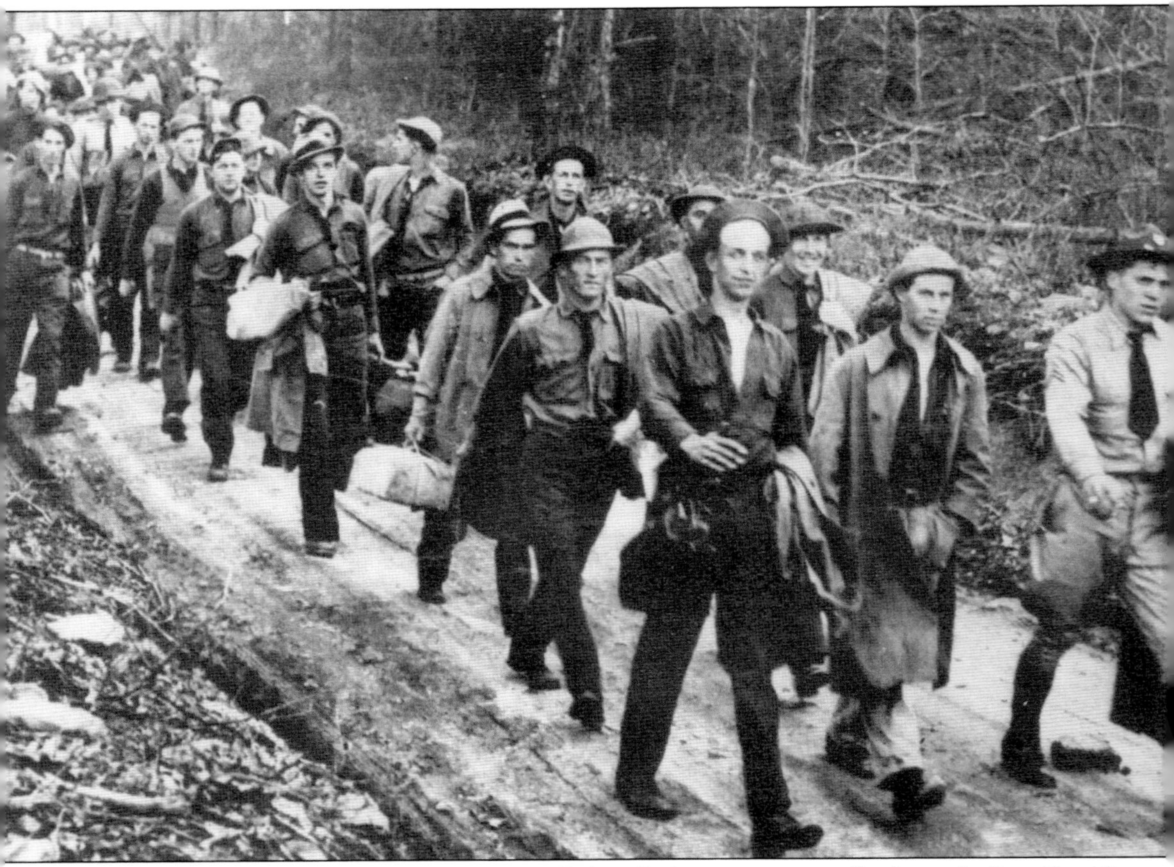

Marching up Massanutten Mountain. Robert Fechner was personally chosen by Pres. Franklin D. Roosevelt as administrator of the CCC and appointed by executive order on April 15, 1933. Two days later, the young men arrived at an isolated clearing, hungry and muddy, to build Camp Roosevelt NF-1. "We Can Take It," the unofficial motto of the CCC, was coined during those first hard days. The CCC Legacy has its national headquarters in Edinburg. (USDAFS.)

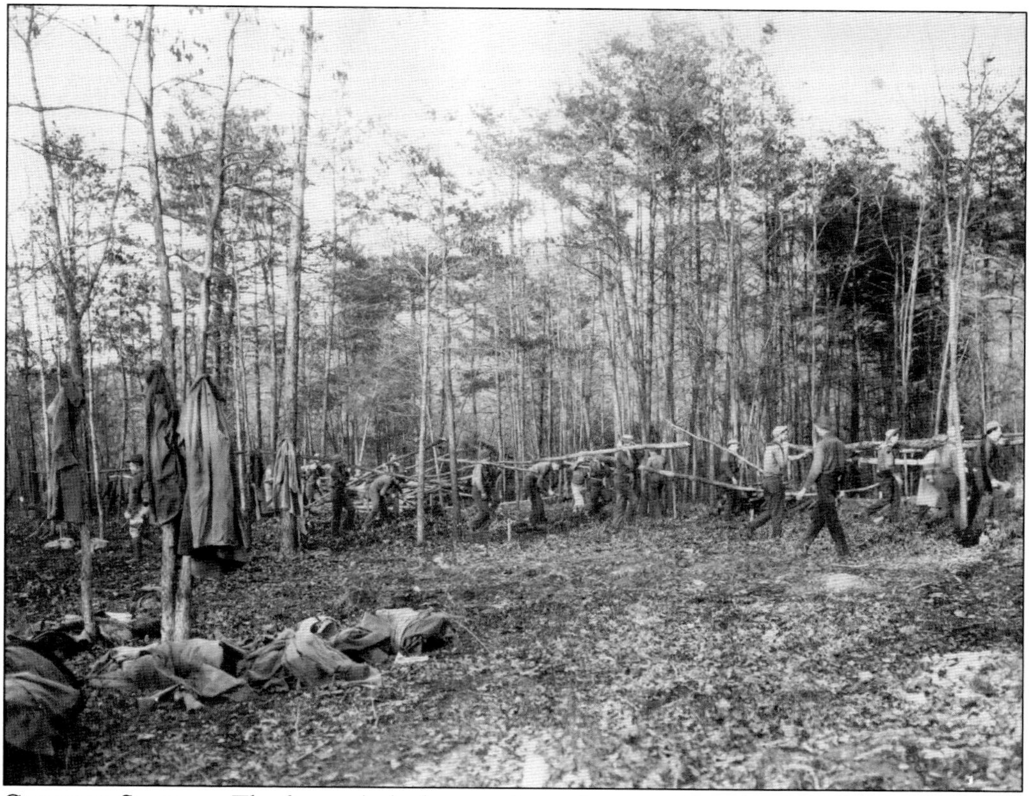

Carrying Saplings. The first task the boys performed was to clear a level place for tents. In the forest early in April, the air can be chilly. The boys took off their jackets and hung them on the trees or tossed them on the ground. Some are cutting saplings and others are carrying them to a designated location. The boys were learning to follow a plan of action. (USDAFS.)

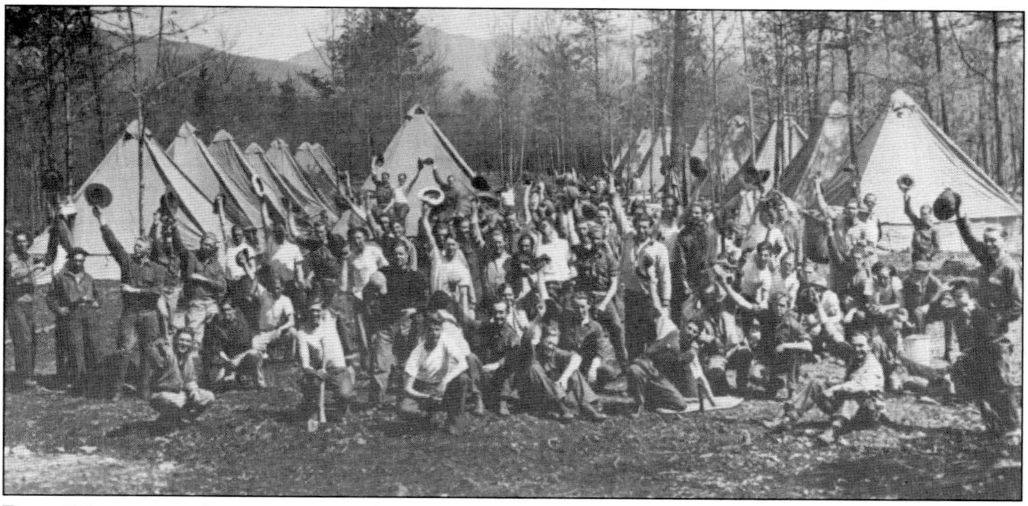

Boys Waving on Second Day. After having arrived in camp about 5:00 p.m. the night before, hungry and with little equipment, the boys cleared the area to make a place to sleep. The moving vans with food and equipment had finally arrived in camp at 11:40 p.m. As rain fell early the next morning, they began to organize the camp. The ground had been cleared, lumber unloaded, and platforms built for tents that were set up in a predetermined formation. (USDAFS.)

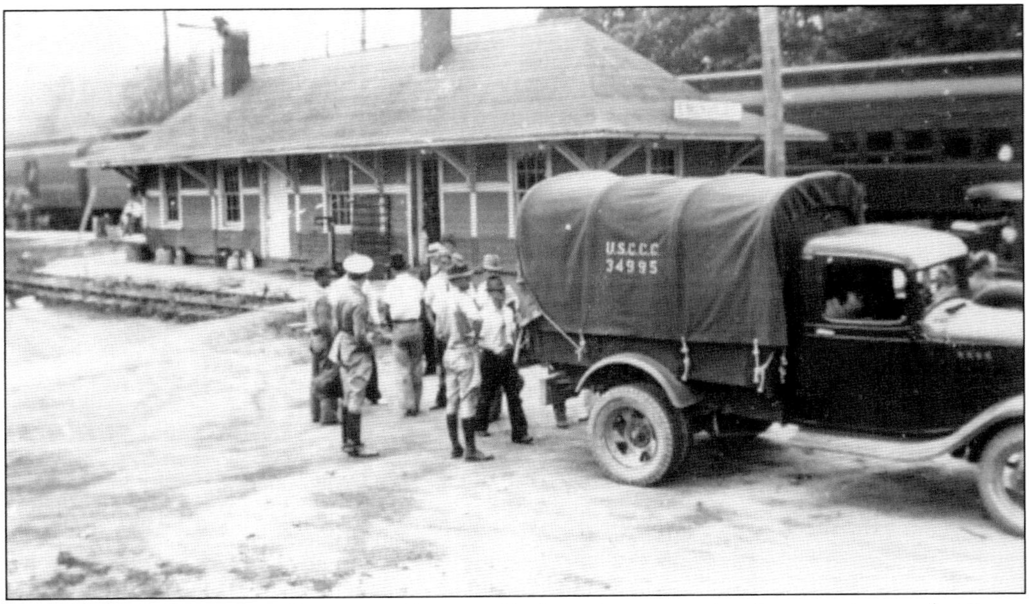

CAPT. PAUL O. TUCKER AT EDINBURG DEPOT. Edinburg depot was the closest train stop for Camp Roosevelt. The first day, the boys got off their caravan of busses and trucks at Luray. Later the new enrollees arrived by train in Edinburg and were met by stake body trucks. Shown here is infantry captain Rev. Paul O. Tucker with a truck that has a canvas cover draped over it and secured with ropes. (USDAFS.)

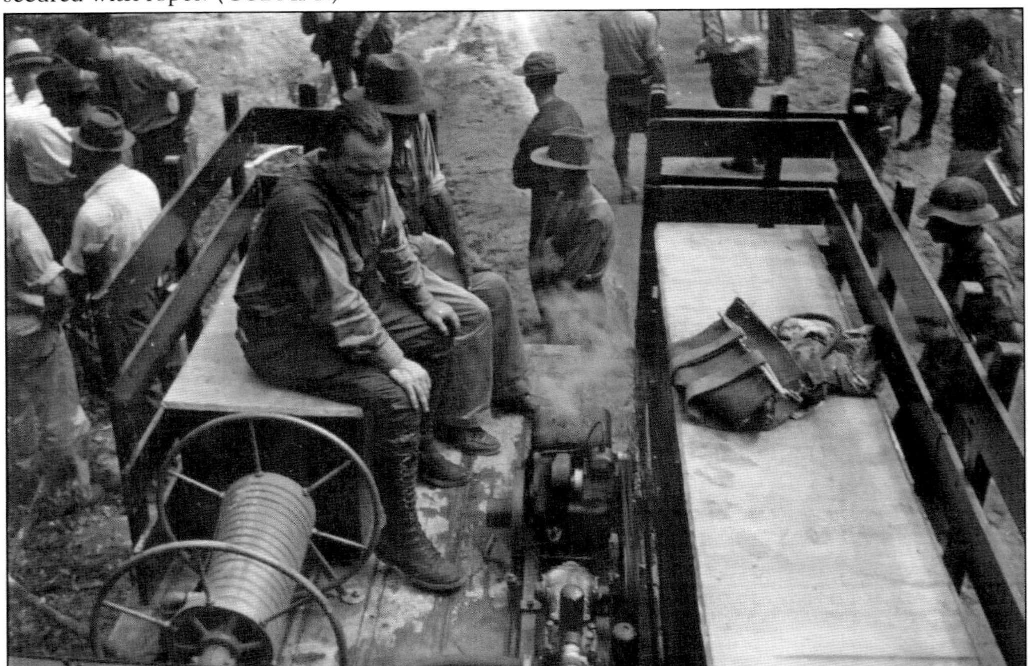

BACK OF TRUCK. This truck shows the staked sides and rear doors made of wood. The seats or benches line both sides, and this truck is equipped with a reel for winding a hose or cable. The trucks carried army equipment and had removable canvas covers, although this one is not covered. A canvas knapsack is on the right bench, and an enrollee and another sit on the facing bench. (USDAFS.)

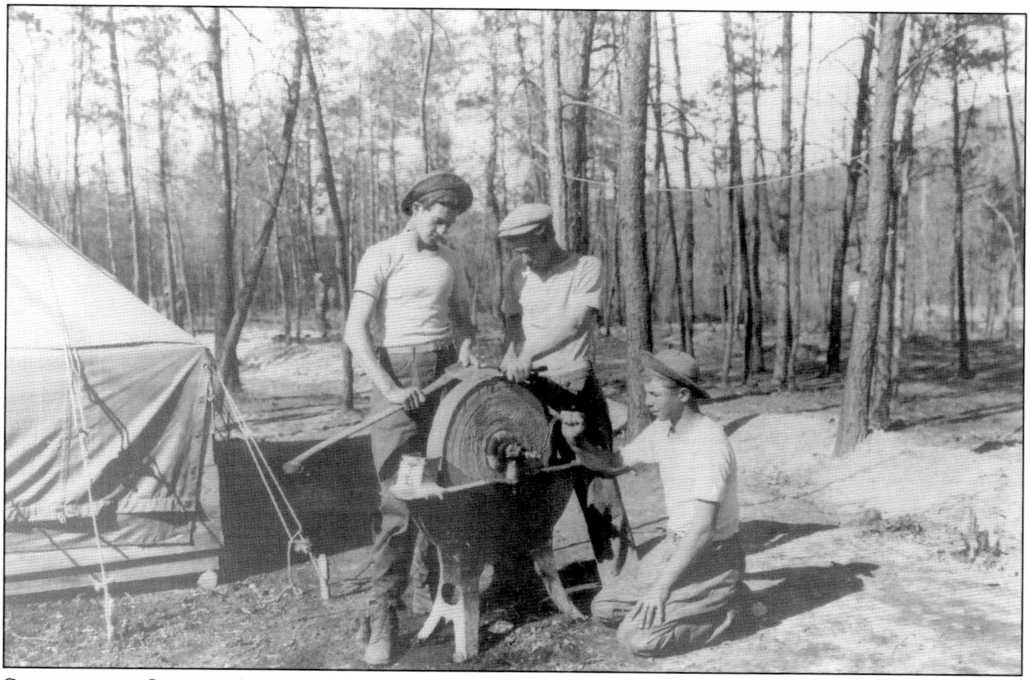

Sharpening Stone. A variety of tasks were assigned each day, and equipment was kept in good working condition. Time was assigned to make handles for axes and mallets, and the blades had to be sharp. These young men are having a demonstration on sharpening an axe. The round sharpening stone may have been pedal-driven or turned by a crank. Only manpower powered the tools, as there was no electricity. (USDAFS.)

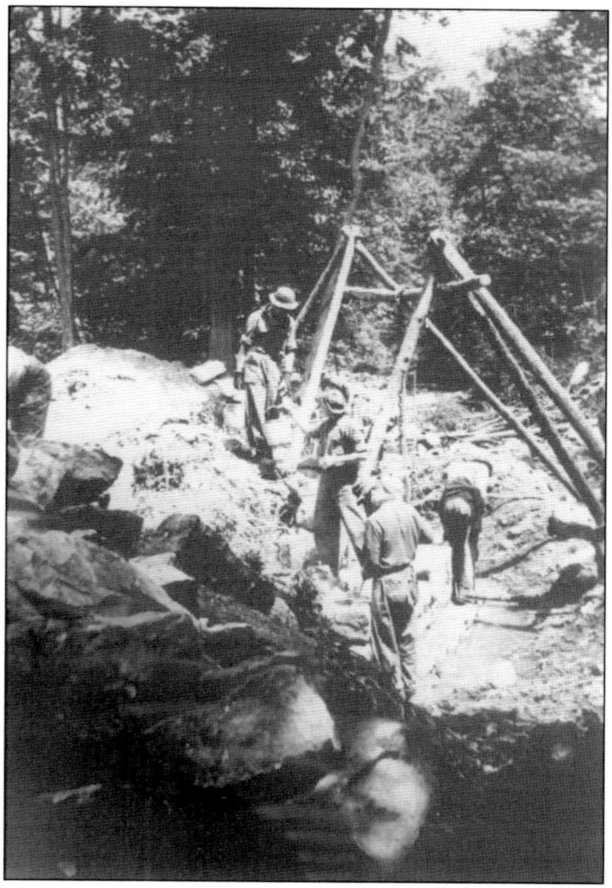

Rock Hoist. This ingenious piece of equipment was made from recently cut small, straight trees. They are pegged together at the top to create two tripods, which support a cross pole. The chain is attached at one end to the pole, with the other end attached to a sling to assist in lifting and moving the rock. The rock from this ditch is being removed to clear the area for a path or foundation. Other rocks are piled at left. (USDAFS.)

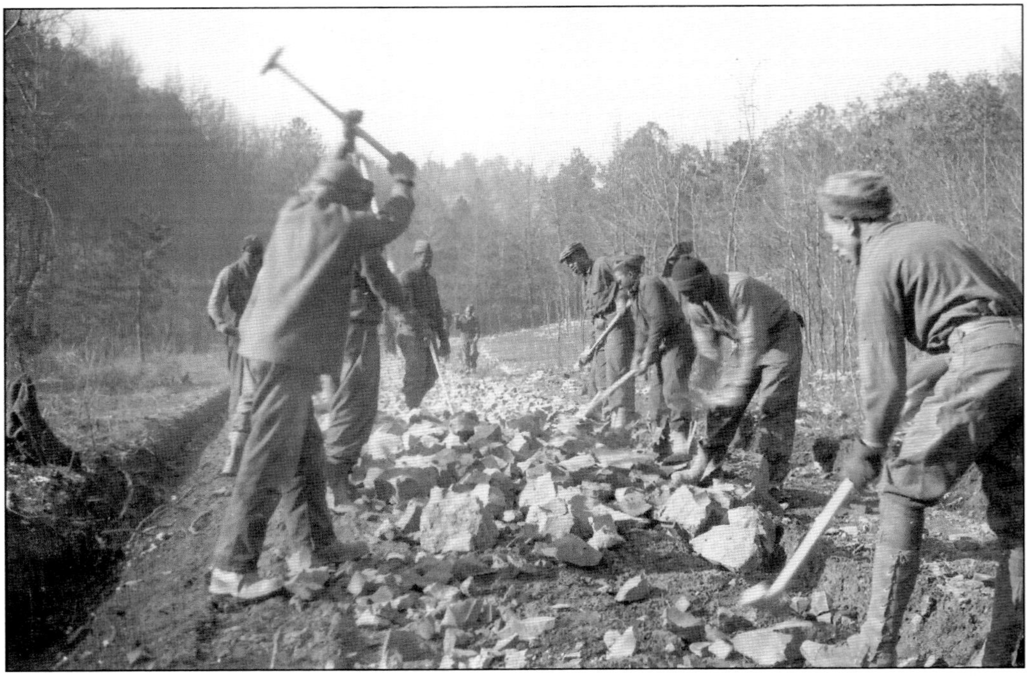

Rock Smashing at Wolf Gap. National director of the newly created CCC was Robert Fechner. Pres. Franklin D. Roosevelt appointed him on April 5, 1933. The first commander of the first camp, Camp Roosevelt, was Capt. Leo Donovan. The only other camp in Shenandoah County was built at Wolf Gap close to West Virginia. Both were segregated camps, with Wolf Gap for the black youth from the large cities. (USDAFS.)

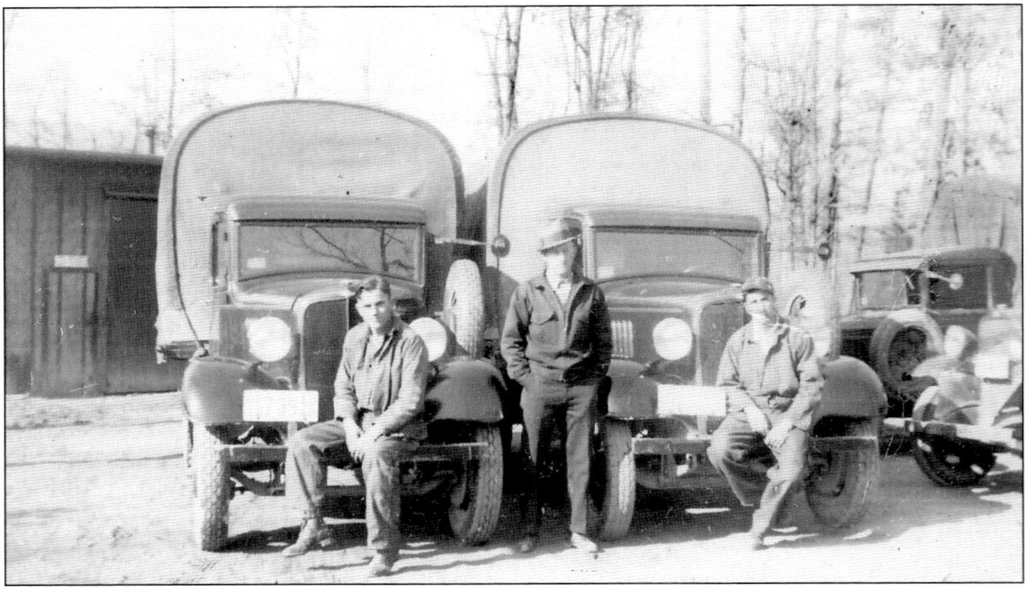

Locally Experienced Men. The first person on the left is unidentified; he, Mertie McClanahan, and Charlie Bledsoe "Moon" Mullins were three of the men from the community employed to oversee and train the boys. Their expertise was maintenance of the trucks. Other skills taught by the locally employed men (LEM) were telephone installation, road and bridge building, tree planting, firefighting, stocking streams with fish, and cooking. (USDAFS.)

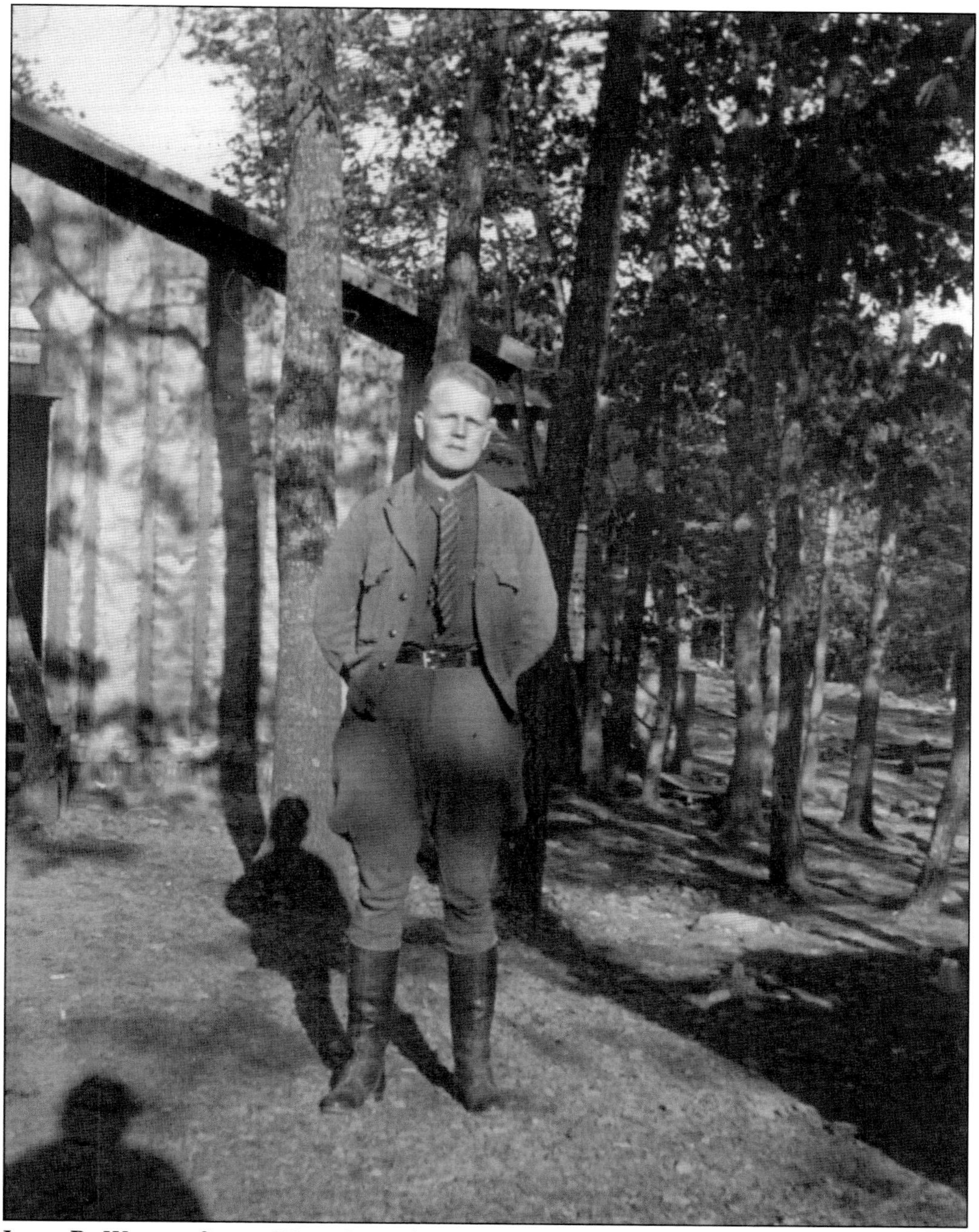

James R. Wilkins Sr. at Wolf Gap. This photograph is from Garland Hudgin's scrapbook. It was donated for the new CCC exhibit at the Lee Ranger District in Edinburg. James R. Wilkins Sr. started with the CCC at Natural Bridge, where he was a U.S. Forest Service employee. On May 1, 1933, he began his first assignment at Glasgow Company 354, and a month later, he went to Wolf Gap, Camp NF-7. He held the title of project supervisor at both camps simultaneously. It was he who began the practice of using local men with experience in needed skills to train the boys. The new Interpretive Center in Edinburg will be named in his honor. As Wilkins said, "We worked long hours, and we put our heart and soul into it, and we loved it. With memories like those, how could they forget?" (USDAFS.)

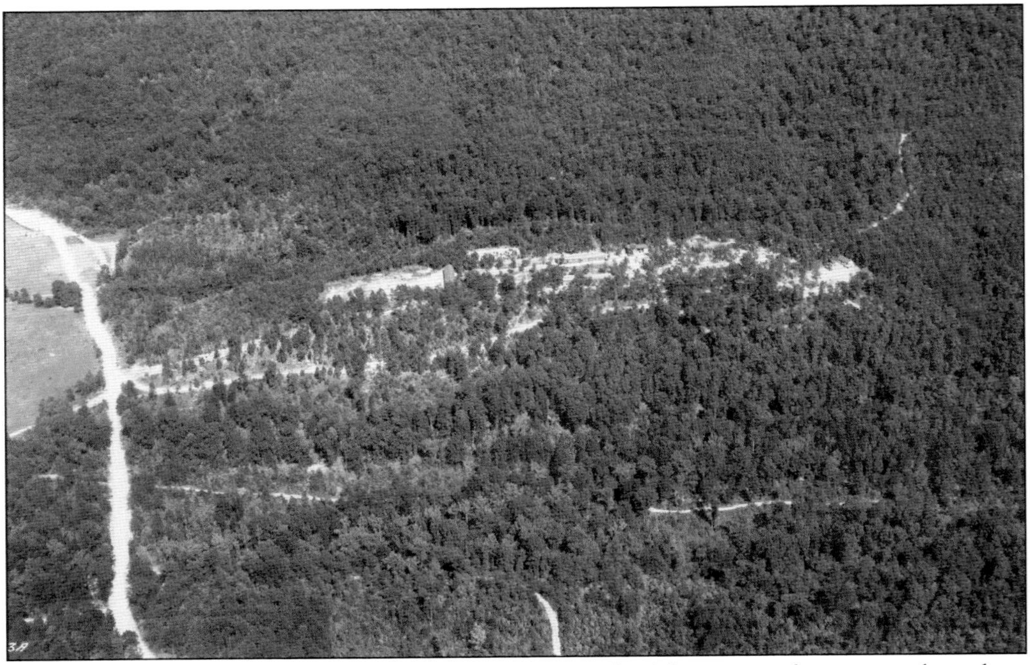

Aerial Views of Camp Roosevelt and Wolf Gap. Both of these views from an airplane show the George Washington National Forest. The image above is of Camp Roosevelt after it was fully constructed. To the left of the camp is Fort Valley Road. The beauty of nature surrounded the residents of these camps. These isolated places were far from the squalor and din of the struggling cities from which most of these men had come. When they left these camps at the end of their time, they were forever changed; they had learned discipline and respect for teamwork. They either went on to become the foundation and leaders of the military units soon to fight in World War II, or they kept America running while the country they loved fought for freedom on the seas and the battlefields of Europe. The image below shows Wolf Gap. Although the layout of the camps is similar, the camp at Wolf Gap has a more complex topography and the roads are not straight. (USDAFS.)

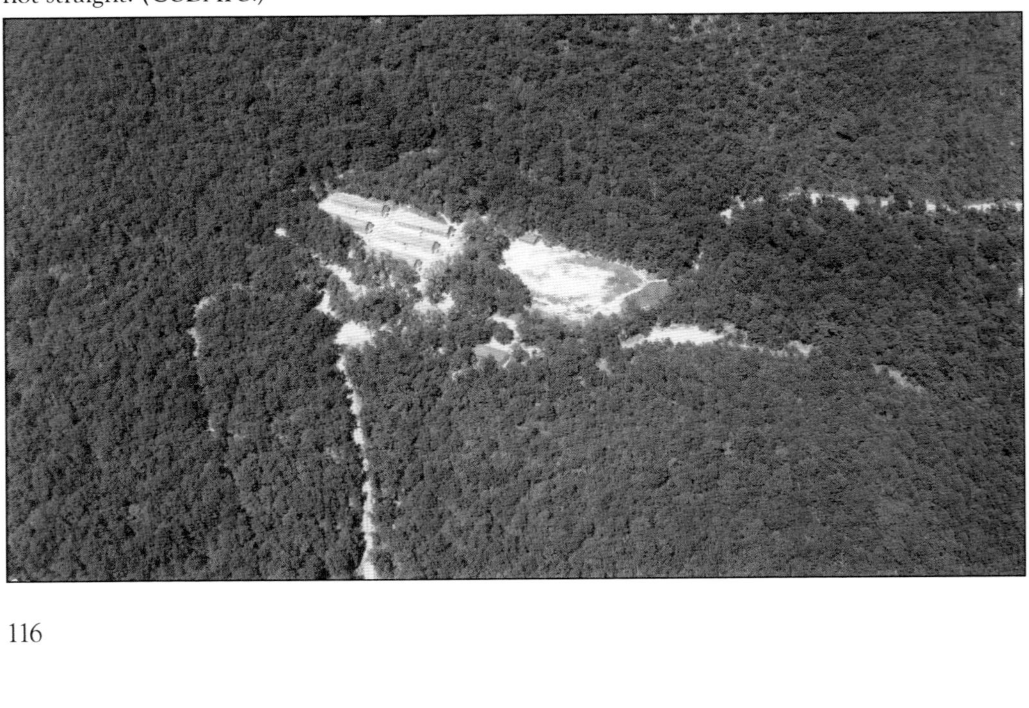

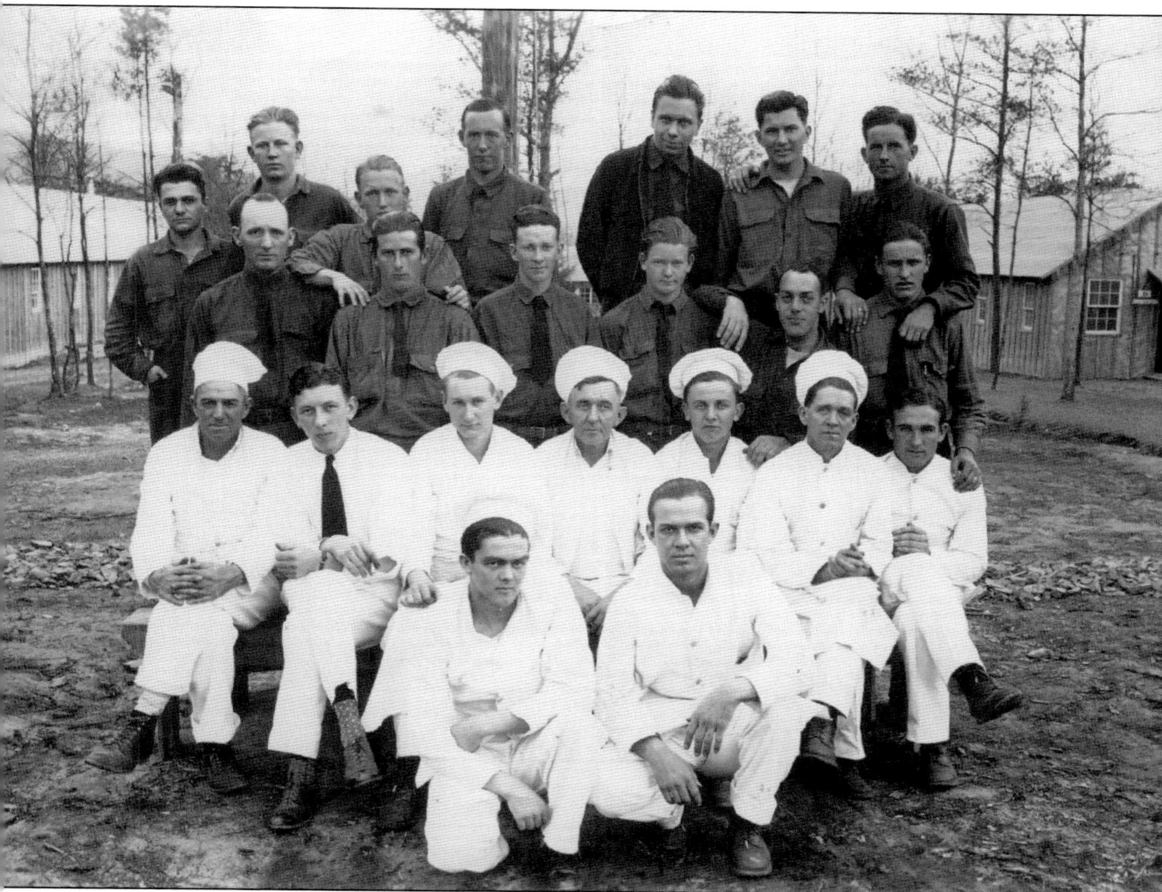

Cooks in White. Capt. Leo Donovan first saw Camp Roosevelt on April 17, 1933, three days after he was briefed about the program. As first in command, his report was on the establishment of this camp. It included problems solved, disciplinary actions, weather, and food. He said, "The only CCC men assigned to the company were cooks who had worked in a short-order restaurant at one time. It is a long step from this kind of cooking to the preparation of meals for 200 men . . . as to the chow situation, there has never been assembled any group of men who could eat more than a Civilian Conservation Corps Company." The average enrollee gained 12 pounds during their time at camp. Locally purchased food made CCC meals nutritious. In this photograph, two cooks are identified: Bill Pillow is wearing the tie, and Shorty Long is in the first row on the left. (USDAFS.)

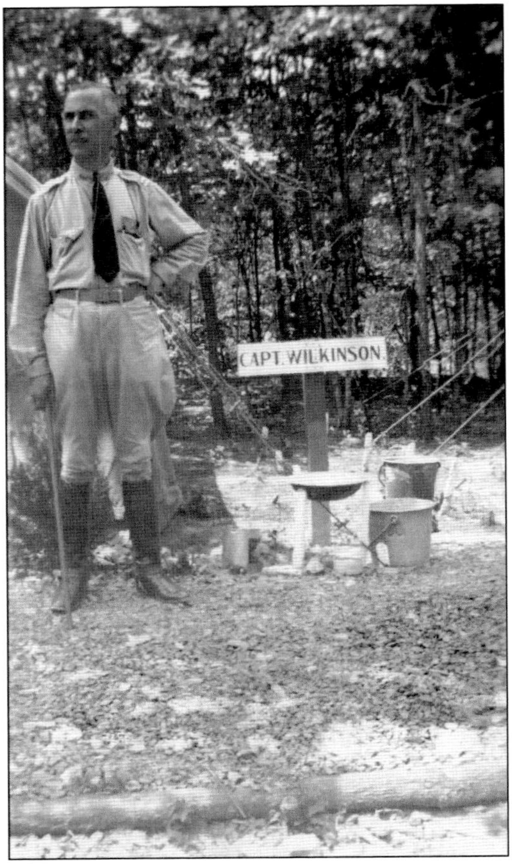

SUPERVISOR IN CAMP. Foremen received $140 per month as on-the-job supervisors. Army officer Capt. Wilkinson was responsible for daily operations. The men worked in crews of 48. Each crew had a leader and an assistant leader in charge in the barracks and job sites. These men received $45 and $46 per month, respectively. Group foremen had attended CCC training school and been assigned to a camp as technical staff. (USDAFS.)

MR. NEWMAN, CASHIER. Unemployed and unmarried men not in school between the ages of 17 and 25 were eligible for enrollment, and their pay was $30 a month. Of that, $25 was sent home to their family or put into an account if they had no family; it would be paid at the end of their service. They had $5 left each month to spend at the CCC canteen. (USDAFS.)

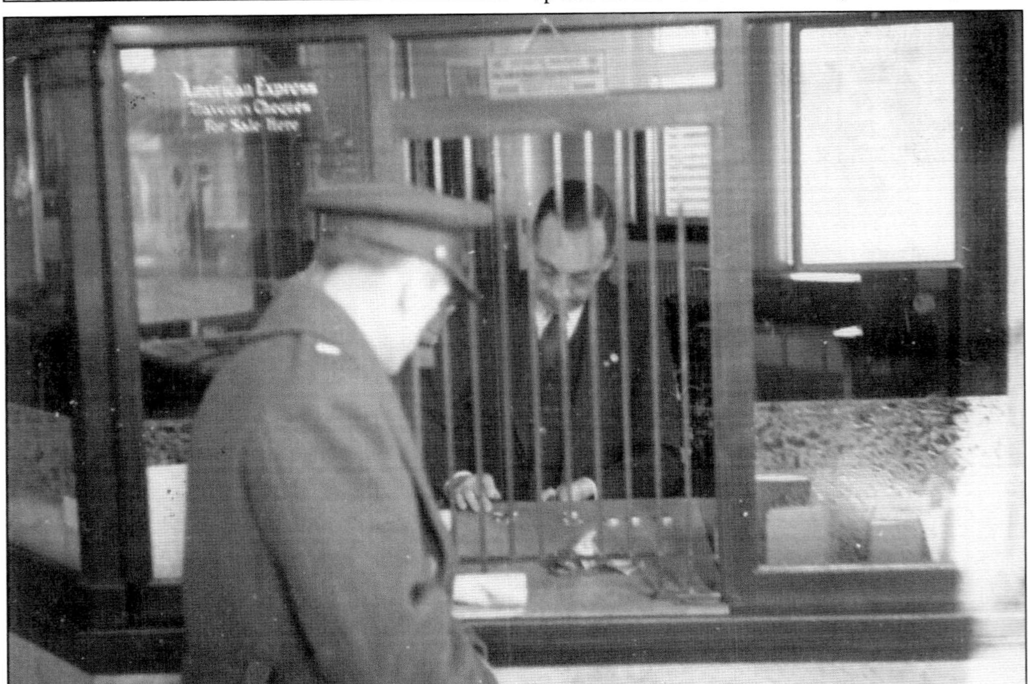

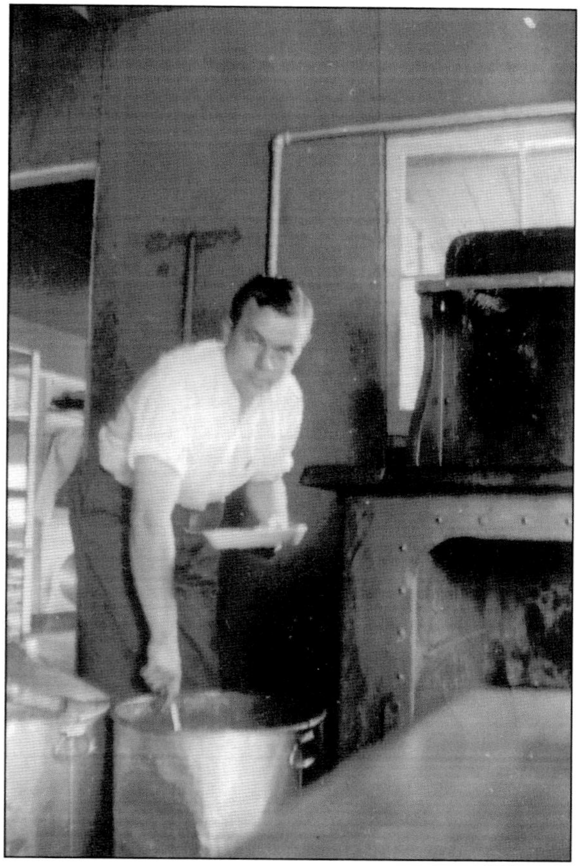

Henry Rich Cooking. The first CCC enrollee heard that applications were being taken while he was on the street in Washington, D.C. Every six months, 200 new junior enrollees arrived and were supervised by a staff of 40. The overhead men were military, LEM, and CCC personnel. The recruits were employed for a term of six months minimum and two years maximum. (USDAFS.)

Henry Rich and Harmonicats. Henry Rich (first row, far right) and his friends formed a band and entertained the men after dinner. Three of them played the harmonica, and three played stringed instruments. Behind them is the mess hall and on the right is the kitchen. (USDAFS.)

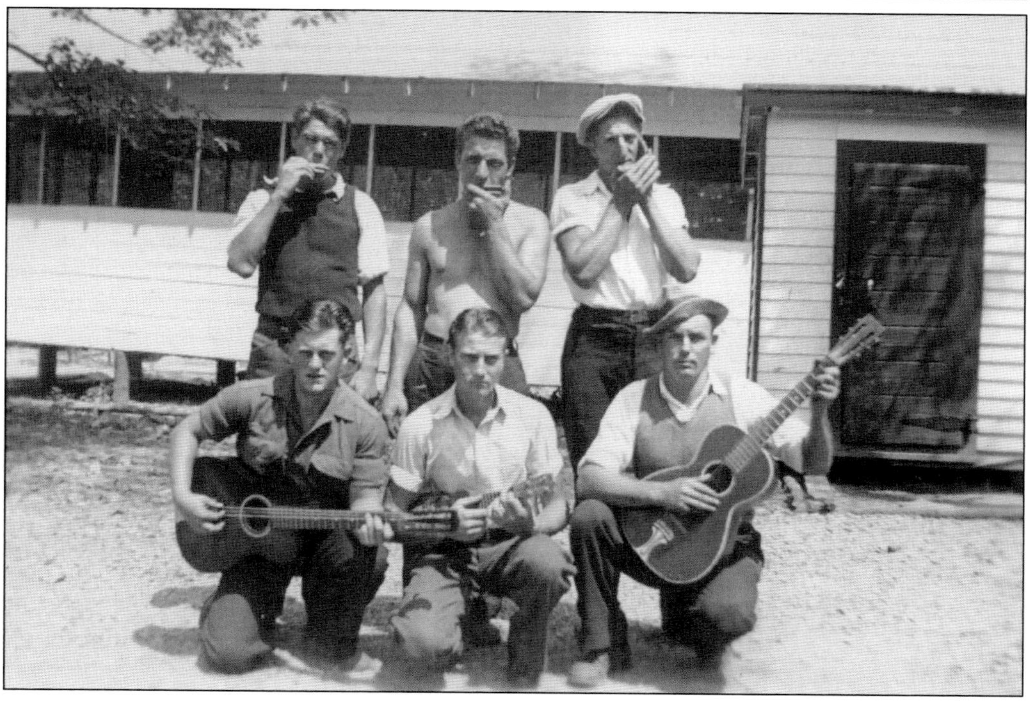

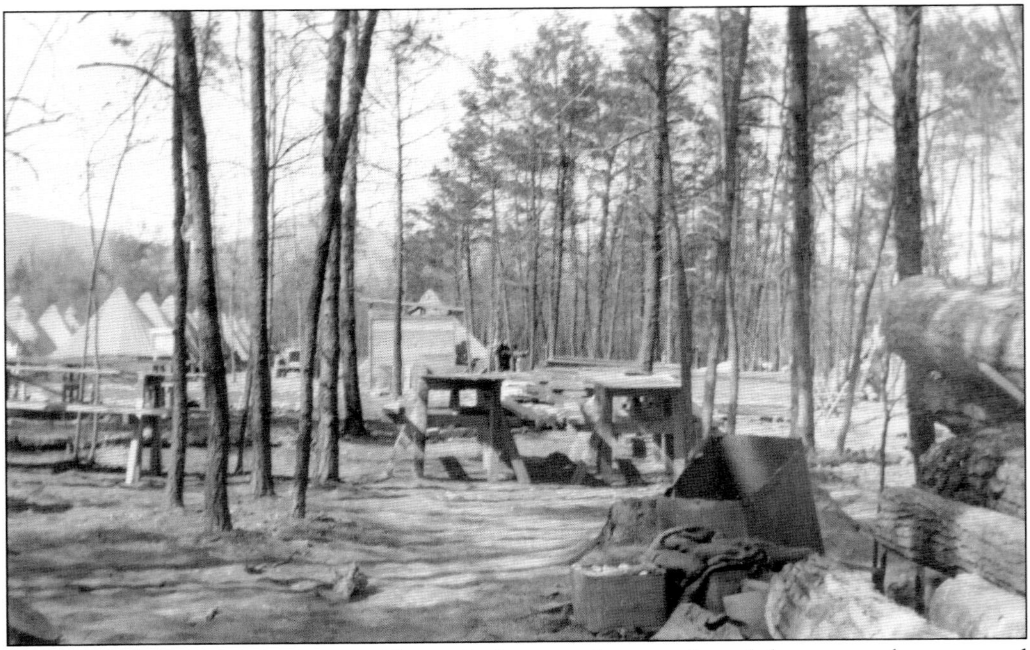

Camp Roosevelt Tents through Trees. Right away, the men cleared the trees and constructed their tent city, or Company Street, to the layout designed by Lieutenant Train. The camps each had a similar pattern with a flag pole at the center; starting with the eight-man pyramid tents on platforms. They were lined up with precision in two rows. Through the trees, the camp is seen here. (USDAFS.)

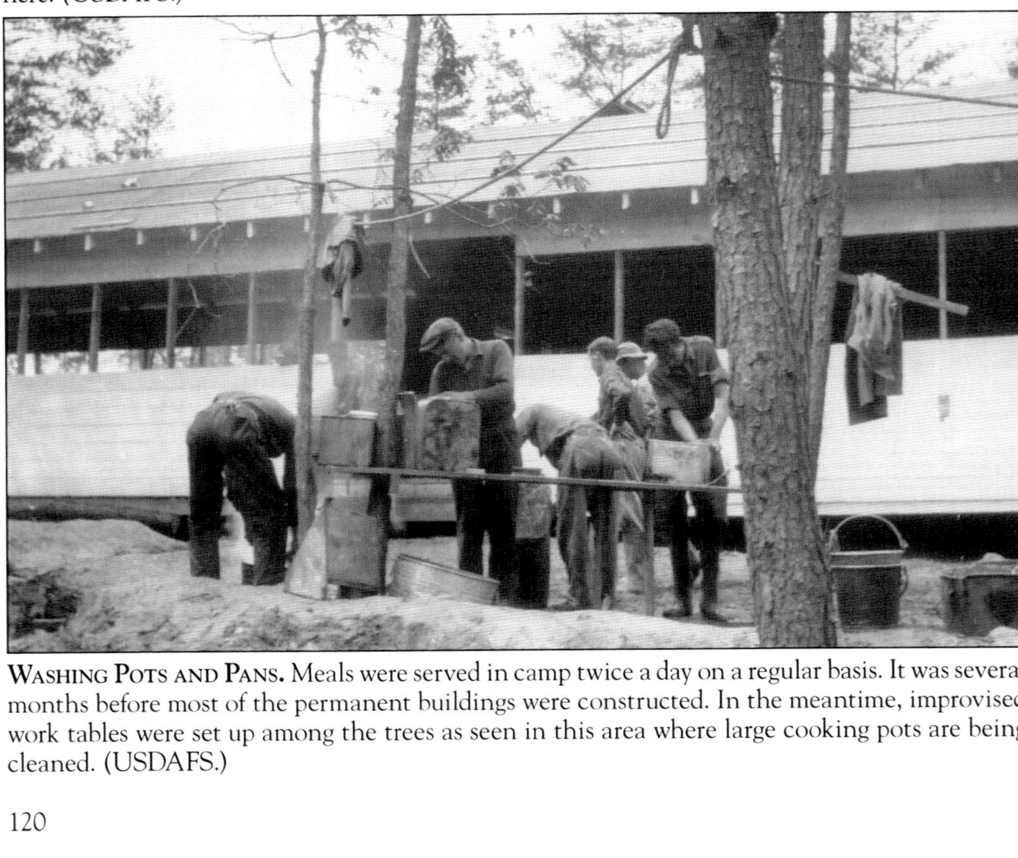

Washing Pots and Pans. Meals were served in camp twice a day on a regular basis. It was several months before most of the permanent buildings were constructed. In the meantime, improvised work tables were set up among the trees as seen in this area where large cooking pots are being cleaned. (USDAFS.)

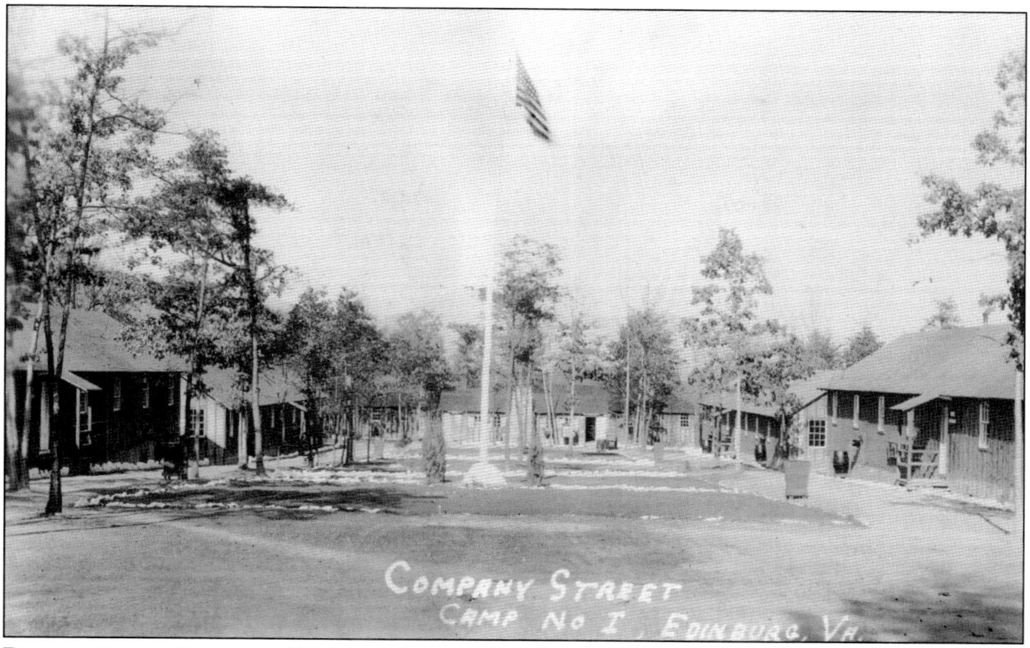

Parade Field, Company Street. The reveille whistle blew at 5:45 a.m. After breakfast, the company formed and proceeded to the U.S. Forest Service Headquarters for assignments. As the men passed the assignment board, a nail was moved to the "out" column. Those failing to check out lost a day's pay. They were divided into details under their respective supervisors and transported in trucks to the work sites. (USDAFS.)

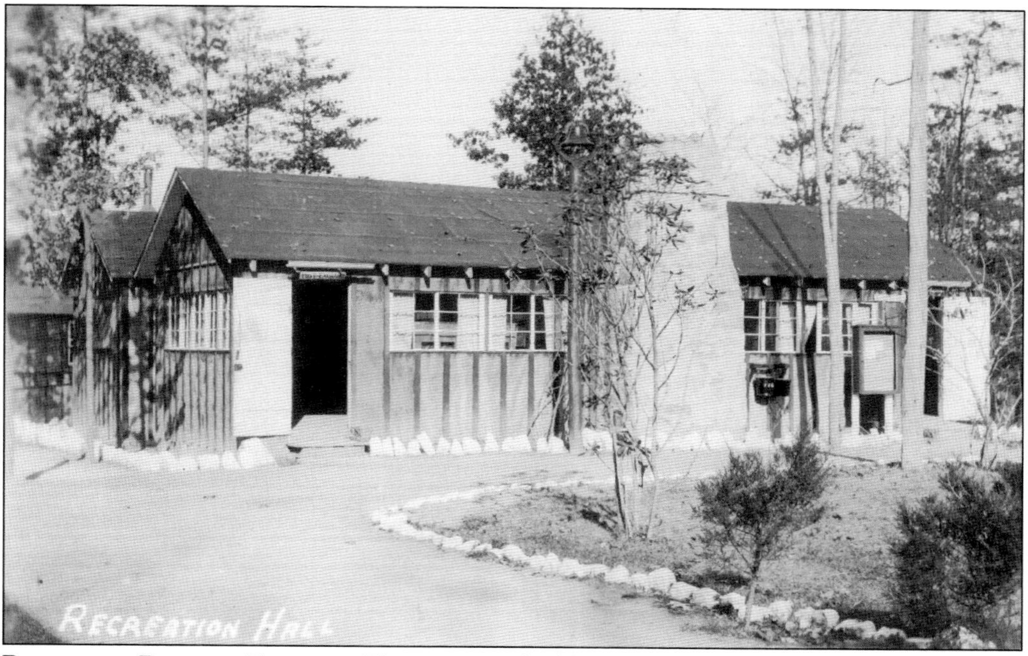

Recreation Building Exterior. The recreation building is seen at the end of Company Street. It had a large stone fireplace for heat. The men had free time after dinner to go swimming in Passage Creek or come to the recreation hall to sit by the fireplace, shoot pool, and play cards. Liquor was not allowed in the camp. Notices were posted on the company bulletin board. (USDAFS.)

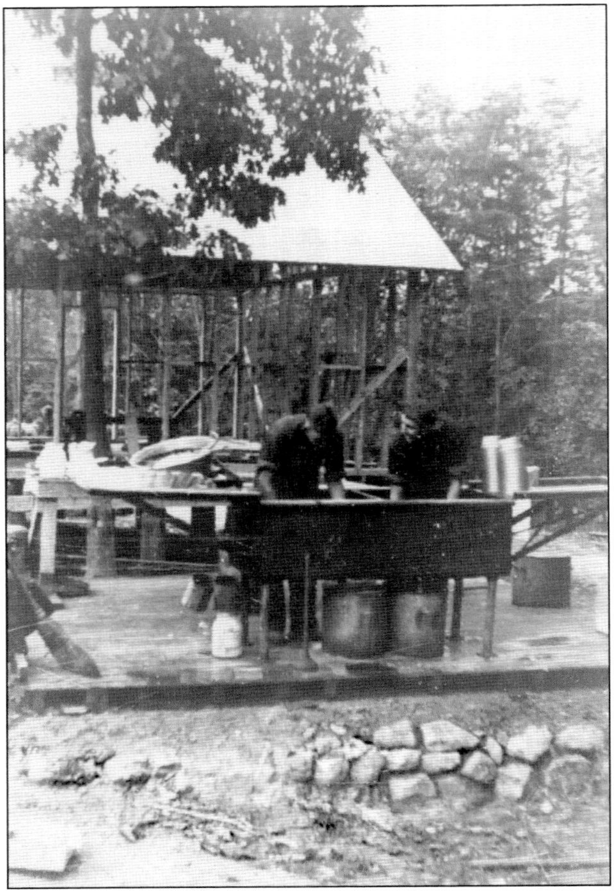

MESS HALL AND KITCHEN. Although the mess hall was not completed, a typical breakfast consisted of oatmeal, milk, bacon, eggs, potatoes, coffee, and bread. Lunch was served wherever the men were working that day. Dinner was Irish stew, coleslaw, mashed potatoes, string beans, bread and butter, pudding, and coffee or iced tea. The regular army was feeding its troops at 45¢ per day; Camp Roosevelt was allowed $1.50 per day. (USDAFS.)

BARRACKS INTERIOR. After weeks living in army bell tents during construction of buildings on Company Street, the men moved into the barracks. By 1934, there were four barracks, each holding 48 men. By 1942, there were six barracks heated by coal stoves. A sentry was appointed to stay awake through the night to tend the coal stoves. Barracks were inspected every morning to make sure all was in order. (USDAFS.)

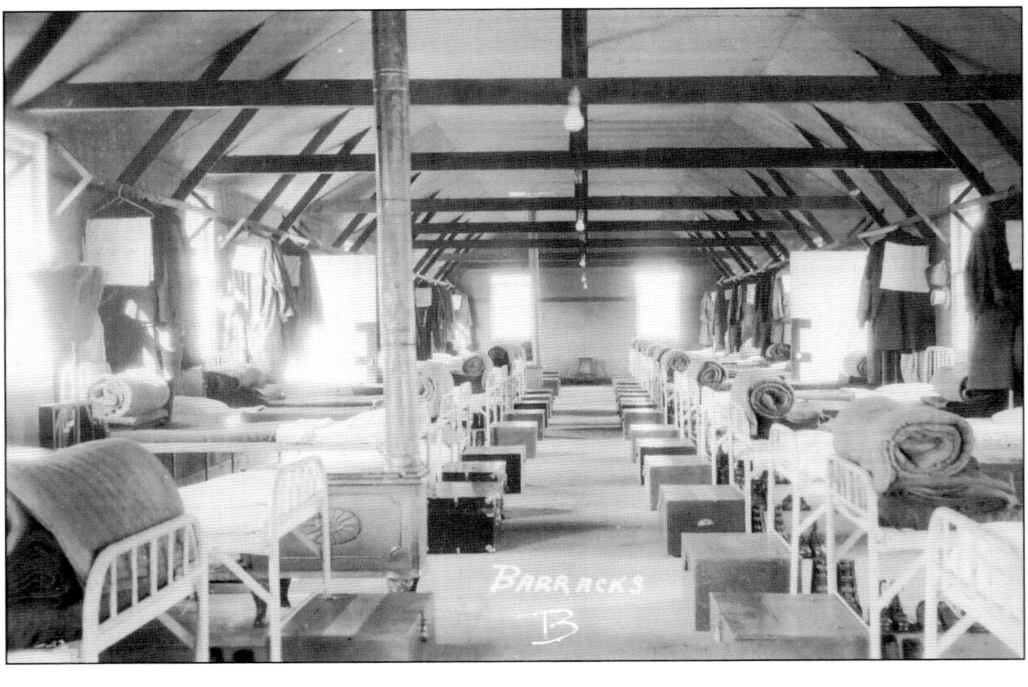

ROLAND STANLEY AND CHARLIE MEAD. The work of this camp consisted primarily of road construction and improvement. They began work at 8:00 a.m.; breaks were given through the day for smoking and resting. The lunch hour was on the road from 11:45 a.m. to 12:45 p.m., and they returned to camp at 4:00 p.m. for a free hour. The men could play sports or swim in the pool created by a dam they made across Passage Creek. The evening meal was served at 5:30 p.m. Seen at right, Roland Stanley, who won a Purple Heart in World War II, and Charlie Mead were considered to be the camp clowns. (USDAFS.)

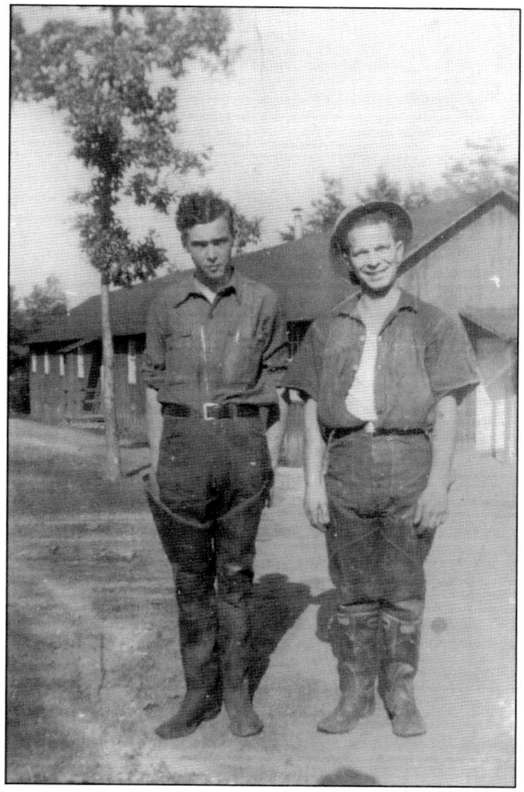

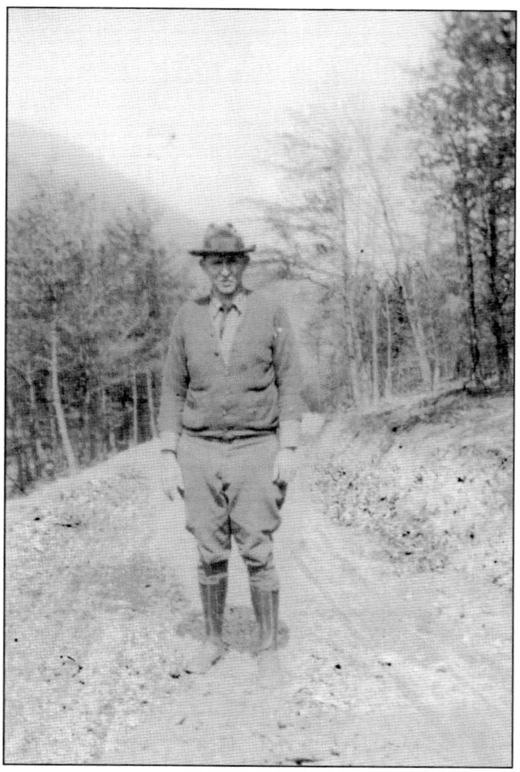

JOHN CHRISMAN. John Chrisman was a forest ranger for George Washington National Forest; he chose flat ground for Camp Roosevelt. He is seen here on the road under construction, wearing his uniform with boots and leather leggings. (USDAFS.)

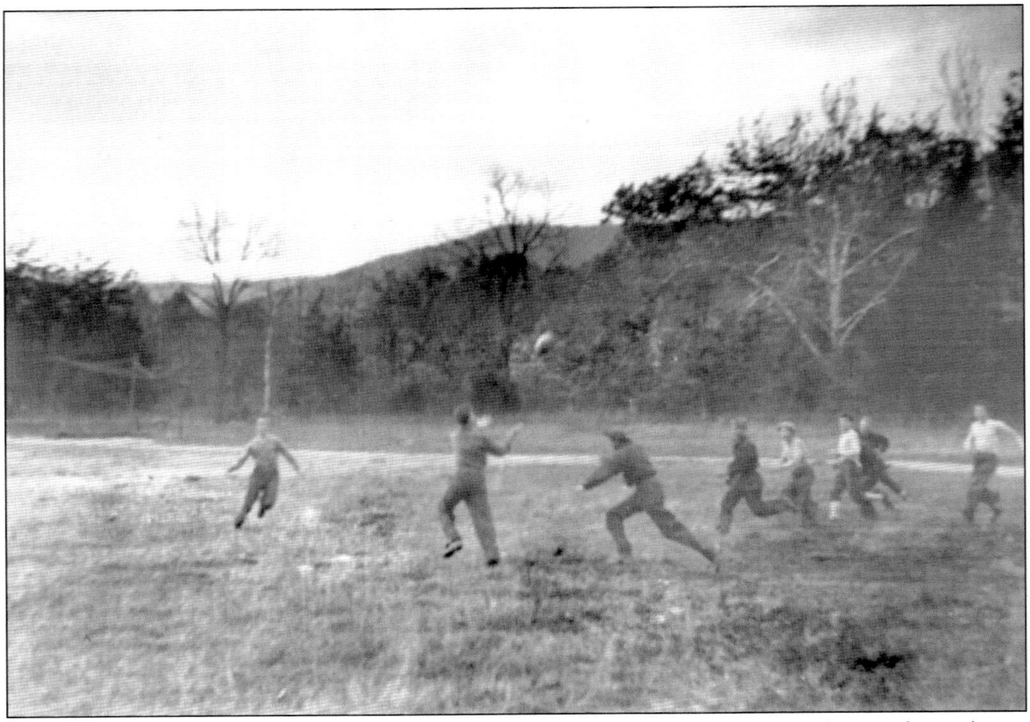

Football in Air and Baseball with Extra Bats. After the evening meal, men formed into teams to play either football or baseball. The teams played games with Luray, Woodstock, Stanley, and other CCC camp teams. The games were scheduled Saturday and Sunday, and local people as well as CCC men attended them. The communities nearby were glad to have Camp Roosevelt because of the economic benefits, and their work projects included building roads and firefighting. Before Camp Roosevelt, people who lived in the area were very isolated. After the roads were built, they could get their children to school and become more a part of the nearby communities. Relations were improved through competitive athletic events. (USDAFS.)

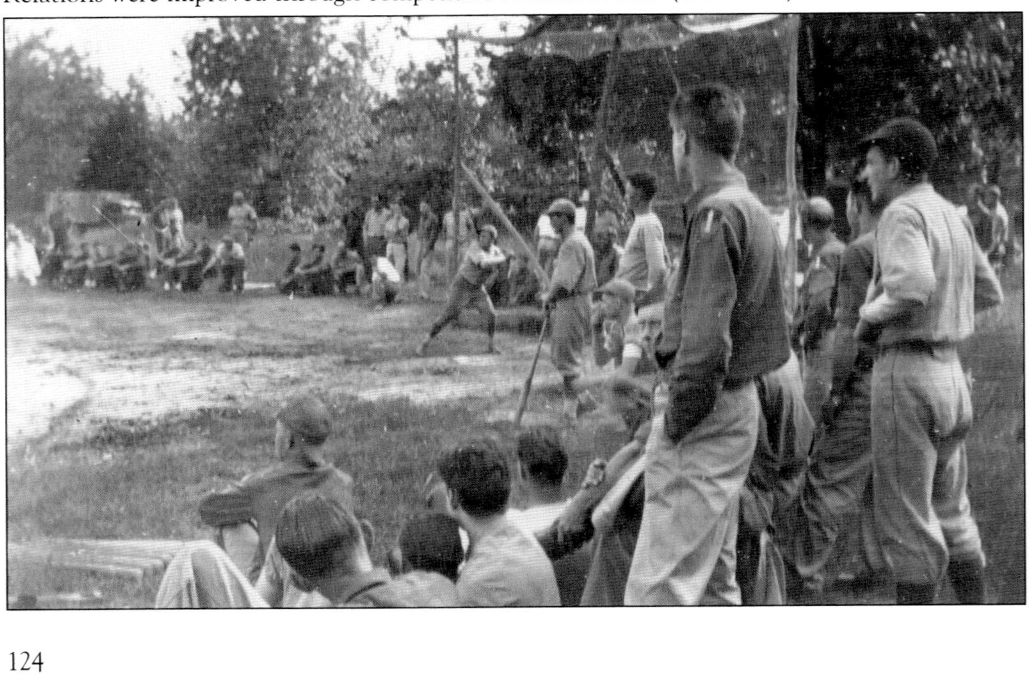

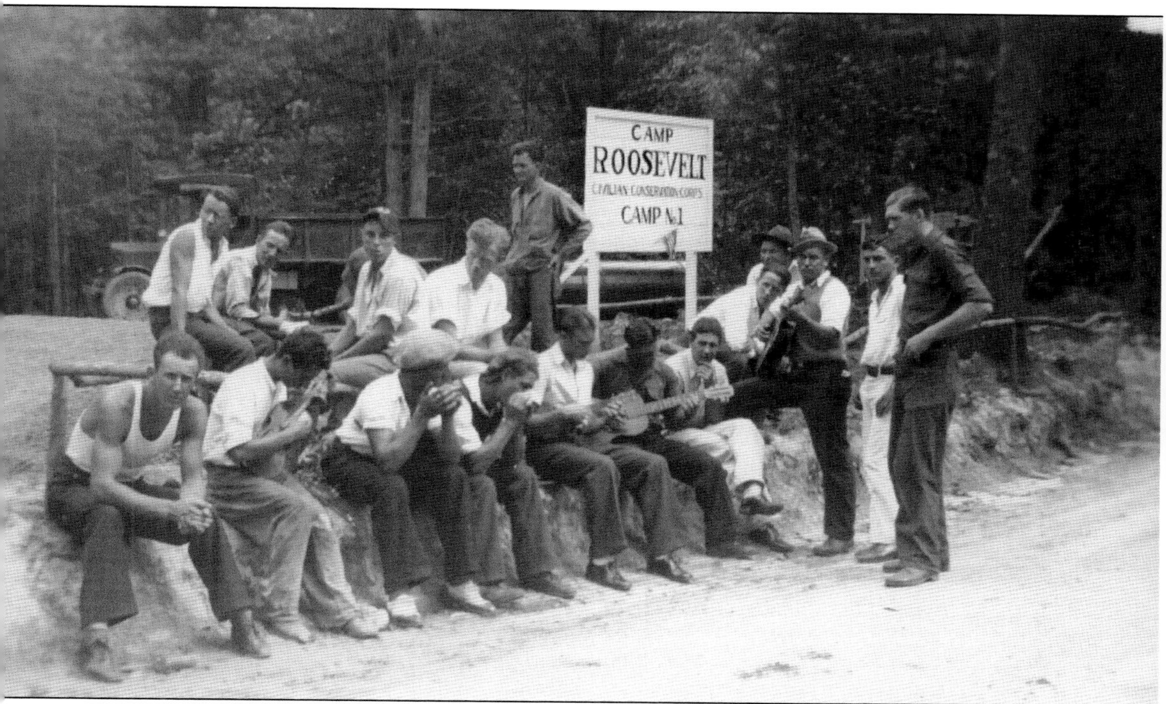

CAMP ROOSEVELT SIGN. After working an eight-hour day, six days a week, the boys enjoyed their free time in the evenings. After the evening meal, the camp offered school lessons given by camp enrollees and officers, as well as lectures given by local school principals, town mayors, and forestry officials. There was also scheduled entertainment provided for the men. The whistle for lights out was at 9:15 p.m., and lights were extinguished at 10:00 p.m. One night a week, the men were able to dress in civilian clothes and drive down the mountain to Edinburg, where they could go to the movies or visit friends. By 11:00 p.m., the trucks returned to camp. It was a 9-mile walk back up to the fort if one missed the ride. These boys are ready for an evening out; some have their harmonicas. (USDAFS.)

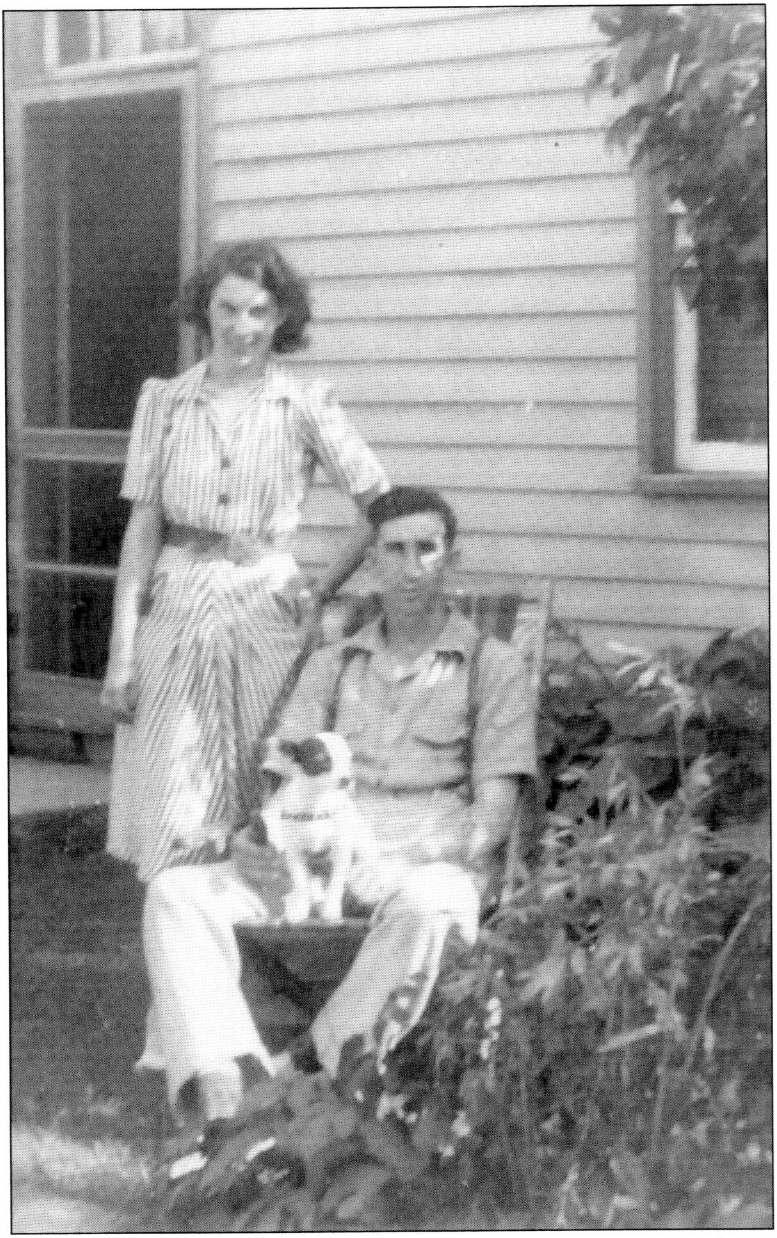

Moon and Pearl. Charlie Bledsoe "Moon" Mullins, from Alberene, joined the CCC in 1934. He was sent to Camp Roosevelt by train and then by army truck to the camp. He stayed for six years, first as an enrollee and then as a LEM. When he arrived at camp, there were 250 men. He participated in local activities and met his future wife, Pearl Markley, through the Edinburg Church. They married and settled in Edinburg, along with many of the other former enrollees from Camp Roosevelt. In his recollections of Camp Roosevelt, Mullins recalled, "You felt lonesome when you got over there in the mountains . . . it took awhile to get accustomed, but the longer you stayed the better you liked it." He stayed in Edinburg for the rest of his life. The Mullins did not have children of their own, but they considered the CCC "boys" to be their family. They were instrumental in getting the Camp Roosevelt Recreation Area built, and he helped organize the annual reunions that still meet there. (USDAFS.)

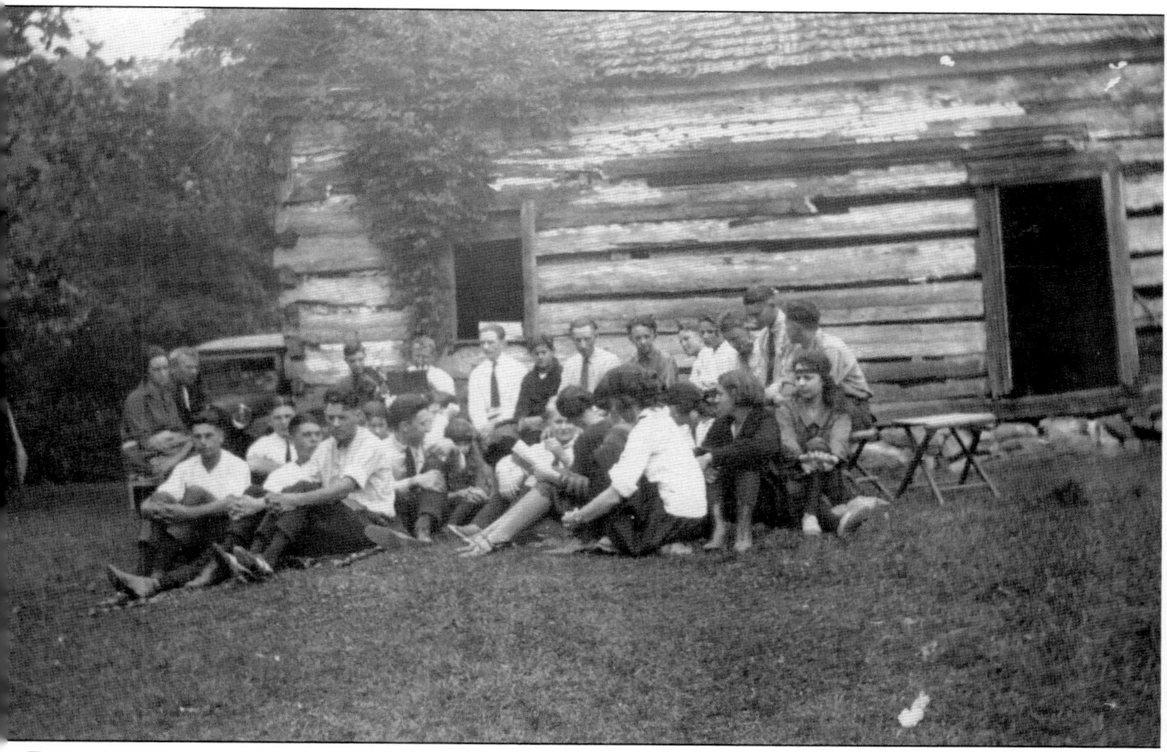

ELIZABETH FURNACE CABIN ON SUNDAY. Only on Sunday did the routine in any CCC camp vary. After six days of toil, the enrollees wore a white shirt and dress slacks rather than work uniforms. The small crowd gathered outside of the log cabin built on the furnace complex included friends from the surrounding area or family. They worshiped together in prayer, read the Scriptures, and heard a sermon by a local minister. At the end of every day, the men reported to the parade ground in full uniform to retire the flag. They placed their right hand over their heart and recited the "Pledge of Allegiance." The flag was lowered, folded, and carried to its resting place for the night. The boys proceeded out of the parade ground to their barracks or to the recreation hall for a few minutes before retiring for the night, knowing they had worked hard and supported their family and their country for one more week. No one is identified in this photograph. (USDAFS.)

Consistent with our mission to preserve history on a local level, this book was printed in South Carolina on American-made paper and manufactured entirely in the United States. Products carrying the accredited Forest Stewardship Council (FSC) label are printed on 100 percent FSC-certified paper.

MADE IN THE USA